More Advance Praise for
Willie Pietersen's *Reinventing Strategy*

"We've had the pleasure of working closely with Willie Pietersen and have seen firsthand what Strategic Learning can do for a company. My advice to other business leaders: Get to know Strategic Learning—before your competitors do."

> —Marty Homlish
> President & CEO, SAP Global Marketing

"Willie Pietersen is that rare commodity, a thoughtful scholar of business with a wealth of practical experience actually running global companies. In *Reinventing Strategy*, Pietersen distills the lessons of a lifetime of business success into a working methodology that any leader can use in the creation and implementation of winning strategies."

> —David Finn
> Chairman, The Ruder•Finn Group

"Anyone leading a corporation—or hoping to do so—should absorb *Reinventing Strategy* and keep it within close reach for continuous reference. Pietersen's chapter on 'Winning the Battle for Insights' is worth the price of the whole book. Never have I come across a clearer guide on how to generate insights that ignite business breakthroughs."

> —Rob Hawthorne
> President & CEO, Ocean Spray Cranberries, Inc.

"Willie Pietersen's Strategic Learning process is able to consistently produce breakthrough strategies. No one concerned with succeeding in today's competitive environment can afford to ignore it."

> —Gunilla Nordström
> Corporate Vice President, M2M Com,
> Sony Ericsson Mobile Communications

"Everyone senses the importance of organizational learning. But until now, there has been no pragmatic method for using learning to drive value creation. Willie Pietersen's insights fill that gap. *Reinventing Strategy* is a great addition to the small shelf of truly useful management books."

—Michael Harper
President, Harper Consulting and
co-author of *Hope Is Not a Method*

"In *Reinventing Strategy*, Willie Pietersen brings deep insight to the challenges of working *fast* and working *right*. The results achieved by the companies Willie has worked with speak for themselves."

—Victoria Marsick
Professor of Adult Education and Organizational Learning
Teacher's College, Columbia University

"Willie Pietersen's years as a successful businessman provided him with a wealth of practical, pragmatic insights into what works and what doesn't. I'm delighted he has gathered these insights into *Reinventing Strategy* so that thousands of others can benefit as I have."

—Jerry L. Marlar
President, Sulzer Biologies, Inc.

REINVENTING STRATEGY

Using Strategic Learning to Create and Sustain Breakthrough Performance

WILLIE PIETERSEN

John Wiley & Sons, Inc.

Published by John Wiley & Sons, Inc., New York
Published simultaneously in Canada.

Library of Congress Cataloging-in-Publication Data:

Pietersen, Willie.
    Reinventing strategy : using strategic learning to create and sustain
  breakthrough performance / Willie Pietersen.
      p.   cm.
    Includes bibliographical references and index.
    ISBN 0-471-06190-5 (CLOTH : alk. paper)
    1. Organizational learning.   2. Strategic planning.   3. Leadership.
  4. Knowledge management.   I. Title.
  HD58.82 .P53   2002
  658.4'012—dc21   2001006725

CONTENTS

ACKNOWLEDGMENTS

The Strategic Learning concept presented in this book owes a lot to the two great learning laboratories that have shaped my ideas.

The first was my two decades as a CEO. These years infused in me a strong sense of pragmatism. Life in the trenches, I discovered, is always messy. So the most important question to ask about any business idea is simply, *Does it work?* In these pages, I've tried to capture some of the ideas that *do* work, so that my colleagues in business leadership may benefit from them.

My second learning lab has been the five years I've spent at Columbia Business School as a teacher, consultant, and researcher— an opportunity to step back from the fray and try to make sense of it all.

Columbia has been the avenue to a second career for me and a catalyst for my personal reinvention. I've received wonderful support and encouragement from many colleagues at the school. In particular, I'd like to thank my good friends Bill Klepper and Mike Fenlon for their rich and generous contributions to my thinking, as well as Victoria Marsick of Teachers College, Columbia University, especially for her scholarly guidance on learning theory.

For the past five years, I have also had the great privilege of serving as chairman of the board of trustees of the Institute for the Future. This has been an education in its own right, for which my thanks go especially to the Institute's president, Bob Johansen. Bob's inspiring ideas, unstinting support, and wise advice have contributed enormously to this book.

As every teacher knows, teaching is the greatest way to learn. I have learned a lot from the participants in the many programs I have taught, ranging from young and eager MBAs with their probing questions to seasoned executives with their no-nonsense challenges. I owe them all a debt of thanks, but I'd like to express my appreciation especially to the people from CGNU, Chubb, Deloitte Touche Tohmatsu, Ericsson, Henry Schein, Inc., International Specialty Products, SAP, and Sony. Strategic Learning has been applied, battle-tested, and honed in workshops with executives from all these companies.

Responsibility for the content and ideas in this book is entirely my own. However, I could not have written it without the professionalism, dedication, enthusiasm, and tireless work of a wonderful creative team.

On the writing side, I initially had the expert help of journalist Alex Prud'homme. With Alex I formed the basic structure of the book and set out its key ideas. I am indebted to Alex for constantly pushing me to develop the stories and examples.

After Alex left the project to join the staff of *Talk* magazine, Karl Weber, who had been serving as an editorial advisor, seamlessly took up the task of assisting me with the writing. Karl's admirable writing skills helped him do a marvelous job of turning the work in progress into a final manuscript. He also developed a keen understanding of the concepts involved and proved to be a valuable sounding board and intellectual sparring partner.

On the research side, I had the invaluable help of Jeff Kuhn, an adjunct professor of organizational learning at Teachers College, Columbia University. Jeff and I often work together on Strategic Learning workshops. Thus, Jeff was also able to bring a keen professional eye to the shaping of the manuscript. I'm grateful for his insights and suggestions. In addition, Jeff provided skillful work in developing many of the case studies.

Thanks also go to my literary agent, Judith Ehrlich of Linda Chester & Associates. Judith has been a wonderful and very caring ally. She expertly steered the project from the development of a proposal to finding the right publisher and has remained engaged and committed throughout the process.

My editors at John Wiley & Sons have been a pleasure to deal with. At the start, I worked with Karen Hansen, who provided superb guidance. Later, Airie Dekidjiev took over the project with enthusiasm and expertly piloted it through to publication. Her help and advice have been invaluable.

I leave till last the support of family. Writing a book, I've discovered, is an all-consuming project. One's personal life must often go on hold when wrestling yet another revision into shape. Without the help of family, the effort would be nearly impossible to sustain. Many thanks to my grown-up kids, Chris and Sally, who kept rooting for me all the way. For more than a year, every conversation we had included a "How's the book going, Dad?" (I think it's done now, kids.) Even my sister Phoebe in far-away South Africa has been cheering me on from the sidelines. This affection and support from my family has sustained and inspired me.

Finally, there is my wife Laura. Herself an author, Laura has been a pillar of support and understanding. She has also demonstrated a wonderful knack for injecting just the right idea at just the right time. And her sense of humor keeps me on an even keel, never letting me become too discouraged when things go wrong. Thank you, Laura.

WILLIE PIETERSEN
New York, NY
November 2001

FOREWORD

Willie Pietersen's *Reinventing Strategy* fills a genuine void between organizational learning and strategy, without the cumbersome jargon of either field.

In these early years of the twenty-first century, it has become increasingly clear that the old ways of creating and implementing strategy no longer work. At the Institute for the Future (IFTF), we're reminded daily about today's frenzied pace of change, most obviously in technology but also in the social, economic, and political spheres. No wonder traditional methods of strategic planning, which tend to assume that the future is more predictable than it really is, have largely failed.

Consequently, finding ways to transform companies into *adaptive organizations* able to respond intelligently to an ever-changing environment has become the top priority for business leaders. *Reinventing Strategy* offers a proven process for doing just that. It is a wonderful mix of theory and practice, plus commonsense reasoning that works—for all the right reasons.

Willie Pietersen's background makes him an ideal guide to this new process. He is both a gifted teacher and a practitioner—a professor of the practice of management at Columbia Business School with decades of experience at the helm of global companies. Think of Willie Pietersen as a player-coach. Having played the game of business at the big-league level, he has the respect of current players and understands the realities they face each day. Thus, *Reinventing Strategy* has the feel of a coach's notebook, an energizing guide to the creation and implementation of winning strategies—not just once, but repeatedly.

I got to know Willie Pietersen at a time of intense pressure for both of us. Willie was the chairman of the board of trustees of IFTF, while I was leading the largest research program at the Institute. An emergency forced the then-president of the Institute to leave us abruptly. I was the only easy choice for his replacement, but at first I was not enthusiastic about being president. During the accelerated search process that followed and the first months after I accepted the presidency of IFTF, I *really* got to know Willie as well as the principles of Strategic Learning he presents in this book.

I learned that Willie is guided by principles. I once called him for advice about a sticky issue involving confidential information concerning two competing companies that were both clients of IFTF. Willie helped us articulate the issues, reminded us of the bedrock principles involved, and guided us in the process of learning how to draw the line between competitors clearly and fairly—without sacrificing the business interests of any party involved.

Perhaps the most valuable lesson I've learned from working with Willie Pietersen has to do with the crucial importance of insight. At IFTF, we focus on *foresight*—the art of forecasting the always uncertain future. Willie Pietersen is all about translating foresight into *insight*—understanding today's business environment better and faster than competitors, so as to gain a crucial strategic edge. Most important, Willie has created a practical process to turn insights into *action*.

Reinventing Strategy is an insights-to-action guidebook, leavened with engaging, revealing stories drawn from real-life companies in many industries that vividly illustrate key concepts. In its pages, Willie Pietersen will teach you how to learn, focus, align, and execute—the essential steps in his Strategic Learning process. Today, more and more global companies are discovering the power of Strategic Learning, both through Willie's own coaching and through its important role in Columbia Business School's executive education programs, which were recently ranked number one in the world for the second consecutive year by the prestigious *Financial Times* of London.

No matter what kind of organization you are in, *Reinventing Strategy* will coach you to develop your own insights and then transform those insights into action—again and again, as our ever-changing world demands.

BOB JOHANSEN
President, Institute for the Future
Menlo Park and San Francisco
August 2001

PROLOGUE

The New Leadership Challenge

The September 2001 terrorist attacks on New York and Washington and the unsettling world events that followed them have profoundly changed the context in which leaders must lead. In a seismic shift, many of the things we took for granted—the seeming certainties on which we once relied—were drastically undermined. Our personal security, many of our freedoms, our confidence in the continuity of our way of life—all were apparently shattered.

This new sense of dislocation has caused people everywhere to pause and search for fresh answers to life's big questions: What do I stand for? What is really important? How should I live my life? There is a new desire to get in touch with the spiritual dimensions of life, to rediscover community and values, and to make a commitment to what really matters.

As we examine the implications for leadership, one important aspect now looms much larger than before. More than at any time in the recent past, people are seeking meaning in what they do. To respond to this quest calls for a high order of leadership, one that is able to engage people's hearts and minds, offering them a sense of purpose in the work they do. Leaders of organizations must be able to create meaning if they hope to energize their people.

This book is anchored in the reality that leaders cannot live by strategy alone. In today's environment, it is strategy and leadership working hand in hand that will make organizations great. The Strategic Learning process is offered as a holistic, practical method for integrating and mobilizing these two vital and interdependent elements. Now that the leadership dimension has become more important than ever, I hope that the leadership principles and tools offered in this book will be of real value to all those who are called upon to lead.

These testing times have also given us new role models to emulate. Perhaps the most notable leader to emerge from the tragedy has been Rudolph Giuliani, then the mayor of New York City. Within hours of the attack, Giuliani provided a vision of hope as he stood amid the dust and rubble at Ground Zero. "New York," he said, "will not only recover, but will rise up to become even greater than before. We owe this to those who died, so that they will not have sacrificed their lives in vain." Amidst the shock, anguish, anger, and confusion of millions, he provided meaning for the huge task that lay ahead. In subsequent weeks, he was constantly visible and engaged, organizing, inspiring, communicating, and empathizing, even while showing the essential qualities of toughness and resolve.

Rudy Giuliani was faced with a momentous leadership challenge and rose magnificently to the occasion. Where did the inner resources to meet the challenge come from? Did they just appear out of the blue? Of course not. We know that life doesn't work that way. When we are tested, our response springs from the foundations we have established over a lifetime of learning and applying that learning, which defines who we are and what we stand for.

This, I believe, is the most important lesson of all: that leadership is a lifelong journey, calling upon the best of the human mind, will, and spirit. Whether the challenges we face are as stark as those confronted by our national leaders in the wake of terrorist violence or as subtle as those involved in directing the daily decisions of a growing business, we owe it to those who depend on us to bring all our strength and wisdom to the task. In some small measure, I hope this book will be of help.

INTRODUCTION

A Journey
of Discovery

A New Game

When I was a globe-trotting CEO, I wrestled with a common dilemma—how to spend more time with my kids, Chris and Sally. I developed a weekly ritual with Sally, then eight years old. Every Saturday morning, we'd sit down to play a game of checkers. It was our quality time together. Sally was a rather good player for such a small child, and she wouldn't tolerate my attempts to help her with an extra checker or two; she wanted to win on her own skill. But she never quite managed to beat me.

Then early one Saturday morning she dragged me out of bed to play a new game. I was jet-lagged after a long trip, but happy to play with her. Sally's new game was a Nintendo video soccer game, and within minutes she had vanquished me. Her peals of triumphant laughter filled the house. Chagrined, I tried my hand at the new game again, and then again, but she beat me every time. In fact, I was never able to beat Sally at video soccer.

I share this story because it neatly encapsulates a powerful lesson for all of us, one that's as true for organizations as it is for individuals. No matter our age or background, *we are all born in one era and must learn to adapt to another.*

From One-Time Change to Continuous Adaptation

We often hear that the central challenge facing business leaders today is "the need for change." In fact, this idea has been repeated so often that it has become accepted as a truism. But it's only half true. And a half-truth, like a little learning, is a dangerous thing.

The problem with this idea is that it strongly implies that change is a *one-time* event; that a company only needs to go from point A to point B in order to succeed. This A-to-B approach is at the core of traditional strategy, but in today's economy it is potentially lethal for corporations. One-time, A-to-B change will only get you stuck in a new rut, and in the meantime the market will roar ahead and leave you behind. As the American humorist Will Rogers used to say, "Even if you're on the right track, you'll get run over if you just sit there."

Instead, change must never stop. In today's global, fast-changing economy, companies must keep making the leap—to adapt from checkers to video games to Web-based adventure games and to whatever games will succeed these—over and over again. Because the environment in which we operate is continuously changing, we must respond by continuously innovating and adapting to it. Thus, the central challenge facing managers today is to *create and lead an adaptive enterprise*—an organization with the built-in ability to sense and rapidly adjust to change on a continuous basis.

Indeed, one of the biggest headaches facing executives is the struggle to *repeatedly* mobilize their companies behind new ideas. This is a much harder task than one-time change. Sustainable competitive advantage cannot come from any particular product or service, no matter how good it may be. Those things have a short shelf life. In today's marketplace it is the *organizational capability to adapt* that is the only sustainable competitive advantage.

The twenty-first century's global, networked economy confronts all organizations with disruptive technologies, high levels of uncertainty, and a demand for insight, speed, and innovation. This has created a near-revolution in the way successful companies are run, and it presents managers with both opportunity and peril. The following statistics (adapted from *Creative Destruction* by Richard Foster and Sarah Kaplan) provide a call to action:

▼ By 1987, 61 of the companies listed in the original Forbes 100 in 1917 had ceased to exist. Of the remaining 39, only 18 had managed to stay in the top 100.

▼ In the 1920s and 1930s, the turnover rate of the S&P 90 (the original Standard & Poor's list of major U.S. companies) averaged about 1.5 percent per year. Thus, a new member of the S&P 90 list could expect to remain on the list, on average, for over 65 years.

▼ In 1998, the turnover rate in the S&P 500 was close to 10 percent, implying an average lifetime on that list of only 10 years.

▼ Of the five hundred companies originally making up the S&P 500 in 1957, only 74 remained on the list through 1997.

While a few fast-moving entrepreneurs like Jeff Bezos at Amazon.com, Scott McNealy of Sun Microsystems, and Steve Case at AOL Time Warner have been quick to exploit the environmental shifts that have been fatal to others, many large, established companies find themselves bewildered by the speed and complexity of today's marketplace.

This book is written for all kinds of businesspeople, but it is particularly aimed at managers in large, established companies who are trying to compete in the new economy. For these managers, I want to offer this thought: In today's turbulent environment there is no more powerful tool for the development of winning business strategies than superior insight. And to achieve such insight and use it to create and implement breakthrough strategies again and again, a company must have a practical and proven process.

Consider this analogy. Over a century ago, industry was being revolutionized by the advent of systematic research and development (R&D). Beginning with Thomas Edison, who founded the first industrial research lab in Menlo Park, New Jersey, in 1876, and continuing with such German firms as I. G. Farben, the development of new technologies was taken out of the realm of serendipity and made into a deliberate focus of time, effort, and resources. "As a result, technical advances no longer happened randomly but could be systematically planned," economist Lester Thurow has noted. "In the twentieth century, economic leadership would become a matter of systematic investment in R&D to deliberately invent new technologies."

In the same way, strategic innovation is too important to be left to chance, or to random, ad hoc initiatives. Just as companies invest in R&D processes to deliberately spur *technical* innovation, we need a systematic process to mobilize *strategic* innovation.

Henry R. Luce, the entrepreneurial founder of the great Time Inc. media empire, once remarked, "Business more than any other occupation is a continual dealing with the future." Strategy—either implicit or explicit—is the means by which companies create that future. Unfortunately, the traditional ways of developing strategy no longer work. Based on a static planning model, they are hopelessly out-of-date in a world characterized more by shifts and discontinuities than by predictable patterns. We need to reinvent strategy as a process to generate *continuous renewal* in times of constant change.

This book offers a set of operating principles and a leadership process aimed at accomplishing this, which I call Strategic Learning. It is designed to provide a practical way to transform staid, established organizations into fleet, adaptive ones.

Strategic Learning has four key steps—*learn, focus, align,* and *execute*—which form a self-reinforcing cycle that combines learning, strategy, and leadership into one organic process. This cycle is designed to produce specific outputs: to generate insights, create focus, and translate focus into action, and then to repeat the cycle of transformation again and again. In its entirety, it offers a new way of leading companies.

In writing this book, I have set out to combine my experience as a CEO of multibillion-dollar businesses with the academic theory I've studied and taught at the Graduate School of Business of Columbia University and what I've learned in observing and working with businesses from a wide range of industries. The concept of Strategic Learning has deep intellectual roots that originate in work done by scholars in learning theory, strategy, systems thinking, and organizational behavior. I have attempted to integrate and build on the best of this thinking.

I believe that two features distinguish Strategic Learning from other approaches. First, it aims to pull all the elements of strategy creation and implementation together into a unified leadership process. Second, its purpose is to go beyond the rhetoric and provide a set of tools for creating breakthrough strategies on an ongoing basis. Above all, this is a *practical* book.

The Need for Practical Tools

There is a real hunger among businesspeople for tools that will help them transform their organizations. Unfortunately, much of the business literature offers advice on what companies should do without explaining *how* to go about doing it.

I recently bought a management book in an airport shop, hoping to glean a few keen insights while en route to my next meeting. The book had an attractive cover and was filled with provocative thoughts, but after reading it I was left feeling empty. The advice it gave—couched in clichés such as "think out of the box" and "move out of your comfort zone"—was too vague to be of any use in the real world. What, I wondered, is a manager supposed to do with these ideas when arriving at the office on Monday morning—run down the hall shouting, "You've got to think out of the box!"? I don't see how that can help anyone.

The point is not that the advice in the book was wrong. In one sense, it was completely correct. No one could argue with "thinking out of the box" and "moving out of your comfort zone" as necessary actions for companies seeking breakthrough strategies. The problem is that we've heard this advice a hundred times and have little to show for it. What's missing is the *How*: *How* are we to learn to think out of the box, act creatively, transform our companies, and so on? This is the void that Strategic Learning seeks to fill.

In 1997, Arie de Geus, a one-time Shell Oil strategy guru and author of *The Living Company*, gave us the germ of a great idea: In the future, "the ability to learn faster than competitors may be the only sustainable competitive advantage."

This was an arresting thought, but perhaps it didn't go far enough. Learning for learning's sake—which is where this idea might lead us—will not provide a sustainable edge. The real challenge is to learn *strategically*, to build an organization that continuously learns new things and translates them into *breakthrough strategies*.

Strategic Learning has been offered in numerous executive programs by Columbia Business School and in many workshops I've conducted with executive teams. It has been taught and applied at companies like Ericsson, SAP, Sony Corporation, Deloitte Touche Tohmatsu, Chubb Insurance, Henry Schein, Inc., CGNU, ASEA Brown Boveri (ABB), Sun Microsystems, and Progress Energy. The Sony Corporation credits Strategic Learning with turning around a loss-making division, its Sony Media Solutions Company. And many other organizations—from the Institute for the Future, a research-based think tank in Menlo Park, California (where I am chairman) to a nonprofit youth orchestra, an urban housing program, and a Florida drug-rehabilitation project—have applied it to their own specific needs.

The process has also shown itself to be a valuable framework for personal growth and leadership development, as I discuss at some length in Chapter 11, "Strategic Learning as a Path to Personal Growth."

Thus, Strategic Learning is proving to be a powerful tool not only for creating winning business strategies but also for developing personal leadership effectiveness. I don't claim for a moment that it is a silver bullet or an instant strategy-in-a-box. As we all know, those things don't exist. Strategic Learning is not a mechanical ritual but a leadership process based on a set of fundamental principles. In the end, it is the quality of leadership that determines its effectiveness.

From the Front Lines to the Classroom

One day early in my teaching career at Columbia, I stood in front of a large class of high-powered senior executives. A few minutes into my lecture, as I was explaining the need for knowledge sharing in companies, a stubby finger at the end of a hairy arm shot out at me in challenge. "But that's *not new*!" a voice boomed across the classroom.

Fifty pairs of eyes swiveled down at me in the teacher's pit, as if to ask: "What do you say to *that*, Mr. Professor?"

I spluttered out a vague answer, and was able to keep the class moving along, but the stubby finger and booming voice lingered with me.

To this day, I am grateful for that executive's challenge, because it forced me to clarify my own thinking. Now, when someone in a class says, "That's not new," my answer is: "Our issue here is not *what's new*. It's *what's important*."

The biggest decisions we make in business, and in life, are identifying what's important. We tend to assume that old thinking is somehow bad and new thinking is axiomatically good. But this assumption is false. It's a cop-out from critical thought, and it can be a dangerous trap. While some new thinking provides real breakthroughs, much of it represents old ideas dressed up as new, or is simply faddish. Many of the lessons that have withstood the test of time, however, are eternal truths that can be applied to many different situations. This book aims to critically examine both the old and the new in the light of today's challenges and to offer a view on what's important.

My own sense of what's important has been shaped by 20 years as a CEO and my current work as a professor, researcher, and corporate coach. This wonderfully rich combination of learning experiences has enabled me to pursue the quest that we all share—trying to discover what works, what doesn't, and why. From this fertile mix of practice and theory has grown the Strategic Learning process, and the book you hold in your hands.

Reinventing Strategy is full of case studies and examples taken from the real world. Some are based on my own experiences as a

CEO or on situations faced by companies I work with. Where necessary, I've disguised or fictionalized details out of respect for my clients' confidentiality. The stories, however, are essentially true, and the lessons they teach are absolutely valid. I hope they'll help you understand the power of Strategic Learning for generating insights and breakthrough strategies as a source of ongoing renewal—both for your organization and for yourself.

The New Playing Field

Running a business today is harder than ever before. Why? Because of the speed and complexity of change in the so-called new economy. By "new economy," I don't simply mean the high-tech sector or the dot-com bubble; the phrase has taken on a much wider meaning than that. It refers to the new rules of competition and how they are affecting everyone, everywhere. Indeed, the most profound effects of the new economy are being felt in large, well-established, old-economy businesses.

To succeed in the new economy there are three questions every business leader must be able to answer.

The Three Leadership Questions in the New Economy

1. *What is the environment in which our organization must compete and win?* What are the underlying forces that are driving our industry in the new economy? We need to understand the environment in which leaders must lead. Until we

have achieved insights into these shifts, we cannot answer the next question.

2. *What are those few things our organization must do outstandingly well to win and go on winning in this environment?* Have the rules of effective leadership changed in the new economy? What are the key things that leaders must do to drive success in their organizations?

3. *How will we mobilize our organization to implement these things faster and better than our competitors?* Knowing *what* to do is important, but that will never be enough to put you in front. To win, you must also know *how* to do it. You must be able to move beyond the rhetoric and actually implement your strategy. As Henry Ford put it, "You can't build a reputation on what you're *going* to do."

This book aims to answer all three of these questions. Let's begin with the first question: What is happening in today's business environment?

It is a leader's first duty to understand the field the company is playing on. Obvious? Maybe. But many executives simply throw up their hands and say, "The market is complex and changing fast," and leave it at that. That's not good enough. One of the most important roles of today's business leader is to be *chief sense maker* for his or her organization—the person to whom others look for a clear understanding of the competitive environment on which a sound winning strategy can be based.

To create a winning strategy, we must understand better than our competitors the forces driving the new economy, how they affect us, and how we can use them to our advantage. Doing this is the first stage of Strategic Learning—an insight-generating process called the situation analysis (see Chapter 5). To gain such insights, every company will have to scan and interpret its particular environment. There are, however, a number of universal forces—such as the Internet, globalization, deregulation and privatization, convergence, and disintermediation—that are radically altering the way *all* business is conducted today (see Figure 1.1).

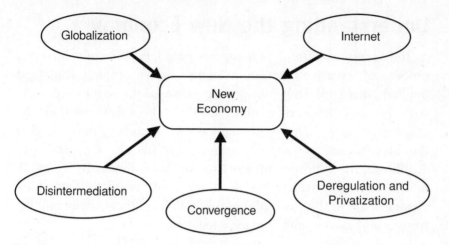

Figure 1.1   Five Discontinuities Are Shaping the New Economy

While each of these forces is distinct, they all interact with one another. Consider the Internet and globalization, the two most powerful forces of change at work today: The Internet connects people and promotes globalization, while globalization of the marketplace pushes people to connect and do business via the Internet. When we step back to consider these major discontinuities as parts of a larger, epochal transition, then we begin to understand how they affect our businesses and what we must do about it.

"New economy" has become a nearly ubiquitous buzzword. While buzzwords can help us get a quick handle on things, they can also become a crutch, a substitute for real thought. In the pages that follow, I attempt to define the significance of the new economy by explaining the nature of the changes taking place around the world at the dawn of the twenty-first century. Rather than offering a long, bland description of these forces—forces that you are probably aware of—I have tried to distill the chief *consequences* of what we call the new economy and how the changes underway have altered the rules of competition. Only with this understanding can business leaders understand and meet the challenges they now face.

Understanding the New Economy

As the economist Joseph Schumpeter noted, capitalism is largely a process of "creative destruction": One era creates new tools and methods that supersede and destroy those of the previous era. As with the agricultural revolution and the industrial revolution, the changes being wrought by the new economy today—most notably the Internet—are not simply extensions of the old ways; they are significant, revolutionary breaks from the past. Today we are in the information age, which has seen the most rapid and complex change of all. At the dawn of the twenty-first century, we are moving from asset-based to knowledge-based competition.

Sense Making in the Information Age

Knowledge is power, the old saying goes. But in the so-called information age, the distinction between true *knowledge* and mere *information* has become more important than ever before.

Thanks to modern technologies such as the digital computer, electronic communications, and especially the Internet, information has become a commodity, and a cheap one at that. As the world becomes networked, mere facts are now more mobile than ever before—they can come *from* anywhere and go *to* anywhere almost instantaneously. The result is that information is becoming an abundant, cheap, and rapidly transferable commodity.

But despite the flood of information in which we are all daily immersed, true knowledge is as rare and valuable as ever—perhaps more so. Knowledge makes distinctions among kinds of information, winnowing the valuable, practical, and important from the useless, unnecessary, and insignificant. In an age when everyone has instant access to infinite information, sense making—the ability to turn floods of information into real knowledge—has become today's scarcest and most valuable resource and the key leverage point for value creation.

A company's primary source of wealth is therefore derived from its insights, knowledge, and ideas. Its success depends on how it leverages its intellectual capital. But leveraging intellect is quite different from leveraging assets, and the business world is still coming to terms with what that means.

Power Shift

For the majority of executives I come in contact with, the Internet is the big question today—a huge, knotty issue that many feel they are not properly addressing. On the one hand, the Internet is simply a tool; it happens to be a very fast means of distributing information—from one desk to the next, or across town, or around the world. On the other hand, the Internet ruthlessly squeezes out inefficiency. Indeed, the Internet is shaking up entire business categories, forcing companies to reinvent themselves and enabling ordinary individuals to accomplish extraordinary tasks.

The Internet is a double-edged sword. It has shifted the balance of power from sellers to buyers, even as it has given sellers better tools to find and serve buyers. One result is that buyers now have a much wider range of choices and lower switching costs than ever before, which has created a fiercely competitive environment, one in which innovation is the key to success.

The most revolutionary aspect of the Internet is that it gives virtually everybody access to the same information. It is this transparency that has caused the shift in power from sellers to buyers—a massive, revolutionary change, which puts a premium on knowledge-based services rather than on products.

This power shift is upending many established relationships. Consider the balance of power between doctor and patient, for example. Traditionally, doctors have been the keepers of specialized knowledge (a form of power), while patients have been their supplicants. Today, however, patients can research their conditions on the Internet, learn about possible treatments, and scour multiple web sites for resources; when they arrive at their doctors' offices, they may know more about what ails them than their doctors do. This puts pressure on doctors to provide extra service in order to retain their patients.

The Internet has also afforded producers much better tools to find and serve customers. Indeed, a number of traditional companies have used the Internet to reinvent themselves and make their core competencies the best in the world. Perhaps the best example of this is General Electric. Traditionally a paradigm of the old, asset-based economy, GE is now a leader in the information age. Under former CEO Jack Welch, the company reconceived itself as a "learning laboratory" that uses the Internet to provide efficient products and services to its customers.

When GE sold a jet engine in the old days, it would sign its client up for a maintenance program that produced a steady annuity. Today, GE Engine Services offers customers like Southwest Airlines "power by the hour," an online service that monitors engine performance in flight and tracks all maintenance and repair data in real time. Customers use GE Aircraft's Customer Web Center to purchase spare parts and to access technical publications and warranty records. Airlines also gain access to online remote diagnostic systems that allow GE engineers to pinpoint engine problems from thousands of miles away without having to make on-site visits. "That's an information-based service as much as a product," Welch told *Fortune* magazine. "I think it's a better game."

Although some old-economy stalwarts might like to think that the dot-com shakeout of the past two years signals an end for the new economy, in fact the new economy is still in its infancy. Historically, new technologies have always spawned cycles of rapid experimentation led by start-up players, followed by periods of absorption by those mainstream firms that survive the discontinuity. As GE's ongoing reinvention suggests, the Internet is no longer a business fad reserved for entrepreneurs. It is a massive enabler, every bit as profound in its effects as the introduction of electrical power was around the turn of the last century.

Margin Squeeze

The unprecedented efficiency of the Internet is driving down purchasing costs for all kinds of goods and services. This is true in both consumer and B2B (business-to-business) markets. For an example of the former, consider CNET, the Web-based service that offers instantaneous price comparisons among hundreds of suppliers of computers, cameras, stereo equipment, and other high-tech products. The effect is to make it extremely hard to compete for business in these categories unless you're willing to match the lowest price in the market.

Similar processes are at work in the B2B arena. Companies in almost every business are using the Internet to connect themselves closely with suppliers around the world, making it fast and easy to buy raw materials, machine parts, or manufactured equipment in just the amounts needed at the lowest possible cost. The effect is the same: to drive prices down to rock-bottom levels.

The inevitable result is a margin squeeze that is steadily moving up the supply chain. The personal computer (PC) maker that is forced to sell its products at bare-bones prices can do so only by demanding the lowest possible prices from its suppliers—chip makers, fabricators of plastic cases and electrical wiring, makers of cardboard shipping cartons, and so on. These companies, in turn, must maximize their own efficiencies while putting the squeeze on those who supply them with raw materials, manufacturing services, and so forth. Little by little, excess costs are being wrung out of the entire system. Thus, sellers seldom get to keep the benefits of the lower costs; they must be passed on to buyers in the form of lower prices if the sellers hope to remain in the game.

The first challenge for any company doing business in this merciless environment: to improve your own efficiencies fast enough to maintain your profit margins—and to keep from being squeezed to death. But such improvement alone merely allows you to remain in the game. You'll never save your way to success. To win, you must go beyond cost cutting to produce genuine strategic innovation that creates new and better ways of serving customers.

The Resurgence of Brands

As a result of these forces, the battle for the customer has grown much more intense. The big question in customers' minds is: *Whom do I trust?* The broad array of choices on the Internet can be liberating, but it can also be confusing, and increasingly customers are looking for guidance.

One consequence of this that some may find surprising is a resurgence in the importance of brands. Robert Reich, the former secretary of labor, points out in his book *The Future of Success* that the "distribution oligopolies" that dominated the first half of the twentieth century are now giving way to what he calls "oligopolies of trustworthiness." In the twenty-first century, superbrands like Walt Disney are becoming our guides to what is good and trustworthy for a wide range of products and services. Such companies are increasingly filling the role of knowledge brokers for consumer audiences. They can prescreen information for us; they can function as a catalog or a showroom; they can subcontract, or forge partnerships with others in the value chain. Many consider Disney, for example, their trusted guide to all sorts of family entertainment, not all of which it directly produces or controls.

Multichannel Marketplaces

As an instantaneous, incredibly flexible medium for interactive communication, the Internet is opening up new channels for sales, marketing, and customer service. Consequently, distribution networks in industry after industry are being reshaped. In many industries, the challenge will be to move from a single-channel to a multichannel approach. Hence, the rush to launch online sales and marketing venues to complement traditional retail outlets—the so-called "clicks and bricks" strategy.

But here's the rub: To remain competitive today while also preparing for tomorrow, it's not simply a question of getting out of one strategy and into another. Rather, you must decide how to maintain your *existing* business, your "installed base"—the existing customers, revenue stream, technological competencies, and other assets you've built up over the years that are still profitable but becoming obsolete—long enough to buy the time needed to adapt to a *new* model at the same time. Sometimes, it's simply not possible to maintain your existing business indefinitely; the challenge then becomes to maintain your overall profit stream and avoid sudden collapse. This is a tricky balance, one that Harvard's Clayton M. Christensen has dubbed "the innovator's dilemma."

Avon Products, Inc., for example, is the largest direct seller of beauty products in the world: 98 percent of its revenue comes from the sale of lipsticks, perfumes, and powders by the famous "Avon ladies" directly to women. Today, however, that business model—which has been successful since 1886—is in the midst of its own makeover.

The Avon Lady Goes Online

When she was named Avon's CEO in 1999, Andrea Jung faced a classic reinvention dilemma. In the United States, Avon's growth was flat, and niche players were nibbling away its market share. Sephora, the French-based firm whose huge stores selling an enormous array of cosmetics and fragrances had successfully imported the "category-killer" concept into beauty retailing, had launched an invasion of the U.S. market. Furthermore, given that three-quarters of American women now work outside the home, Avon's door-to-door sales model was in danger of becoming obsolete. Jung's dilemma was: How could Avon develop new sales channels without alienating its famous sales representatives, the Avon ladies, and undermining its existing sources of revenue?

But it was the advent of the Internet and the development of e-tailing that posed the most direct challenge ever to Avon's traditional direct model. After all, the Internet made possible a variety of direct-to-consumer sales interactions that were even more flexible, customized, and immediate than those practiced by the Avon ladies. For example, the Internet is available 24 hours a day and can be accessed in the evening by a busy homemaker or during a coffee break by a deskbound female executive. As other beauty-products companies established footholds on the World Wide Web, it was increasingly obvious that Avon couldn't afford to ignore this new marketplace.

Understandably, the Avon ladies felt threatened by the Internet, fearing that an Avon e-strategy could hurt their livelihoods. In 1997, the company had launched a bare-bones web site that offered only a limited number of products—for fear of upsetting its sales force. This fear was well founded: Even innocuous acts, like printing "www.avon.com" on product brochures, were met with great hostility; many Avon ladies simply covered that label over with their own stickers. Meanwhile, Avon's Internet policy prohibited the sales reps from setting up their own web sites, and many of them quit in frustration.

Others in the cosmetics industry had embraced e-tailing. By 1999, when Andrea Jung was named CEO, it was clear that Avon's head-in-the-sand approach to the Internet could continue no longer.

In a speech given to industry analysts in December 1999, Jung acknowledged the new realities. While door-to-door sales will "continue to be a very relevant mode of buying beauty and related products for women around the world," she said, the company must also create a new business model—one "with the potential to appeal to a much broader consumer base in a broader range of distribution channels." In other words: Avon had no choice but to adopt a multi-channel approach.

Jung outlined a best-of-both-worlds strategy designed to grow Avon's customer base without disenfranchising its field reps. From now on, she said, Avon products would be distributed through five channels: through its three million Avon ladies in 137 countries; through middle-market retailers, such as JCPenney; through mall kiosks franchised to local Avon representatives; through chic, company-owned Avon Centers; and through the company web site, Avon.com.

"No one has the direct-to-the-consumer relationships that we have with tens of millions of women in the United States through our sales representatives," Jung said. "We intend to leverage that unique competitive advantage in bold new ways using Internet technology."

Jung quickly earmarked $60 million over three years to build a new Internet site to provide a direct sales channel for Avon's full product line, while at the same time moving to help the Avon ladies sell online through personalized web pages developed in partnership with the company. For $15 a month, any rep can become what Avon calls an "eRepresentative" who can sell online and earn commissions ranging from 20 percent to 25 percent for orders shipped direct or 30 percent to 50 percent for orders they hand deliver. Indeed, the new Avon web site allows eRepresentatives to conduct all aspects of their business online, including customer prospecting, ordering, getting account status, and making payments. The site even has a message board where reps can exchange selling tips.

The jury is still out on the ultimate success of Jung's initiatives, but she has shown enormous courage in placing her bets. In just the first five days of Avon's e-commerce initiative, 12,000 Avon reps had created personal web pages. Currently 20 percent of product orders are input online by eRepresentatives. The 2002 target is 35 percent.

So don't be surprised if the familiar *"Ding-dong . . . Avon calling"* is soon replaced by a new Avon greeting from your computer: "You've got mail!"

What Andrea Jung has created is not necessarily a perfect or lasting solution, but it is a bold and intelligent response to the new realities of the marketplace, one that adapts to the forces of the new economy and allows Avon to learn its way to success.

Likewise, to remain competitive in the new economy, every company must formulate a well-thought-out response to the Internet. But don't wait until you've figured out a perfect solution. The key is to make a start. Only then can the real learning begin.

Disintermediation

Certain businesses are more vulnerable than others. In the past, intermediaries like insurance brokers or travel agents helped clients get the goods and services they needed. Today, many of these niche players are being "disintermediated"—squeezed out of the game—by the harsh new efficiencies created by the Internet. As the distance between producers and consumers is shrinking, highly specialized experts are emerging as the new intermediaries. These "reintermediaries" are helping people conduct business more efficiently while adding value through knowledge services.

With the advent of cheap online ticket sales, for example, travel agencies can no longer survive as mere ticket brokers: They must now provide extra value to make their services worth paying for. The smartest have begun to do this by arranging scholarly tours, providing unusual access to remote regions, or organizing groups of people with specialized interests—things that typical tourists wouldn't have access to if they were buying a cheap flight to London from Virgin.com.

From Products to Services

As customers become empowered by the access to information, and suppliers sell directly to customers, we're seeing a shift from products to services, and from simple services to superservices. To understand this shift, consider the dilemma of a medical-supplies company that I'll call Med-Surg Supply Corporation.

Retooling Med-Surg

Med-Surg is a billion-dollar medical supplies distributor based in the Southwestern United States. For more than 30 years, the company has been highly successful in selling basic medical and surgical supplies to dentists and doctors, but lately its profits have been dropping off. Why? First, some buyers have begun to bypass intermediaries like Med-Surg and buy directly from the manufacturers (Med-Surg's suppliers). Second, they are using the Internet to compare prices and handle transactions, which squeezes margins and emboldens customers to squeeze Med-Surg for better prices and value-added services.

But an even more fundamental threat is looming over Med-Surg. Sophisticated new entrants have used the Internet to offer doctors and dentists high-end value-added services—Internet-based office systems such as inventory control, scheduling, and office management. These high-end services, it turns out, are near the top of customers' hierarchy of needs, and are far more important than Med-Surg's low-end distribution of things like rolls of gauze, boxes of surgical masks, or tubes of ointment. Indeed, one of these companies that provides excellent high-end office services could enter the product distribution game (perhaps through an acquisition) and steal customers from Med-Surg by offering end-to-end solutions.

In short, the Internet has changed Med-Surg's world: It compels the company to be efficient in its internal operations to protect margins, while at the same time forcing it to retool its business from being solely a supplier of *products* to being also a supplier of Internet-based *services* (much as GE has done with its jet engines). This is a large transformational challenge. The good news is that Med-Surg has the technology to exploit the Internet. But it must also change its culture and the competencies of its sales force. Today the company is making good progress in its change efforts, even as the clock of marketplace transformation continues to tick.

The Networked Enterprise

Web-based outsourcing is creating a new business model: the networked enterprise able to work interactively with its suppliers, distributors, and service providers around the world, thus creating a finely tuned business ecosystem. This approach is much more dynamic and efficient than old-economy outsourcing, which kept vendors at arm's length. For example, a company like Nike, Inc. manufactures nothing: The Portland, Oregon–based athletic equipment company, which is the world's leading supplier of athletic shoes, creates brilliant design and highly effective marketing, then uses its computer networks to make design alterations with production partners around the globe, virtually in real time. Nike's 21,000 direct employees are supported by more than half a million indirect employees who work for Nike's manufacturing partners. And thanks to its excellent supply-chain technology, the system is so tightly interconnected that Nike's partners are not simply contract outsourcers—they are an integral, vital part of its business.

Convergence

In the new economy, traditional industry boundaries are disappearing. The days when distinct borders existed between products or between industries—say telephones, television sets, computers, consumer electronics, media and entertainment—are long gone. You may find yourself competing against new rivals from disparate fields bringing unique skills or products into your arena. Everyone is facing this dilemma, and it's becoming much more unrealistic to go it alone. This has led to some innovative new strategies.

For example, Cisco Systems—the leading producer of Internet networking gear—grew throughout the late 1990s using a simple but powerful acquisition strategy: It created some of its new technologies in-house, but it also routinely made 15 to 20 acquisitions a year, typically of small, pre-IPO start-up companies that were developing promising technologies. (As I write, Cisco is scrambling to adapt that strategy to a new environment of diminished stock valuations and a slower-growth economy. Will it succeed? The smart money isn't betting against Cisco.)

To keep your hand in the game, you may have to jump into someone else's business, buy an existing segment leader, or form a joint venture with an active player. Or you'll simply have to learn to compete against your new rivals, who, left unattended, will nibble away at your business with all the relentlessness of piranha. Indeed, a new chess game is emerging. Companies that compete *against* each other are also forging partnerships or joint ventures together. It's a complicated game, as Encyclopædia Britannica, Inc. learned the hard way.

Fatal Convergence

The *Encyclopædia Britannica* was first published in 1768, and by 1989 its sales reached an all-time high of $627 million. But since then, sales of the distinctive multivolume set have plummeted 80 percent. What happened? In short: convergence. A new product was introduced by an indirect rival, which stole the encyclopedia business away from Britannica.

The product was the CD-ROM, which could hold an entire set of encyclopedias on one small, flat, relatively inexpensive disk. At first, Britannica didn't take this new technology seriously. After all, its indirect competitor—Microsoft's Encarta—used inferior text licensed from Funk & Wagnalls, poor illustrations, and low-quality sound recordings. The leaders of Britannica were unimpressed. How could a computer software company hope to compete in a knowledge-based product arena against one of the world's oldest and most respected reference book publishers?

Nonetheless, the Encarta Encyclopedia proved to be an enormous hit. The convenience, low cost, and speed of access of the CD-ROM product outweighed its content weaknesses, and Microsoft's enormous marketing clout ensured that hundreds of thousands of copies of the Encarta would find their way onto the hard drives of students, families, and professionals around the world. Soon Britannica sales slumped—at first slightly, then massively.

Britannica responded slowly. To produce a competitive CD-ROM, Britannica realized it would have to cut its text from 40 million words to 7 million. To make matters worse, its vaunted sales force began to revolt against the loss of lucrative commissions. Britannica eventually produced its own CD-ROM, but by then it was too late. In 1996, the company was sold for $135 million, significantly *less* than its book value.

Globalization

Along with the Internet, the globalization of the marketplace is the major driver of the new economy. "Globalization," like "new economy," is an all-encompassing buzzword that means different things to different people, so we need to clarify what we mean by it. When you analyze it, it emerges that globalization has not one but three interrelated components—the globalization of markets, business functions, and knowledge, each of which has a different set of consequences.

First, there's the *globalization of markets*. Most executives tend to think of globalization in terms of massive geopolitical shifts—such as when the Russian, Eastern European, and Chinese markets suddenly opened to the West in the 1990s, or the gradual dropping of trade barriers throughout the European Union and among the American members of the North American Free Trade Agreement (NAFTA). The world is now open for business to an unprecedented degree. This aspect of globalization creates great opportunities to enter new markets and increase volume.

Second, there is the *globalization of business functions*. The opportunity to consolidate worldwide R&D, procurement, manufacturing, and information systems, for example—while maintaining local responsiveness—can create great new global efficiencies.

Third and most significant, there is the *globalization of knowledge*, which puts a premium on global best practices. Caused by today's unfettered mobility of ideas, this has produced the most profound changes of all.

The Death of Local Competition

Today, virtually every business in every part of the world—from the local pizzeria to DaimlerChrysler, or even the rogue oil barons of Iraq—is part of the global economy. Ideas now come from literally anywhere, at any time, from any messenger. The result is a stunning new reality: *Local competition is extinct.*

This may sound like an overly bold or simplistic statement. But the truth is that one of the greatest mistakes a company can make is to ignore the fact that local competition has gone the way of the dodo bird and will never come back. *All* competition is global. If there is a better idea for your business anywhere else in the world it will eventually come into your market, whether you use it first or someone else does.

"I'm not worried about the Taiwanese coming to Cincinnati," a client once said to me. Mark ran an air-conditioning manufacturing business in Cincinnati, and I had been trying to explain why he needed to pay attention to global best practices.

"Okay, fair enough," I said. "You know more about the intricacies of the air-conditioning business than I do. Maybe the Taiwanese have no interest in coming to Cincinnati. But who's your main competitor?"

"Jerry Etheridge. He's across town. We've been competing against each other for 20 years, and I know all his tricks. Nah, I'm not worried about Jerry."

"Does he like to travel?" I asked.

"Oh, yes. He and his wife Debbie take a trip every summer."

"Well, suppose Jerry Etheridge takes a trip to Taiwan, discovers a leading practice used there—such as a way to make his machines quieter and more fuel-efficient—brings it back to Cincinnati, and wipes you out. What then? The Taiwanese themselves don't have to come to Cincinnati. But if they have a better idea, sooner or later it *will* come here and compete against you. You can run from globalization, but you cannot hide."

Thus, companies are faced with the need to shift gears away from being the best locally to being the best globally, wherever they compete. The new game is global best practices, everywhere, all the time. The new cardinal sin is to allow a competitor to steal one of your best ideas and globalize it before you do. As a result, knowledge sharing is becoming the crucial new competency. Philosophically, globalization is more of an *idea* than a *place*.

As we've seen, in the new economy the rules of competition have changed not just for the dot-coms and high-tech players, but for everybody. All these changes call to mind the famous parable of the boiled frog, with which you may be familiar. According to this parable, the behavior of a frog is predictable: If you put a frog into hot water, it will jump out; but if you place it in a pot of cool water and heat it gradually, the frog will slowly grow accustomed to its surroundings, be lulled to sleep, and eventually will be boiled alive.

This may sound like a French culinary lesson, but it's much more. It's a way to explain that companies that grow complacent about change, especially incremental change in their surroundings, will end up as boiled frogs. Those who fail to interpret and respond to the changes swirling around them are at risk of being parboiled by the rising heat of the new economy.

The changes brought by the new economy can be summarized this way.

Eleven Hallmarks of the New Economy

1. Information has become a commodity. It is now sense making that has become the key lever for value creation.

2. The Internet gives buyers more information, wider choices, and lower switching costs. But it is a double-edged sword. While it has shifted power from sellers to buyers, it has also given sellers better tools to find and serve buyers.

3. The Internet is ruthlessly creating a more efficient supply chain, confronting many sellers with a margin squeeze.

4. The battle for customers is becoming more intense. This puts a premium on creativity and innovation, and means that brands are likely to grow in importance.

5. The single-channel business model is dying. Most marketplaces are becoming multichannel games.

6. Purely transactional intermediaries are disappearing.

7. Business models are shifting from products to services and from services to superservices.

8. Web-based outsourcing is creating a powerful new business model: the networked enterprise with the ability to orchestrate.

9. Industry boundaries are disappearing, producing greater complexity and dangerous new competitors for most companies.

10. Going it alone is becoming increasingly unrealistic. A new chess game is emerging that incorporates more partnerships, joint ventures, and other forms of alliances.

11. Local competition has become extinct.

The challenges of competing in the new economy have placed extraordinary pressures for change on companies of every kind. To develop an effective response, it is necessary to understand what these challenges mean at an organizational level. This is the central theme of the next chapter.

2

The Challenge of Change

"Shift Happens"

In explaining how change takes place in a rapidly evolving competitive environment, I like to tell a story drawn from sport: the evolution of high-jump techniques.

Leap to Greatness

Once upon a time in the early 1900s, a little boy (we'll call him Tommy) went to a track meet and was awed by the sight of high jumpers performing graceful leaps over a high bar. Tommy went home and told his parents that he wanted to become a high-jump champion. "All right," they replied, "but you'll have to practice!"

So Tommy found a track coach who taught him the scissors, the preferred jumping style of the day, and Tommy practiced it diligently every day for months. It never occurred to him that there might be some other way to get over the high bar. For Tommy, the scissors *was* high jump.

The boy did well at his new sport. He became one of the best jumpers at his school, and then one of the best in the county. But no sooner had he begun to win gold medals at state meets than the boy discovered that another competitor—call him Mike—was using a completely new technique, quite different from the scissors. It was called the Western roll. Using it, Mike was able to jump much higher than anyone else. At first this caused a tremendous uproar, and Tommy and the other jumpers cried "Foul!" But Mike walked away with the gold medal. "I haven't broken any rules," he observed. "I simply invented a new way of doing an old task. You're only complaining because I beat you."

Mike was right. After the meet, some of the other high jumpers were able to learn the Western roll, but Tommy was unable to adapt to a new way of doing things. He never quite mastered the Western roll, and within a couple of years his jumps were no longer among the highest. By the time Tommy was a college athlete, he was no longer good enough to compete.

Years passed. The Western roll ruled the world of high jump for a number of years, eventually giving way to a variant known as the straddle. But both of these were eventually supplanted by a new style of jumping that broke all the old records.

Richard Douglas Fosbury, a Seattle youth, began competing in the high jump while attending grade school in the 1950s. At first, he used the old-fashioned scissors method, which felt natural to him. However, his grade school and high school coaches worked hard to convert him to the straddle, which was by then the standard style used by the world's best jumpers. Fosbury dutifully practiced the straddle, but it never carried him higher than five feet, four inches—a mediocre performance at best.

Fosbury wasn't satisfied. Gradually, by trial and error, he began to develop an entirely new jumping technique, a weird-looking, backward twist that ultimately became known as the Fosbury flop.

Although the flop enabled Fosbury to jump well over the six-foot mark, the coaches he worked with during high school and college continued to urge him to master the classic straddle. Not until his sophomore year at Oregon State University did Fosbury forsake the straddle permanently for the flop. That year, he cleared the bar at 6 feet, 10 inches; a year later, he had become the most consistent seven-foot jumper in the nation.

Fosbury was still not considered a medal contender for the 1968 Mexico City Olympic Games. Most high-jump fans and coaches reacted to his radical style with amazement and, often, derision; as Fosbury recalls, the crowds would "mostly hoot and holler" when he performed his jumps. But at Mexico City, Dick Fosbury set a new Olympic record of 7 feet, $4^1/_2$ inches—an inch better than teammate Edward Caruthers had managed using the straddle. The revolutionary new jump had proven its worth (see Figure 2.1).

By the 1972 Olympics, many of the world's leading jumpers had adopted the Fosbury flop, as did all three medalists at the 1976 games. It has now been more than 20 years since the world high-jump record was held by a straddle jumper. What's more, the rate of improvement in high-jump performance has increased dramatically since the invention of the Fosbury flop. Between 1900 and 1960, the average annual increase in the world high-jump record was one-sixth of an inch. Since 1960, it has been one-third of an inch.

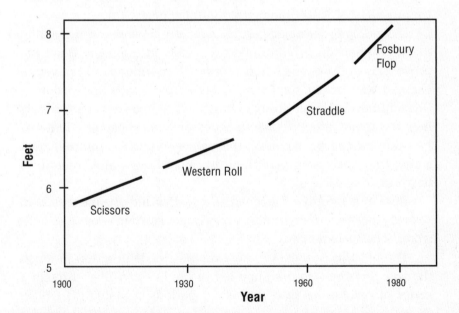

Figure 2.1 High-Jump Records

Today, the Fosbury flop still reigns as the premier high-jumping style. In fact, it has become the new orthodoxy, just as the scissors, the Western roll, and the straddle were in their day. But who would bet that we've seen the last innovation in the world of high jump?

Of course, this story isn't only about the high jump. It explains how progress takes place in *any* field of human endeavor. There are periods of stability, in which continuous, incremental improvements are made, that are periodically interrupted by disruptive, revolutionary changes in which major breakthroughs are accomplished.

This pattern of change is sometimes known as *punctuated equilibrium*. It's a term borrowed from the science of evolutionary biology—specifically, from the work of scientists Stephen Jay Gould and Niles Eldredge, who suggested in the early 1970s that evolutionary change in species tends to occur in just such a pattern. Personally, I prefer the pithy phrase coined by my friend Jerry Marlar, president of Sulzer Biologics: "Shift happens."

Indeed, long-term success in business depends on the ability to do two seemingly contradictory things at the same time: improve existing processes and products (continuous, incremental change) and invent totally new, better processes and products (discontinuous, breakthrough change). The latter is a particularly important, and difficult, task to accomplish. Companies will never become long-term winners through continuous improvement alone; they must also be willing to make large—and sometimes nerve-racking—leaps.

Research by Mike Tushman of the Harvard Business School strongly suggests that virtually every industry, from cement to software, behaves in this way.

The healthcare industry, for example, made progress in much the way that the scissors jump led to the Fosbury flop: through a series of revolutions interspersed by periods of stability. In 1900, the average life expectancy in the United States was 46.3 years for men and 48.3 for women; by 1997, those numbers had increased to

73.6 and 79.4. This transformation is the result of many incremental advances, but is primarily the result of two huge scientific break-throughs. The first was the establishment of basic standards for sanitation and hygiene in the early 1900s. The second was the invention of antibiotics like penicillin at the end of World War II. The next big advance—likely to increase our life spans to 150 years or more—will almost certainly come from the emerging sciences of biotechnology.

The watch industry provides a good example of punctuated equilibrium in action. For centuries, watches had been heavy, mechanical timepieces—intricate metal mechanisms made up of dozens of moving parts powered by a spring. Craftsmanship, beautiful ornamentation, and the prestige of particular brand names were keys to success in this industry, and they remained so for a long time. Now, however, lightweight, battery-driven quartz watches are the name of the game. This has posed a particular challenge for the Swiss, who are justly proud of their long history as among the best watchmakers in the world, and have had to struggle to keep up with the pace of change.

Hayek's Breakthrough

The first quartz watch prototypes were developed by a Swiss laboratory and exhibited at the Basel Watch Fair in 1967. These prototypes set a new standard for lightness and timekeeping accuracy, and were considered a significant breakthrough. And yet, even though a number of Swiss watchmakers embraced quartz technology, it was the Japanese and Americans who popularized—and profited—from it.

The Seiko Astron, the first quartz watch for consumers, appeared in Tokyo on Christmas Day, 1969. These watches had analog dials, were encased in 18-karat solid gold, and sold for 450,000 yen ($1,250), which was about the same price as a Toyota Corolla. By prevailing standards, they were also remarkably accurate—within three seconds per month.

In 1972, HMW Industries of Lancaster, Pennsylvania, introduced the Pulsar, the first all-electronic wristwatch. This "time computer" displayed the hours and minutes in flashing red LED (light-emitting diode) numbers rather than on a round analogue dial. Consumers snapped them up, but they were soon supplanted by LCD (liquid crystal display) watches. Then, in 1976 Texas Instruments (TI) shocked the world by introducing the first wristwatches priced at $20. Competitors began to match that price, and the following year TI cut its price to $9.95.

This brutal war over innovation and price had a devastating effect on the Swiss watch industry. Between the mid-1970s and 1983, Switzerland saw its share of the world's watch business shrink from 30 percent to 10 percent. Hundreds of proud, highly skilled craftspeople were put out of work, and the two largest Swiss watchmakers, SSIH and Asuag, went broke. By not pushing hard enough to exploit quartz technology, Swiss watchmakers had behaved like adherents to the Western roll: They were quickly rendered obsolete by the Japanese and American straddle jumpers.

But no competitive advantage lasts forever.

In the 1980s, a flamboyant Lebanese-born, Swiss-based engineer named Nicolas G. Hayek became the Dick Fosbury of the watch industry when he restructured the bankrupt SSIH and Asuag as SMH, which created the Swatch watch. Hayek built a global empire on a twin insight: First, with quartz technology, precise time-keeping is a given; second, watches are worn on the body, and are therefore fashion accessories.

When Swatches appeared in 1983, they had far fewer parts than any other analog quartz watch; they had low manufacturing costs; they were not designed to be repaired; they came in many eye-catching styles; and they sold for between $25 and $35. By producing affordable, high-tech, stylish Swatches—favored by fashion models and trendsetters—rather than heavy, expensive timepieces, Hayek almost single-handedly saved the Swiss watch industry.

Today, Swatch Group Inc. is searching for the next breakthrough. It owns a stable of traditional, blue-chip brands like Omega, Longines, and Tissot, and is developing a Dick Tracy–like phone wristwatch, an Internet access watch, and a Swatch that acts like a ticket to sporting and cultural events. "First, you must do a nice-looking watch, and then we can talk about the function," Hayek told *The New York Times.*

The inescapable realities of punctuated equilibrium point out three key realities for any industry:

▼ You will never be a long-term winner through continuous improvement alone. You must also seek and create breakthrough changes.

▼ Creating the right balance between incremental improvements and radical innovation is the key to success.

▼ A shortage of resources is not necessarily serious, but a shortage of imagination can be fatal.

Take a look at your industry and map the big breakthroughs in it. What do you think will be the next Fosbury flop? Then ask yourself the really tough question: Who will discover and implement this breakthrough first—you or your competitors—and why?

When a group of software executives worked through this exercise recently, their eyes lit up with recognition. "Aha!" they said. "We've done the scissors and the straddle, but we haven't yet done the Fosbury flop. That's harnessing the Internet—and *that's* the hurdle we need to clear next."

Most breakthrough innovation in business is accomplished by individual entrepreneurs like Ted Turner at CNN, Fred Smith at FedEx, or Anita Roddick at the Body Shop rather than established companies. These innovators are not weighed down by tradition and bureaucracy. Why is it so hard for large, established companies to make these significant breakthroughs?

If we want to make large, established companies more innovative, then we must first understand the inherent barriers they face.

The Sigmoid Curve

Social organizations, from businesses to empires, seem to adhere to a set of inherent natural laws. We need to understand these laws and the barriers they create in order to overcome them.

Life is self-limiting: Generally, a period of growth is followed by deepening maturity, decline, and then death. As the prolific and insightful management thinker Charles Handy has noted, this tendency is illustrated by the sigmoid curve (see Figure 2.2). The word "sigmoid" is derived from the Greek word *sigmoeidēs*, and it simply means "S-shaped."

Consider the empires: Roman? Gone. Greek? Gone. Spanish? Gone. By the fifteenth century, the Portuguese empire was the largest in the world, extending across Asia, Africa, and the Americas; but after reaching its peak, Portugal's decline was rapid. The British invented the Industrial Revolution and long boasted that "the sun never sets on the British empire," but now the sun has set.

I like to joke that some 2,600 years ago, the greatest place for a vacation was beautiful Babylon, with its famous Hanging Gardens. But if you'd waited too long, your travel agent would have told you, "Sorry, ma'am, Babylon is going out of business. It hasn't been the same ever since the Persians took over. But I believe that Athens is still open for tourism—can I book you a room near the Acropolis?"

The business world is equally replete with examples of the cycle of growth, stagnation, and demise. The cases of disappearing brands like Peter Stuyvesant cigarettes (formerly number one in the world) and Pan Am are well known. One that still boggles my mind is the demise of Howard Johnson's.

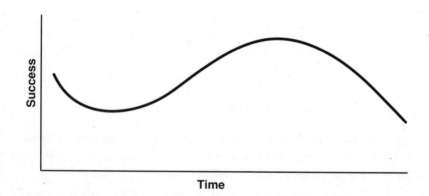

Figure 2.2   The Sigmoid Curve

Death of a Brand

Howard Johnson's, the famous orange-roofed restaurant and hotel chain, was founded in 1925. By the mid-1960s, "HoJo's" was one of the great American brands, boasting 1,000 restaurants and 500 Travelodges spread along highways up and down the Eastern seaboard. By the mid-1980s, however, the company had collapsed. What happened? Fast-food restaurants with specialized menus—hamburgers, fried chicken, pizzas, tacos, doughnuts—had sliced, diced, and deep-fried the food market into smaller and smaller segments. Howard Johnson's was unable, or unwilling, to adapt to these menus and the new pricing, and shriveled to virtually nothing.

How can a successful company and a great brand like Howard Johnson's fall so far, so quickly? Let's explore this question.

The sigmoid curve teaches two important rules that are as powerful as gravity:

▼ Nothing lasts forever under its original momentum.

▼ Success contains the seeds of its own destruction.

Why does this happen?

If you were to diagnose the cases discussed so far, you'd say that these organizations were suffering from the curse of success. When an organization reaches the top of the sigmoid curve, a set of symptoms becomes entrenched, which leads to a decay of forward momentum. The following characteristics are typical of such a large, mature, "ailing" organization:

▼ *Complacent:* Companies in a mature stage are usually enormously successful—to such an extent, in fact, that they show disdain for their competitors and come to believe they know better than their customers.

▼ *Inward-looking:* Companies of this level have become much more complicated, and it's often a challenge to manage them.

Their tendency is to look inward at their own processes and structures, rather than outward to their customers.

▼ *Political:* Often, mature organizations breed a climate rife with personal agendas, internal competition, and power plays; as people turn inward, they direct their energies toward tremendous battles over fiefdoms.

▼ *Risk-averse:* It is human instinct to want to hoard and protect wealth, assets, and power.

▼ *Forgetful of drivers of initial success:* A strong initial momentum can carry an organization forward for a while after it has taken its foot off the gas. But with time, people begin to forget those things that created the momentum in the first place; they fool themselves into thinking that the bureaucratic game is a way to keep growing.

▼ *Obsessed with entrenched standards and routines:* Working in a large organization, you need standards and routines to operate efficiently. But this can become a trap if you end up merely repeating the past rather than inventing the future.

These are all symptoms of the same underlying disease. These companies feel they have figured out the formula for success. They have stopped learning. This can be a fatal condition.

It's important to understand the lessons of the sigmoid curve so we can devise ways to overcome these barriers. But before we get into answering this challenge, there is one more lesson to take from the sigmoid curve: the importance of launching a second curve.

Leaping to the Second Curve

The most successful companies ride a series of sigmoid curves. Consider Disney, for example, which has evolved its business from simple black-and-white cartoons about a mouse to all sorts of family entertainment–related products—movies, books, theme parks, real estate development, cruise ships, and education, to name a few.

In the second curve diagram (Figure 2.3), the shaded area shows the critical time for change: Research shows that the *best*

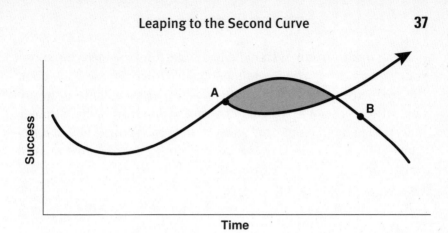

Figure 2.3   The Second Curve

time for a company to change is while it is still successful (soon after point A). Conversely, the *worst* time to change is while a company has already begun to fail (point B). Of course, you hear miraculous stories about companies like Harley-Davidson or Apple Computer that have faced near-death and recovered, but that's no way to run a business.

When a company is successful, the best people want to work there, its profits are high, its stockholders are happy, and its market share seems secure. In such a company, the need for change is not felt; in fact, there is a strong *resistance* to change. However, when profits are falling, talented people are leaving, and the company's stock is being dumped; the support for change is high, but the probability of success is very low. Here is the paradox: *You have the highest chance of success when you have the lowest support for change, and the lowest chance of success when there is the highest support for change.*

The most dangerous words in the English language are, "If it ain't broke, don't fix it." Instead, the words to live by should be, "If you don't fix it, it will break."

The lesson of the second curve is: *Your organization must change while it is still successful.*

However, changing once is not enough; instituting a process of ongoing change is the imperative for success. Innovative companies like 3M or GE succeed year after year because they are constantly pushing themselves to adapt and innovate. Intel succeeds because it is guided by the spirit of cofounder Andy Grove, whose book about the company, *Only the Paranoid Survive*, urges a constant awareness of the possibility of encountering what Grove calls "strategic inflection points," moments "when change is so powerful that it fundamentally alters the way business is done." Indeed, this urge toward constant self-improvement is what the late David Ogilvy, founder of advertising giant Ogilvy & Mather, liked to call "divine discontent"—the perpetual dissatisfaction with the current state of things and the relentless search for a better way.

In 1997, the then-21-year-old golf magician Tiger Woods was in the midst of a winning streak. When he demonstrated his powerful swing for *Golf Digest* magazine's high-speed camera—the head of his driver moved at 120 miles per hour, about 15 miles per hour faster than most touring pros—he declared his swing "almost perfect." A few days later, he won the 1997 Western Open. Shortly after that, Woods surprised everyone by announcing that he'd decided his swing needed a major overhaul. He spent more than a year lifting weights, altering his diet, and putting himself through hours of practice and drills to reinvent his "almost perfect" swing. During this period he won only a couple of tournaments. Since the reinvention, however, he has won almost half the tournaments he has entered—sometimes by record-breaking scores. Woods has many wondering whether he'll prove to be the best golfer in history.

My favorite business example of divine discontent is the tiny island nation of Singapore (population three million), which for two years in a row was named by the World Economic Forum as "the world's most competitive economy." In reaction, the Singaporean government did not celebrate with a ticker-tape parade or self-congratulatory banquets. Instead, Singapore launched an "urgent" public/private task force to discover new ways of becoming even more competitive. "Our success is the result of anxiety, and the anxiety is never fully assuaged by success," George Yeo, the Singaporean minister of information, told *Fortune*. "It keeps people on the ball."

In the new economy, the duration of a company's success is getting shorter and shorter. This means that organizations must institute change sooner and quicker than ever before.

Where is your firm positioned on the sigmoid curve? You'll know where if you're a start-up (near the bottom and on the way up) or if you're standing on a burning platform (at point B or beyond). Otherwise, it may not be easy to tell. Suppose that sales growth has recently stalled after several years of strong performance. Does this mean you've peaked and entered your phase of decline, or are you experiencing a temporary glitch that will soon give way to more years of growth? In some cases, you won't know for sure until after the fact, when it may be too late. Furthermore, in a large, complex organization, different divisions or product lines may be at different places on the graph, further complicating the question.

However, there are very few cases of companies that suffered because they pursued experimentation or innovation too early. The more common problem is waiting too long to move. Therefore, when in doubt, the safest rule of thumb is this: Assume that you are at point A, and act accordingly.

So far in this book, we've dealt with the changes being wrought by the new economy, and we've looked at the lessons of the high jump and the lessons of the sigmoid curve. All of these help to clarify the nature of the environment in which we're now operating and the realities we now face—the first key question we listed at the start of Chapter 1.

Next we need to begin to consider the second and third questions: *What are those few things our organization must do outstandingly well to win and go on winning in this environment?* and *How will we mobilize our organization to implement these things faster and better than our competitors?*

Our search for answers begins in the next chapter.

The Search
for an Answer

As the sigmoid curve teaches us, creating an adaptive organization—one that is capable of continuous change in response to our ever-changing environment—is perhaps the most important challenge any business faces. This chapter will consider the most prominent attempts that have been made to meet this challenge, analyze why they have failed, and offer an answer that has worked in practice.

Starting with Strategy

We tend to define a company's success or failure in terms of its strategy. "Look at IBM's turnaround," we say. "What a great strategy Lou Gerstner devised!" Or, conversely, "Isn't it sad what's happened to Xerox? Their leadership just couldn't come up with an effective strategy."

We assume, then, that strategy makes the difference between the successful company and the failure. But what, exactly, is strategy? That isn't always so clear. The word is derived from the Greek *stratēgia*, meaning "generalship," which itself is compounded from two words, *stratos*, meaning "army," and *agein*, "to lead." (Note the implicit connection between strategy and leadership, a theme to which we'll return throughout this book.) In military science, *strategy* refers to the large-scale plan for how the generals intend to fight and win a war. (The word *tactics*, in contrast, refers to small-scale operations like the conduct of a single battle.)

Your company's strategy, therefore, defines *how you will win*.

More specifically, your strategy determines how you will use your scarce resources in the best way possible. If resources were unlimited, then there would be no need for strategy; we could survive indefinitely by throwing time and money and people at our problems until our obstacles and competitors were simply overwhelmed. But in the real world, resources are limited. Even the world's greatest corporations have only so much cash, so many employees, so many factories. Strategy means deciding how to use each of your resources for maximum impact in the competitive arena.

Consider chess, the classic game of strategy. The players begin the game with virtually identical situations: They have the same number and assortment of pieces arranged on the board in the same fashion. Yet over time one player gradually manages to capture control of more and more of the board, until finally the opponent is forced to resign the game. How does this happen? The details of chess strategy are complex, but the overarching explanation is a simple one: The winner is the player who has used his or her scarce resources more effectively.

If you play chess, try to imagine what would happen if the rules of the game were changed to permit each player to add new pieces at will. Lost one of your bishops? No problem, add another—or two if you like. Is your king backed into a corner? Never fear, throw in a new queen or two to defend him. (Of course, your opponent would be free to multiply his or her forces as well.) How would chess strategy be affected? The answer is obvious. No real game would even be possible under these circumstances—because once the players have access to *unlimited* resources, there can be no winner or loser. And the game of chess would no longer bear much resemblance to real-life strategic competition, in which resources, no matter how great, are *always* limited.

Geopolitical competition amounts to strategy on a grand scale. The advantage goes to the country or system that makes best use of its limited resources. During the Cold War, a debate raged over the merits of the free enterprise and socialist systems. Both sides made strong cases for their ideologies, and both sides were guilty of rampant propaganda; the real merits and demerits of each system were often drowned out in the cacophony. But in 1989, when the socialist system ran out of resources, collapsing under the weight of its own inefficiency, debt, and stagnation, it became clear that the debate was over—free enterprise had won.

Of course, no analogy is perfect. In a board game like chess, the goal is to *preserve* one's resources—the pieces with which one starts the game, especially the all-important king. In business, resources are not only to be preserved but to be *leveraged and multiplied* in the creation of value.

If strategy is about winning, we need to be clear about the measures of success. In business, success means winning the competition for value creation on two fronts:

▼ Greater value for your customers.

▼ Greater profits for your company and its shareholders.

These two goals are distinct but closely related. Unless you create greater value for customers, you won't retain their business for long, and the resulting loss of revenues will soon make it impossible to generate profits for your company and its shareholders. Conversely, if you create value for customers but do so without generating greater profits, investment capital will flee and you'll sooner or later run out of resources. Thus, an effective strategy is one that provides answers for how and where to use your limited resources in the pursuit of both goals.

At the heart of an effective strategy is what I call the *winning proposition*. When I work with executive teams, I ask them to banish the conventional term *value proposition* from their vocabularies. A value proposition is no more than table stakes—something you need simply to be in business. And if you ask your organization to devise a value proposition, that's all you'll get—a me-too approach to business. The real challenge is to find and leverage a *winning* proposition, one that produces *greater* value than your competitors' proposition. You won't get one if you don't aim for it.

Strategy as Making Choices

Because strategy is about the intelligent deployment of limited resources, the formation of a winning strategy requires that we make a series of difficult choices. In fact, the point of strategy is to create an intense focus on the *right things*. After all, in the words of the personal productivity guru and author David Allen, "You can do anything. But you can't do everything." Or, as Sir Basil Hart, the British military scientist, put it, "All the lessons of war can be reduced to a single word: CONCENTRATION."

Thus, as a CEO your challenge is simple: *where* and *how* to focus your scarce resources.

First, *where* should we focus our scarce resources? That is:

▼ Which businesses will we compete in?

▼ Which geographies will we focus on?

▼ Which customer segments will we pursue?

▼ What products or services will we offer our customers?

Then, *how* should we focus our scarce resources? That is:

▼ How will we deliver our product or service offerings?

▼ How will we create superior value for our customers?

▼ How we will generate superior profits?

▼ How will we align our organization and motivate our people behind the chosen strategy?

Strategy, then, is the art of making the most intelligent choices—those that will help us use our limited resources to win the competition for value creation. This, along with leadership effectiveness, is the most crucial element in business success. Yet the strategy process as traditionally practiced in many corporations has hampered rather than helped the development of winning strategies. Let's consider why.

The Dead End of Strategic Planning

At many companies, people groan when they hear that the "strategic planning" season is at hand. Frankly, I don't blame them. Far too often strategic planning is an empty ritual rather than a process of discovery. It involves gathering sales, financial, and other data, extrapolating them into the future, and then adding detailed projections about future hiring, investment, and other expenses. Plenty of minutiae are captured in the process, but there's very little evidence of creative, long-term thinking about changes in the competitive environment and how the company must deploy its scarce resources in response to those changes. The end product is a five-inch-thick binder full of data that collects dust on top of the CEO's bookshelf. This isn't strategy—it's planning, which is a very different thing.

When I begin work with a new organization, I'll generally ask to have a look at its current strategy. A binder is pulled from the shelf, and I study the document to try to find where in the 500 pages of tables and projections it explains how the company plans to win. Usually the explanation is nowhere to be found. The reason is simple. What I have been given is a planning document—often an excellent one—but not a strategy.

Henry Mintzberg, author of the classic management text *The Rise and Fall of Strategic Planning*, has studied what really happens under the guise of strategy development. His findings are eye-opening. As shown in Figure 3.1, fully 90 percent of the results projected in most companies' formal strategic planning processes never come to fruition. Instead, they fall by the wayside, vanishing into the limbo of "unrealized strategy" as seen on the lower left-hand side of Mintzberg's diagram.

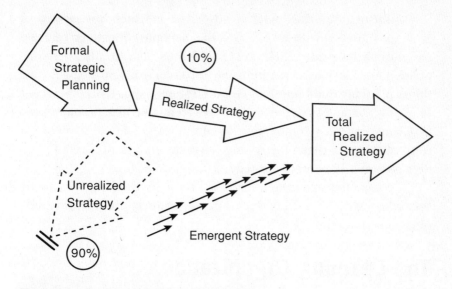

Figure 3.1 Traditional Strategic Development

Source: Reprinted with the permission of the Free Press, a Division of Simon & Schuster, Inc., from *The Rise and Fall of Strategic Planning* by Henry Mintzberg. Copyright © 1994 by Henry Mintzberg.

Only 10 percent of most companies' actions arise out of their strategic planning ("realized strategy"). But what is the source of the other 90 percent of what companies do? Mintzberg calls it "emergent strategy." This describes the series of ad-hoc initiatives, reactions, decisions, and choices that managers make in response to daily pressures, without guidance from any overarching strategic concept. Taken together, they amount to the *real* strategy that most companies follow.

Of course, the executives running the big companies that Mintzberg studied aren't fools, or blind. They recognize the huge gap between the formally planned strategies they developed at such great expense and the realized strategies their companies actually followed. In frustration, some companies decide that they haven't tried hard enough or taken strategic planning seriously enough. They vow to buckle down and devote even more time, energy, and money to strategic planning.

Unfortunately, the usual result is to heighten the agony of strategic planning without bridging the disconnect between realized and unrealized strategy. The real problem is that, as Mintzberg has pointed out, strategic planning is an oxymoron. Strategy is one thing; planning quite another. Great strategy begins with *divergent thinking*. Planning excellence is above all an exercise in *convergent thinking*. For most companies, the attempt to combine them in the form of strategic planning produces a result that is 90 percent planning and only 10 percent strategy.

If companies are to mobilize the creativity to achieve strategic breakthroughs, it is vital that they separate strategy from planning—and put strategy first.

The Learning Organization

Recognizing the failure of traditional strategic planning, many companies, as well as the consultants and business theorists who advise them, have been searching for ways to forge a more vital connection between corporate *thinking* and corporate *action*. One positive result has been the creation of a body of research and theory on what has been called the "learning organization" (i.e., an organization with an enhanced ability to generate, capture, and share knowledge).

At first glance, the concept of the learning organization might seem to offer a solution to the strategy dilemma. After all, one of the reasons that traditional strategic plans wind up gathering dust on executive bookshelves is the fact that they fail to capture the dynamics of the competitive marketplace—how customers are changing, which new competitors are entering the field, the effects of emerging technologies, and so on. A learning organization might be expected to have its antennae finely tuned to such changes and therefore to be well prepared to recognize and respond to them, shifting strategy nimbly rather than blindly following an obsolescent plan to defeat.

It's a reasonable expectation, and in fact the learning theorists have produced some valuable insights into how individuals and groups learn, and how to convert this knowledge into organizational action. I've already quoted Arie de Geus's observation that a company's "ability to learn faster than competitors may be the only sustainable competitive advantage." This captures the central insight of the learning organization movement, and it's an important concept as far as it goes.

However, as a guide to the creation of breakthrough strategies, I would argue that it is incomplete. Remember our definition of strategy: Your strategy defines how you will win, based on best deployment of scarce resources in the creation of greater value for your customers and greater profit for your company. Learning alone doesn't produce such an outcome. Only when learning is specifically targeted toward the creation of a plan to win, and when the information generated through learning is used to support the creation and implementation of such a plan—only then does corporate learning produce real value.

Many learning theorists seem to position learning as an end in itself rather than as a means to an end. Is this a merely theoretical difficulty? Not really. Hundreds of organizations, inspired by this idea, have struggled to incorporate learning into their operating philosophies. The results have been mixed at best. While much potentially useful information is being gathered, it tends to languish in corporate databases and intranets, often failing to reach the people who could make good use of it in their daily work, as well as in strategy creation and implementation. Although some progress has been made in finding ways of sharing such knowledge in organizations and making the information more practically useful, the vital connection of learning to strategy has yet to be made.

Furthermore, the learning movement has done little to help business leaders figure out how to regulate and harness the ever-growing floods of data being generated by the new information and communication technologies. Paul Saffo, director at the Institute for the Future, has said it well: "Our predicament is the growing gap between the volume of information and our ability to make sense of it." There's nothing wrong with the notion that organizations must learn how to learn. But it's even more crucial to develop a process for deciding *what* we need to learn and *how* we will apply that knowledge to the creation and implementation of our strategy—our plan to win. The company that uses such a process will have converted knowledge from a *potential* asset into an *actual* one.

As we'll see, Strategic Learning seeks to make organizational learning more purposeful and productive by introducing *strategy* as the pivotal factor in the learning equation.

Complexity Theory

Another reaction to the failure of traditional strategy has been a growing interest in complexity theory—a concept borrowed from biology and other natural sciences—as a new way to think about corporate behavior.

Led by such brilliant thinkers as Steve Kaufman of the Santa Fe Institute (and popularized by writers like James Gleick, M. Mitchell Waldrop, Roger Lewin, and Margaret J. Wheatley), the complexity theorists have emphasized the rapid, unpredictable, apparently random quality of environmental change today. It's easy to scan the history of the past 10 or 20 years and tick off the technological, political, economic, social, and cultural changes that almost no one predicted accurately, from the fall of the Iron Curtain to the rise of the Internet. In this kind of nonlinear world, characterized more by discontinuities than by incremental changes, it's almost impossible to forecast the future correctly. Therefore, the complexity theorists argue, the idea that companies can plan ahead is fundamentally an illusion—at best a waste of time and resources, at worst a road to oblivion.

For the business leader, this might seem to be a counsel of despair. But the complexity theorists take heart from their observations of nature, and in particular from the way in which the mechanisms of biological evolution—variation, natural selection, and survival of the fittest—have enabled individual species and entire ecosystems to evolve and adapt to changing environmental conditions: floods and droughts, ice ages and heat waves. Flocks of geese, for example, migrate together successfully over routes thousands of miles long, even in the apparent absence of mechanisms for developing, communicating, and enforcing travel routes and flight patterns. Similarly, ants, bees, and other social insects create complex and highly adaptive societies through a combination of instinct, trial and error, and natural selection. The complexity theorists refer to such naturally occurring organizations as *complex adaptive systems*, and they posit that such systems inherently tend toward order rather than randomness.

According to the complexity theorists, human organizations are also complex adaptive systems. Such systems, they say, instinctively "know" how to act purposefully and strategically. Thus, the job of a company leader is to create conditions that will allow strategy to emerge naturally, through a process the complexity theorists call *self-organization*.

What sort of working conditions will encourage this kind of self-organization? The complexity theorists talk about the importance of individual expression, decentralization, and even chaos as crucial success factors. Top-down controls, they insist, are doomed to failure in a world no single mind or team of minds can fully understand. Therefore, virtually all controls should be eliminated, allowing a hundred voices to suggest new ideas and new directions. Out of this diversity, they say, the best strategies for survival and competitive advantage will gradually emerge, just as they do in the complex adaptive systems we observe in nature.

There's much that's attractive in the writing of the complexity theorists. Their emphasis on freedom and creativity, their scorn for mechanistic processes, and their recognition of the need for flexibility in the development and implementation of strategy are all valuable insights (as well as necessary correctives to the rigidly hierarchical thinking that still dominates too many corporations). When the complexity theorists argue that most organizations are filled with potentially creative people whose insights and fresh ideas ought to be liberated to refresh the corporate wellsprings of innovation, I agree and applaud.

But it's also easy to carry this argument too far. Human organizations are not flocks of birds, schools of fish, or swarms of bees, after all. People have free will, and they often make self-interested choices that are at odds with the larger goals of the organization. Humans regularly resist change, sabotage strategy, and even go on strike. If people always behaved like a flock of geese flying south in an orderly manner, relying on emergent strategy might work. Unfortunately, they don't.

In a small, entrepreneurial organization made up of 30 to 40 employees with deeply shared values, objectives, and ideas, a highly informal process for creating and implementing strategy may suffice. Over morning coffee, someone says to the gang, "Hey, I had an idea on my way to the office today. What do you think?" If the idea is approved, they can start work on it the same day. It's an exhilarating way to run a small company, or perhaps a single plant or department within a big company. But large, diverse organizations like those in which most of us work simply can't organize themselves or create clarity of focus in this way.

New England is proud of its tradition of "direct democracy," in which all the residents of a village gather periodically in the town hall to make decisions about their local laws. But a nation the size of the United States or even a state the size of Vermont can't be governed in that way. Similarly, a company of 500 or 50,000 employees must have a process for creating and implementing its plan to win. Yes, it must be a fast, flexible process that encourages learning, input, and creativity at many levels of the organization. But it must be a *process*, not simply a soup of chaos from which the plan is supposed to emerge by itself.

The complexity theorists insist that chaos is essential for ideas to flourish. This idea is not so much wrong as incomplete. Creativity requires the right *balance* between chaos and order. You want an environment in which bright insights, unusual perspectives, little-known facts, and contrarian approaches have an opportunity to surface and be recognized. But all these intellectual assets must then be focused on the common goal of answering the strategic question, *How will we win?*

The Adaptive Enterprise: Nature as Teacher

About one thing the learning theorists and the complexity theorists are in agreement: The volatile, competitive, unpredictable business environment in which we now operate places unprecedented demands on our capacity for creating smart and flexible strategy.

They're right. As I have argued, today's primary leadership challenge is to create and sustain an adaptive enterprise. In the current business environment, I believe this is the *only* sustainable advantage. It is not a product or a service; those things have a short shelf life. Rather, it is an *organizational capability*. By definition, an adaptive enterprise is one with the built-in ability to renew itself over and over again. This is important because, as we've seen, to win once is not enough; you must be able to *go on* winning. Mastering the scissors isn't sufficient; you need to be prepared to learn (or, better yet, to *invent*) the straddle and then the Fosbury flop.

When it comes to ongoing adaptation, our best teacher is nature. However, I put a somewhat different twist on nature's lessons than do the complexity theorists.

In *The Origin of Species*, his groundbreaking study of biological evolution, Charles Darwin noted a wonderful example of how "plants and animals . . . are bound together by a web of complex relations." In England, he wrote, the common red clover (*Trifolium pratense*) has developed a flower with a unique feature—a long, thin funnel leading to the nectar at its base. Many species of insects might be attracted to the sweet-smelling and nutritious nectar, but only bumblebees, which have unusually long tongues, can reach it. As the bee reaches into the flower to retrieve the nectar, pollen collects on its legs; the pollen is then transported to other flowers, and thus fertilizes them.

The beauty of this arrangement is that bees can fly farther than most other insects. Thus, they ensure that the plant's pollen is distributed more widely than that of other plants. This gives the red clover a crucial competitive advantage that promotes its long-term survival.

In effect, the common red clover has formed an exclusive alliance with bumblebees. This strategy is not without risk, however. What happens if another plant produces a sweeter-tasting nectar, and the bees "switch brands"? What if the bees' enemies, field mice, destroy the bees' combs and nests, and the bees are forced to relocate or are wiped out? The risk/reward trade-off is hard at work here. Nonetheless, the alliance strategy between the common red clover and the bumblebee has so far captured a significant advantage that no other plant has yet been able to challenge.

How does the natural world create such brilliant strategies? Put simply, nature is constantly conducting a massive set of experiments through the genetic process known as natural variation. These variations, apparently random in nature, test a wide range of survival strategies—changes in size, shape, color, mating behaviors, food preferences, internal chemistry, and much more. Most of these variations are failures, but a few of them succeed. The lucky few— those gifted with favorable variations—will live longer, reproduce in greater numbers, outcompete other species, and eventually come to dominate future generations.

The key to this process is that nature never sits still. Because the process by which genetic information is transferred from one generation to the next produces constant, random variations, millions of experiments with survival are constantly taking place in every plant and animal species. Thus, when the environment changes, whether massively and rapidly or gradually, the chances are good that one or a few individuals already exist who are well adapted to life under the new conditions. For example, if the climate changes so that average temperatures increase by one or two degrees over a century (which represents a dramatic shift), individual creatures adapted to the change (mammals with less shaggy coats, perhaps) will be favored and will gradually come to dominate their niches in the ecosystem. To paraphrase Darwin, it is not the largest, the strongest, or even the most intelligent of species that survive but the most adaptable to change.

In all of this, nature is brilliantly creative. Undirected by any overarching intelligence (so far as science can know), nature generates an unending stream of adaptive solutions to the survival challenges thrown up by a constantly changing environment. But there's a problem with nature's approach. Because variations are generated without apparent design, evolution is a low-odds game: 99 percent of all the species that ever existed are now extinct. All the current successes have come from the remaining 1 percent.

Nature, in effect, suffers from two massive learning disabilities. When nature fails, it doesn't know why; and when it succeeds, it doesn't know why.

How does this analogy play out in the business arena?

As in nature, the rules of survival in the marketplace are Darwinian: You must never sit still; you must continually generate favorable variations in your business or run the risk of extinction. But here's the twist: Human organizations don't suffer from nature's learning disabilities. We humans are able to think about what we are doing and to learn from our experiences. By harnessing lessons from this learning, we can make smarter strategic choices, deploy our limited resources with greater skill, and thereby increase our chances of success.

In the world of organizations, therefore, *strategic learning is at the heart of successful adaptation*.

The Killer Competencies

Having defined the essence of strategy, explored some of the most prominent attempts to respond to the question of how to develop winning strategies, and looked at the key lessons regarding adaptation taught by nature, we're now in a position to consider the second question we posed at the start of this book:

What are those few things our organization must do outstandingly well to win and go on winning in this environment?

Specific answers to this question will vary from company to company and from industry to industry, of course. But I believe we have learned that there are certain common elements that all successful adaptive businesses must master—what I call the "killer competencies." They are the skills crucial for mobilizing the collective intelligence and creativity of your people and for forging the integrated system of strategy and leadership that you'll need to succeed in today's business environment.

The five killer competencies are:

1. Insight. First and foremost, in a world of increased speed, complexity, and uncertainty, your company will need a superior ability to make sense of the changing environment. This is where the competition begins. Indeed, the competition for superior insight is perhaps the most decisive battle today. For example, consider a company like Royal Dutch/Shell Group, justly famous for its use of scenario planning as a way of envisioning possible futures and developing insights about how it will win in each of those futures.

2. Focus. Throughout the ages, no lasting success has been built without an intense focus on the right things. Thus, you'll need the ability to translate your insights into such a focus—to make the most intelligent strategic choices about where and how to deploy your scarce resources in support of your plan for winning. A classic example is the Walt Disney Company, a far-flung media and entertainment empire that has succeeded because of its single-minded dedication to one vision: using imagination to make people happy. Every strategic choice made by the Disney leadership is tested against that vision.

3. Alignment. You'll need the ability to align every element of your entire organization—measurement and reward systems, organizational structures and processes, your corporate culture, and the skills and motivation of your people—behind your strategic focus. This is a monumental leadership challenge; without success here, no strategy can succeed. Look at Southwest Airlines, which has developed a very clear focus on low-cost, point-to-point air travel and defended its position as the most profitable airline in the industry by aligning every aspect of the organization behind that focus.

4. Execution. You'll need the ability to implement your strategy—fast. Speed in carrying out your strategy expands the gap between you and your nearest competitors and improves your ability to take advantage of the next shift in the environment—which is likely to happen sooner than anyone expects. You'll be able to do this only when the first three competencies are in place. A company like Cisco Systems is a great example of the power of effective execution. Using the communication power of the Internet, a corporate culture single-mindedly devoted to rapid innovation, and its unique ability to acquire companies and absorb them quickly, Cisco has managed to remain ahead of the competition in the networking gear business, one of the fastest-moving industries in history. On a different scale, GE offers an equally impressive example of the power of execution. The conglomerate has shown how adroitly executed initiatives, such as Six Sigma and Destroyyourbusiness.com, can be used to focus an entire global corporation on adaptations (quality improvement and harnessing the Internet, respectively) that are crucial to the company's future.

5. Renewal. Finally, you'll need the ability to do these things over and over again, without ever stopping. Winning once is not enough; the real challenge is to create an ongoing cycle of learning, focusing, aligning, and winning. Motorola is an excellent example of an organization that is able to continuously renew and reinvent itself. Founded in 1928, the company has evolved from a humble battery-repair business into a manufacturer of car radios, televisions, semiconductors, integrated circuits, and cellular phone systems. Today, Motorola is harnessing the power of wireless, broadband, and the Internet to deliver end-to-end network communication solutions for individuals and work teams in offices, homes, and vehicles.

Note that the first four competencies are aimed at producing specific outputs, while the fifth—the ability to repeat the first four ad infinitum—is different. The fifth killer competency creates *an ongoing cycle of renewal*. The ability to constantly renew your organization separates truly dynamic organizations from those that are doomed to become dinosaurs. It is the ultimate killer competency.

These, then, are the competencies necessary to create the adaptive enterprises of the future—the companies that will dominate the business arena in the coming century. Thinking hard about the five killer competencies and honestly measuring your company's current capabilities against them can be a valuable starting point for assessing your organizational strengths and weaknesses.

Still, we've so far been examining the quest for adaptation in fairly general, abstract terms. And any idea, no matter how profound, is without value until it is put into practice.

What we now need to do is to address the third question:

How will we mobilize our organization to implement these things faster and better than our competitors?

Strategic Learning offers a practical process for mobilizing the five killer competencies to create and lead an adaptive enterprise. The next chapter will begin to consider that process.

4

The Strategic Learning Process

Strategic Learning is built on the proposition that the ability to build and lead an adaptive enterprise is the only sustainable competitive advantage in today's complex marketplace. Merely saying this is not enough, however. Executives need a practical method for generating innovative strategic ideas and then turning them into effective actions.

As we've seen, the increasing pace of change means that the A-to-B approach of traditional strategy no longer works. To succeed, companies must generate insights, create focus, achieve alignment, and motivate change continuously, in a dynamic cycle of renewal. This cycle is the essence of Strategic Learning.

The Four-Step Process

As shown in Figure 4.1, the Strategic Learning process has four linked action steps—learn, focus, align, and execute—which build on one another and are repeated (as the fifth step, if you will) in a continuous cycle of learning and renewal.

Learn
Generate insight into
changing environment and
learn from own actions.

Strategy
Creation

Execute
Implement the strategy
and experiment with
new ideas.

Focus
Make strategic choices.

Strategy
Implementation

Align
Align organization behind
strategic focus.

Figure 4.1 The Strategic Learning Cycle

These action steps embody the killer competencies explained in Chapter 3. The first two steps form the basis of a firm's strategy creation. The third and fourth steps are the foundations of strategy implementation. Thus, strategy creation and implementation are integrated in a mutually reinforcing process.

The key is to think cycle—not straight line. Simply following the process once is not enough. The challenge is to repeat it over and over, so that your organization continuously learns from its own actions and from scanning the environment, and then modifies its strategies accordingly. The more often an organization repeats this cycle, the better it will become at doing it, thus enhancing its adaptive capacity. The result is the kind of process of ongoing renewal that characterizes the truly adaptive organization.

Implementing Strategic Learning as a Leadership Process

How can organizations make the Strategic Learning cycle operational so that it becomes integrated into the way they function? When aiming to achieve something vitally important, the key to success is to create a process that will take you there. The challenge of ongoing renewal is too important to be treated as a side issue or relegated to random actions and ad hoc initiatives. Just as companies employ systematic research and development to generate technical innovation, so too they need a deliberate, systematic process to drive strategic innovation. In essence, Strategic Learning amounts to a new way to lead companies in a world of unpredictable change.

Figure 4.2 illustrates how the four-step cycle is converted into a practical leadership process for creating and implementing breakthrough strategies.

The remainder of this chapter will briefly outline the leadership process and its key outputs, giving you a bird's-eye view of the entire cycle. It's a prelude to the much more detailed examination of the process that you'll find in the subsequent chapters.

One important caveat: Although, for clarity's sake, I'll describe the steps of the Strategic Learning process sequentially, reality is a bit more messy. Thus it is often necessary to repeat a stage or loop back in an iterative process. For example, you may find yourself immersed in the second step—making your strategic choices—when a fresh insight into the changing marketplace is

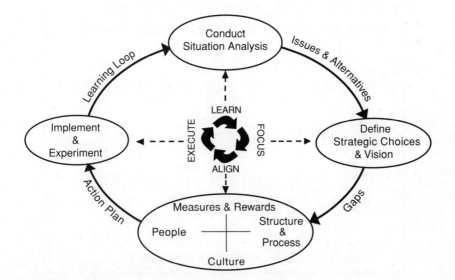

Figure 4.2   Strategic Learning: The Leadership Process

uncovered that suggests an important shift in your strategic focus. If that's a problem, it's the kind of happy problem any business leader would hope to encounter. Accommodate the new insight and move on. In business, as in life, learning, adaptation, and renewal should be a continual, organic voyage of discovery. Being responsive to the learning is more important than completing the process in a neat sequence.

With that said, here, in broad brush strokes, is what's involved in each step of the Strategic Learning cycle.

Step One: The Situation Analysis (*Learn*)

Strategic Learning always begins with a situation analysis. It's a systematic way for an organization to develop a set of *superior insights* that will form the basis of its strategic choices (see Figure 4.3).

Objective:	Win the battle for superior insights.
Technique:	Ask and answer the right questions.
Focus of Inquiry:	• Customers.
	• Competitors.
	• Own realities.
	• Industry dynamics.
	• Broader environment.

Figure 4.3   Step One: The Situation Analysis

What is an insight? A later chapter will discuss this question in detail, but for now you can think of an insight as a truth about customers, the marketplace, the competition, or your company that you understand earlier or better than your competitors. In today's business world, superior insights are a key source of competitive advantage. In fact, the battle for unique insights is increasingly where the competition really begins.

The key to conducting a good situation analysis is to ask and answer penetrating questions that provoke meaningful insights. While each company must come up with the right questions depending on its own circumstances, every company needs to cover the following areas: *its customers, its competitors, the firm's own realities, industry dynamics*, and the *broader environment*.

A major defect in traditional strategic planning is that there is often no divergent thinking—no process to challenge existing assumptions and explore alternatives. Instead, strategic planning typically involves ritualized analyses that tend to reinforce existing mental models of how the world, and your business, works. By contrast, the situation analysis is deliberately designed as an exercise in divergent learning—a crucial stimulus to creativity. It is a process of discovery that aims to shake off outmoded mental straitjackets and examine the world afresh.

In conducting a situation analysis, you'll use a combination of analysis and creative brainstorming to scan and interpret your company's environment and its internal realities. Your goal is to challenge existing assumptions and produce new ways of thinking. An effective situation analysis will combine market research, analysis, critical thinking, and creative brainstorming, drawing on the talents of cross-functional teams that include people from many levels of the organization. This helps to create a sense of ownership of the new ideas that will emerge.

The insights you discover through this process will be crystallized into concise diagnostic statements that can readily be understood by everyone in the firm. Simplicity and clarity are crucial virtues, since these insights will be the basis for the strategic choices that the entire company will soon be charged with implementing.

Step Two: Strategic Choices and Vision (*Focus*)

As we've seen, strategy is about making choices. The situation analysis (step one) is designed to ensure that you make the most intelligent choices possible, based on hard-won insights rather than guesswork, assumptions, or a vision that's untethered to reality. The next step is to translate these insights into the key strategic choices of your firm. Figure 4.4 provides a framework for making these strategic choices.

There are three critical elements here. The first, *customer focus*, defines which customers the firm will serve (as well as those it will *not* serve), what their hierarchy of needs is, and what products or services it will offer them. The second, *the winning proposition*, answers the question, "What will we do differently or better than our competitors to achieve greater value for our customers and superior profits for our firm?" The third, *five key priorities*, is a list of the most important steps the company must take to turn its winning proposition into a reality.

As we'll discuss, the second step of the Strategic Learning process also includes the formulation of a compelling *vision statement*. It's a

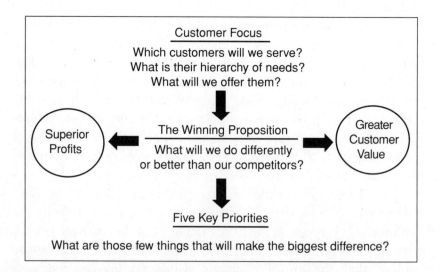

Figure 4.4   Step Two: The Strategic Choices

concise word picture of what your organization aspires to be in the future and provides a clear sense of direction that everyone in the organization can understand and act upon in the present. A good vision is simple, motivating, and realistic, and it should involve stretch. The desired response from the people you lead should be: "Yes, *that's* where we want to go—but we can't get there by doing what we're doing today." A great vision inspires transformation, not incrementalism.

Finally, you'll need to translate your strategic priorities into operational tasks defining what must be done to make your strategy successful. To do this, look at each of your strategic priorities and ask, "What performance gaps must we close in order to achieve this priority?" The resulting series of *gap statements* defines the difference between the current reality and the desired future state for each of your priorities.

Step Three: Align the Organization (*Align*)

Once the strategic choices and the gaps to be bridged have been clearly defined, you're ready to tackle the issue of strategy implementation.

The first challenge is *effective project management*. The right disciplines, measurements, and accountabilities must be applied to closing the gaps. If your service quality needs to be improved, or your research and development (R&D) efforts need to be more sharply focused, or your financial management system needs to be modernized, then people with the necessary talents must be assigned the task and given the resources needed to accomplish it.

Even more important, however—and far too often ignored—is the fact that for implementation to be successful, it is essential that all the key supporting elements of your business system be aligned behind the chosen strategy.

Think of an organization as an ecosystem—a rain forest, perhaps, or an oasis in the desert. An ecosystem functions successfully only when its interdependent elements support one another. When an element does not play its supporting role, or when elements work against each other, then the system will fail. The key elements in any business system are similarly interdependent. Thus, success comes not from a single action such as changing the organization structure. Instead, it comes from orchestrating the right *interactions* so that all the key elements of the business system are working together synergistically to support the new strategy.

Is it always necessary to examine the entire business system when making a change in your company strategy? In a word, yes. After all, your existing alignment was established over time to support your old strategy; if you don't change it, how can you expect to get anything more than business as usual? If you want to move to a new strategy, it's crucial to consider the implications for the whole organization.

The task is to understand the key supporting elements of a firm's business system that must be aligned. Various frameworks for doing this have been suggested by, among others, Jay R. Galbraith, David Nadler, and Michael Tushman. The model proposed here (and shown in Figure 4.5) comprises the following supporting elements,

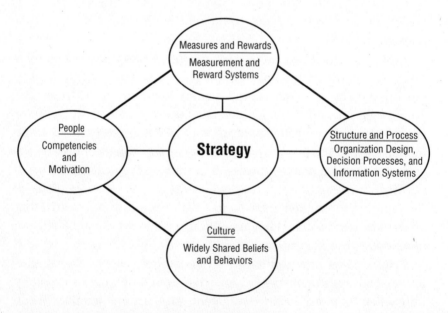

Figure 4.5   Step Three: Aligning the Organization

which must work in unison: *measures and rewards, structure and process, culture*, and *people*. Let's briefly consider each.

Measures and Rewards

Whenever you measure an activity within your company, you are inevitably doing two things: You are gauging its performance, and you are sending the message, "This is important." Conversely, failure to measure something sends the opposite message: "This is *not* important." It's crucial that your measurement and reward system acts in unison with the other elements of your business system in support of your new strategy. You cannot hope to achieve your new strategy if you continue to measure and reward the old one.

Structure and Process

A new strategy often requires important changes in the way a firm is organized and how its decisions get made. Therefore, it's necessary to ask such questions as: *Should the firm be organized by product line, customer grouping, function, geography, or some other principle? What should be the level of centralization or decentralization for each activity in the value chain?* As your strategy changes, it's likely that your answers to these questions will change, too.

Culture

Corporate culture is probably the most misunderstood and mismanaged aspect of the business ecosystem, and yet it is arguably the most important success factor of all. The poor management of culture usually stems from a number of misconceptions. One of these is that culture is a vague and mysterious thing. In fact, as we'll see, culture always expresses itself through specific values and observable, measurable behaviors. Another misconception is that culture is an end in itself and somehow separate from the rest of the business. The truth is that corporate culture is a means to an end. If it does not support the business strategy, that strategy will almost certainly fail. The effective business leader not only can but *must* make an impact on the culture of the firm if he or she hopes to achieve the desired strategy.

People

An organization is not a machine: It will achieve success only if its people are focused, skilled, and motivated. So the first order of business is to make certain that your people have the right competencies to carry out the new strategy. Motivation is an equally pivotal factor, especially in times of transformational change. Human beings by nature resist change. It is important to overcome this natural tendency and inspire active support for the new strategy. As we'll discuss, this is perhaps the most difficult of all leadership challenges.

Effective alignment of *measures and rewards, structure and process, culture,* and *people* ensures that your firm's key organizational resources and the energies of your people are concentrated behind the new strategy.

Step Four: Implement and Experiment (*Execute*)

The final step, implementing your strategy, should include a deliberate set of experiments to produce further learning (see Figure 4.6). You'll never know for sure what is going to work, so it is important to try alternative solutions. Like nature, you'll maximize your chances of finding favorable variations through continuous experi-

---

- Implement the strategy.

- Conduct experiments to explore alternatives and fuel new learning.

Figure 4.6   Step Four: Implement and Experiment

mentation; like a scientist, you'll learn as much from your failures as from your successes.

Step four then loops back to step one, the situation analysis, at the top of the cycle. Your firm updates its insights, learning by examining its own actions and by rescanning the environment, and keeps modifying its strategies accordingly. The process of Strategic Learning never stops.

From Bird's-Eye Vista to Ground-Level View

This, then, is a brief description of Strategic Learning. It has probably triggered many questions in your mind, including: *How, in concrete terms, are the four steps carried out? What kinds of resources—in time, energy, and talent—are needed to perform them? What, exactly, should the desired outputs look like? How can we know if our organization is performing the process correctly?*

The next several chapters will be devoted to answering these and many similar questions so as to clarify the process and how it can work. However, before we embark on a more thorough exploration of Strategic Learning, it is necessary to stress a crucially important point—perhaps the most important point of all.

Einstein once said that, if given an hour to solve a challenging problem, he would devote 45 minutes to thinking about how to solve the problem and just 15 minutes to actually solving it. His point was that developing the proper *approach* to a problem is the key to solving it.

The problem we're addressing here is how to create and sustain an adaptive organization—one capable of ongoing learning and strategic innovation. In tackling this problem, my approach has been to start with the *outputs* that an adaptive organization must be capable of producing on a systematic basis. The outputs I have put forward (in Chapter 3) under the rubric of the "killer competencies," are *insight, focus, alignment, execution,* and *renewal*. I would argue that without the ability to systematically generate these outputs, no organization can hope to be truly adaptive.

The significance of the Strategic Learning process is that it is a *means* for creating these vital outputs, not an end in itself. Therefore, the key is to concentrate always on the quality of the outputs. These outputs are what matter—not the steps of the process in themselves.

Therefore, in applying Strategic Learning it is important to see it as a new way of leading organizations, not as a business ritual to be mechanically followed. The key to success is to think of it as a holistic, emergent process and to mobilize the underlying principles creatively, in a discovery-driven, flexible way. Only companies that approach Strategic Learning in this spirit will be able to realize its full benefits.

5

Winning the Battle for Insight: Doing a Situation Analysis

No Substitute for Insight

Every business breakthrough starts with a unique insight.

This is an eternal truth—one that applies equally to the ideas that have spawned enormous businesses like FedEx, America On-line, and eBay as it does to more modest enterprises. Even my friend Commander Noel Evans's fruit farm.

In the mid-1960s, Evans retired from the British Royal Navy, married a South African woman, and moved to her homeland with the idea of becoming a farmer. The fact that he'd spent his career at sea and knew nothing about farming didn't bother him; he'd always been resourceful, and he expected to succeed at his new avocation as he'd succeeded in everything he'd tried. Using his limited pension and some borrowed money, Evans bought a farm in the Elgin Valley, a lush region known for its apples, plums, and peaches, nestled in a beautiful part of South Africa called the Western Cape.

It was planting season, and time was short for the would-be farmer. Evans drove up and down the valley, introduced himself to his new neighbors, and asked their advice on getting started. The farmers all welcomed him and offered a variety of helpful tips. On one point they all agreed: "There's been a glut of peaches this year. If I were you, I'd plant plums."

Evans returned to his new wife and their farm, and set about planting *peach* trees.

Why peaches and not plums? Evans had had a winning insight. He understood that nearly all of his neighbors, frightened by this year's peach glut, were planting nothing but plums, and would therefore produce a surfeit of the purple fruit. Sure enough, when the trees matured, Evans was one of the few with a full crop of peaches. It usually takes new farmers in the Elgin Valley years to break even, but Evans was in the black within two seasons. And just two seasons after that, he had become one of the most successful farmers in the entire valley.

It was his insight about the market, not years of farming experience, that made Commander Evans a winner.

This homespun story makes a deceptively simple point. *The battle for superior insight is increasingly becoming the real starting point of business competition.* Those who arrive at the right insight first, or use it best, enjoy a powerful advantage— whether they are planting fruit trees on a South African farm or managing a global business.

This is why the Strategic Learning cycle always begins with the situation analysis, a systematic process of divergent learning that enables a company to uncover meaningful insights about customers, competitors, its own realities, industry dynamics, and the broader environment. Unfortunately, this kind of exploration is generally absent from traditional forms of strategic planning, which tend to operate from the assumption (explicit or implicit) that tomorrow's business is likely to be a straight-line extrapolation from today's. As a result, anticipation of disruptive change, creative thinking, and strategic innovation are discouraged rather than promoted.

The situation analysis begins from the opposite assumption— that discontinuous change is the norm in today's world, and that a conscious effort to recognize, understand, and respond to such change is a vital precursor to strategy creation. As noted earlier, it is impossible to predict the future with any precision. Attempting to do so is a waste of time. But as the famed cyberpunk novelist William Gibson once wrote, "The future is already here. It's just not evenly distributed yet." In other words, there are many signs and symptoms all around us that indicate the likely future direction of events. The trick, therefore, is not to try to predict the future; rather, it is to seek to understand the future consequences of present realities.

Thus, the situation analysis is the essential first step—what I call the sense-making "engine room"—of Strategic Learning, and it drives every subsequent step of the process (see Figure 5.1).

The goal of the situation analysis is to win the battle for superior insight. But what is insight?

Occasionally, a dictionary definition can shed surprising light on the meaning of even a familiar word. The *Random House Dictionary* uses two interesting clauses to define insight: "seeing into . . . underlying truth" and an "understanding of relationships that sheds light on . . . a problem." Both definitions share the idea of revealing *previously unseen truths*—an idea that is highly relevant to the pursuit of insight in Strategic Learning. In this context, winning the

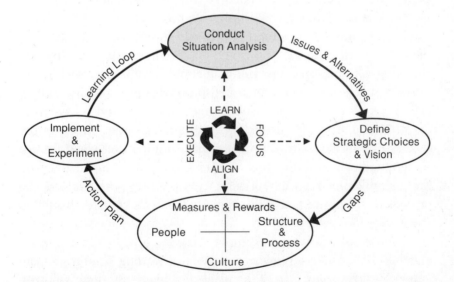

Figure 5.1   Strategic Learning: The Leadership Process—Situation Analysis

competition for insight means seeing the underlying truth *first* or seeing it *better*, so that you can outwit, outmaneuver, and outstrategize your competitors.

The key to a successful situation analysis is to ask the right questions—those that probe and explore the deeper trends at work in relevant areas—and then to answer them better, or faster, than your competitors. This is not easy, and you should spend the necessary time deciding what the right questions are for your particular company.

The situation analysis combines creative brainstorming with rational analysis. It should engage the intellectual and creative resources of people in all levels of the firm, not only those at the top. When multidisciplinary teams from many departments of the company help to generate the insights, the chances of discovering surprising and unexpected truths about your business and the world in which it operates are greatly increased. Furthermore, the involvement of a large, diverse group of employees helps to ensure a generalized sense of ownership of the new ways of thinking that emerge. Few things are harder than trying to impose a new mental model on an organization from the top down. It's far easier to shift the company's ways of thinking when people from throughout the firm have a hand in shaping the new outlook from the start.

Participants in the situation analysis should be encouraged to challenge existing assumptions and explore imaginatively, although the point is to produce new thinking about what is strategically important, not to meander. The net result of this process should be a set of penetrating insights about your company and its environment. The quality of your insights will have a direct effect on the quality of your strategy. By recognizing an important trend first or understanding its implications better than your competition, you are giving yourself a winning edge from the very start. Indeed, the struggle for superior insight is arguably *the* decisive battleground in today's business wars.

I witnessed a powerful example of the importance of winning insights in 1993, while serving as president of Sterling Winthrop's Consumer Health Group. One of the major challenges Sterling Winthrop faced was deciding how to launch the drug Panadol in Russia.

Capturing Russia for Panadol

It wasn't an ordinary assignment. In June 1993 Sterling Winthrop began to focus on ways to launch the drug Panadol (an over-the-counter headache remedy based on acetaminophen) into the newly opened Russian marketplace. That was challenge enough, but we felt that to succeed we had to do our job faster and better than our archrival, Johnson & Johnson, which we'd heard was moving to launch Tylenol (their version of the same drug) into the same market at the same time. The fact that J&J was almost six times as large as Sterling Winthrop at the time ($14.1 billion in annual revenues versus $2.5 billion) made the potential competition into a bit of a David-and-Goliath battle.

The stakes were high. Russia was a huge and potentially lucrative place to do business, but the Russians were still figuring out how capitalism worked while we capitalists were trying to make sense of their chaotic economy. To make matters even more interesting, the fall of the Berlin Wall had set off a wave of privatization in Eastern Europe and China, and our ability to compete in Russia would be an important indicator of how we would fare elsewhere. Finally, this would be the first time we'd compete head-to-head against our rivals in virgin territory: While Tylenol was the dominant over-the-counter analgesic in the United States, Panadol reigned supreme in many overseas markets, and neither of us could make inroads in the other's territory. We suspected that Russia, too, would be a game of winner take all.

What we needed was a "killer" entry strategy. We had endless meetings, racked our brains, and searched high and low for a silver bullet. The regional manager for Eastern Europe, John Mansfield, brought two or three strategies to me in New York, but they were all based on traditional Western models, in which distribution, promotion, and advertising are used to compete in mature economies. After some vigorous discussion, we agreed that to use such an approach in Russia would be like shouting into the void. To succeed, our strategy would have to be tailor-fit to local conditions. "Keep looking, John," I urged him. But the clock was ticking; pressure was high to find an answer and implement it quickly.

This is a situation that most business leaders have faced in some form during their careers, and it is a particularly difficult one to manage well. We concluded that if we got Panadol to market first but did it wrong, we'd just be opening the door for Tylenol. Not only did we need to move *first*, we also needed to do it *best*.

To accomplish this, we systematically asked ourselves a series of questions about the situation that existed before the era of retail pharmacies—"Where did a Russian with a headache go for medical attention?" "Who administered analgesics, how, where, and at what price?"—probing for the insights that would give us an edge. The answers provided the source for a winning strategy.

Traditionally, a Russian who had a headache would go to a state-run clinic and wait (and wait) for an authority figure in a white lab coat to dispense an aspirin or some other pain reliever. Usually, the joke went, the patient would wait all day only to be told there was no aspirin available and that the sufferer would have to return the following week—by which time the headache would probably have cured itself. By 1993, however, free-market pharmacies were sprouting up all over Russia, promising better care. This shift from state clinics to private pharmacies was a radical change—and, we decided, it would be the key to our entry strategy. But it was also abundantly clear that neither the consumers nor the pharmacists really understood how their new economy worked.

We came to the conclusion that in 1993 Russian consumers—conditioned over many years to accept whatever medicines they were given at the clinics—would simply not go up and down pharmacy aisles and choose healthcare products for themselves. Rather, they would continue to go to the authority figure in the white lab coat—now the free-market pharmacist—for medicinal advice. The pharmacists, meanwhile, were hampered by terrible supply and delivery service, and had only a vague idea of how to run a profitable retail business.

Intense debate about these issues distilled our thinking into two linked insights, which in turn provided us with a winning strategy:

▼ Russian consumers would not self-select medicines; they would ask the pharmacist for advice.

▼ The pharmacists were getting terrible service from their suppliers and didn't understand how to run a business.

The conclusion was obvious: If we helped the pharmacists improve their businesses, then they would recommend Panadol to their customers.

Then we had a happy accident. In New Orleans, at a quarterly meeting of regional executives from around the world, we heard a Sterling Winthrop customer service expert I'll call Wendy Smith describe the strategy she had developed for our Canadian subsidiary. In Canada, the company had made the needs of retail pharmacists a major priority. By assisting them with inventory control and product display and by providing them with accurate and timely deliveries, Sterling Winthrop ensured their loyalty. In return, the Canadian pharmacists enthusiastically supported the company's marketing drives and recommended its products to the public. As a result, Sterling Winthrop was one of the most successful pharmaceutical companies in Canada.

As we listened to Wendy, John Mansfield and I looked at each other. We'd been struck by the same thought: *There it was*, our entry strategy for Russia, developed in Toronto, transmitted to us in New Orleans, and now ready for use in Moscow.

Wendy gave her presentation on a Thursday. By Friday morning we had convinced her to pack her bags and fly to Moscow, where she would explain her customer service strategy and help Mansfield's team refine it for local conditions.

The fun and suspense in trying out a new strategy is that there is never just one correct answer that will guarantee success. Business, after all, is a game of risk and probability. But after a certain point we had done as much legwork as time would permit, and now we had to act.

We outfitted two enormous buses as roving Sterling Winthrop retail stores—complete with displays for Panadol, shampoo, and toothpaste—and sent them to visit pharmacies all over Russia. We ran training seminars and showed the free-market pharmacists how to improve their businesses. And we built a new warehouse and delivery system to provide them with accurate, on-time deliveries. These were unheard-of luxuries in Russia.

The result? As we predicted, Russian consumers did indeed rely on pharmacists for advice. The pharmacists, in turn, were inspired by Sterling Winthrop's help in training and equipping them, and they enthusiastically recommended Panadol to their customers. Within six months Panadol had become a leading headache remedy in Russia, while Johnson & Johnson and Tylenol were nowhere to be seen.

Some months later, we had a good laugh when we met a senior Johnson & Johnson marketing executive at an industry conference in Atlanta. Shaking his head ruefully, he asked, "What the hell did you guys do in Russia? We couldn't believe it—it seemed like every pharmacy in the country had a Panadol display in the window!"

Today, looking back at this story, I see that we were unknowingly engaged in the four essential steps of Strategic Learning—learn, focus, align, and execute—and had discovered the importance of doing a good situation analysis by asking the right questions.

While the companies that I work with today are grappling with different issues, they still face the same basic dilemmas we encountered in Russia. Indeed, many of the lessons of the Panadol launch have grown only more important with time—above all, the importance of insight, the wellspring of strategy.

Vision versus Insight

When working with a company, I frequently find that the first thing executive teams want to do is define a new vision for their company. It is a common misconception that a firm can simply invent a new direction for itself in a vacuum, express it in a galvanizing vision statement, and implement it the next day. If only life were so simple.

As we discovered in launching Panadol, it is essential to develop key insights first and *then* develop a vision statement based on those insights. (Where a clear and compelling vision already exists, a thorough situation analysis will validate and reinforce it.) A company's vision and its strategy are intertwined. A vision statement, after all, is an extension of a firm's winning proposition—an aspirational statement of where that winning proposition can take them in the future. To treat them as separate entities is a serious mistake.

Competing on insight is not just a good idea, it is vital to a company's survival. As we've seen, divergent learning is at the heart of successful adaptation. Yet it is a disturbing fact that most companies do not have a systematic process for generating insight. In today's fast-moving environment, managers are often forced to come up with a strategy on the fly, and they find themselves in a mad scramble through a bracken of misperceptions and half-formed ideas. In an ever more complex world, the need for an effective process to generate better and faster insights is more crucial than ever.

In the following pages, we'll examine how to harness such a process of divergent learning by doing an effective situation analysis.

The Golden Rules for Situation Analysis

There are three golden rules for doing a situation analysis.

Produce a Diagnosis, Not a Survey

Making a survey is the easiest thing in the world. The only criterion you need to know is: Leave nothing out. But surveys are useless; all they do is burden you with a glut of information. A *diagnosis*, on the other hand, is a process that allows you to dig beneath the superficial symptoms of a problem and discover its root causes and ultimate consequences.

First you should uncover what is strategically important, then dig deeply into the issues and begin to filter the important from the unimportant. The understanding you gain in this process will help you make the most intelligent choices for your business.

Trends Tell a Story; Snapshots Never Do

A wide-angle snapshot of your firm—a statement like "We're losing millions of dollars"—gives you only a superficial understanding of your business. But mapping trends will help reveal the underlying drivers of this condition.

Every trend tells a story. Whenever you make a significant finding, map the trend, and tell the story it reveals—for example, "Our business looks good today. However, operating costs are rising and revenue is static, which means that we won't be profitable tomorrow."

Simplicity Is a Virtue

The more complex the world becomes, the more important simplicity is. But this should not be confused with superficiality. Simplicity is no shortcut. The reduction of an insight into a clear, distilled, and meaningful statement is very hard work. Once a company has uncovered an insight, managers frequently want to take immediate action. But this is a mistake. It takes real discipline to say no at this point, and to keep digging and sharpening and polishing, until your insight shines like a rare gem—which is precisely what it is.

Searching for the Scoop

A great situation analysis is the result of asking the right questions. Break the team into small groups and present them with a set of guiding questions in each of the five categories—customers, competitors, the firm's own realities, industry dynamics, and the broader environment. Later in this chapter, I'll offer sample guiding questions that you can use in each category, but the best questions for your company and industry may be somewhat different from these. Feel free to revise, subtract, or add questions as needed to focus on the key issues facing your business today. And you may also want to allow your working groups to modify the questions further as they probe for relevant insights. Members of the groups, drawn from different functions and hierarchical levels in the organization, should then work together intensively for the next month to drive out insights in their assigned areas.

Discovering insights takes practice and hard work: There are no cookie-cutter answers to these penetrating questions. To spur the teams on, I like to tell them to pretend they are investigative reporters hunting for a scoop. They must continue to dig and probe the issues relentlessly, until they have discovered a handful of superior insights that could be worthy of front-page headlines.

After a month, the executive team reassembles, and each group reports on its insights. We debate the pros and cons of each group's conclusions and capture common themes. In my experience as a corporate coach, I've noticed that no matter what the company does or who is participating in the situation analysis, the same thing always happens. After they have considered the issues from every angle, different groups start pointing at the same short list of key insights. This is a very interesting phenomenon to witness. In this "Aha!" moment, all of a sudden people begin to make connections or see answers they had never noticed before. This is when the really important insights begin to come into focus, allowing the group to create a consolidated list of well-honed insights. It's an exciting moment for any company.

When we launched Panadol in Russia, as you'll recall, we relentlessly asked questions about our product and our new market, and finally arrived at the following insights:

▼ Despite the rise of modern pharmacies, Russian consumers will still not self-select their medications. They will continue to turn to the authority figure in the white lab coat for advice on what to buy.

▼ The authority figure they turn to is now the free-market pharmacist. Customer service for the pharmacists is terrible, however, and few of them understand how to run a retail business.

▼ The way to reach consumers, therefore, is through the pharmacists. If we provide the pharmacists with superior customer service and education, then they will promote Panadol to the Russian public.

In retrospect, these statements look deceptively simple. The truth is, each one required a significant amount of hard work—first to recognize and develop, then to express clearly. Taken together, they gave us the winning strategy.

How to Do It

The situation analysis probes the following key areas for insights:

▼ Customers.

▼ Competitors.

▼ The firm's own realities.

▼ Industry dynamics.

▼ The broader environment.

The first order of business is to develop a set of questions to ask within each of these areas. The questions will vary depending on the industry and the particular issues your company faces. The following is a set of guiding questions I typically start with when doing a situation analysis with an executive team.

Customers

▼ What are the underlying trends affecting our customers' preferences? How is today different from yesterday, and how will tomorrow be different from today?

▼ What is the hierarchy of customer needs? (These should include customers' hidden needs—those things we must understand before they do.)

▼ How well do we currently serve those needs?

Note how the first question is posed. It doesn't simply ask, "What will your customers' needs be tomorrow?" That's too big a question for anyone without a crystal ball to answer. It can be paralyzing. The trick is to break the question into parts: First define today; then ask yourself how today is different from yesterday; finally, ask how tomorrow will be different from today. In the course of this questioning you will define a trend, and suddenly the larger question becomes much more manageable.

When discussing the hierarchy of customer needs, the challenge is to put yourself in your customers' shoes. First, make an exhaustive list of *all* the things you think your customers consider to be important; then prioritize the list in a hierarchy from most important to least important. This will give you a much deeper understanding of your customers, and of how you can fill their needs.

Some clients ask, "How do we know if we have come up with the right hierarchy?" My answer is: Come out of your shell; ask the people in your organization who deal with customers, and ask your customers directly. Use whatever means you can—market research, focus groups, interviews, or informal discussions—to define what is most important to your customers. That understanding is a critical input for your strategy.

Many companies—particularly high-tech companies, I've noticed—are far more comfortable talking about what they offer rather than what the customer wants. To make a bad situation worse, they often speak in the mumbo jumbo of their specialty, which others find difficult to understand. This is counterproductive. Strategy creation is an outside-in process, not an inside-out process.

The mantra is: Define the benefit you offer your customers, not the product you are trying to sell them—and do it so clearly that even nonexperts in your industry will readily understand.

Theodore Levitt, the Harvard Business School professor who is one of the most distinguished experts on marketing, reminds us that "People don't want a quarter-inch drill; they want quarter-inch holes." Your job is to define the solution you're offering, not simply the product or service you're selling.

Nicholas Hayek of Swatch understood this brilliantly. With the development of quartz technology, accurate timekeeping became a given. Hayek recognized that an overlooked benefit of quartz watches was that they could now be a fun, creative, and easily affordable fashion accessory. This was a stunning insight, one that mattered very much to a lot of people, it turned out. And Hayek saw it *first* and understood it *better* than any of his competitors. Indeed, he used this simple insight to revolutionize and revive the entire Swiss watch industry.

"Discovery consists of seeing what everybody has seen and thinking what nobody has thought," said Albert Szent-Gyorgyi, a 1937 Nobel laureate in biochemistry. Japanese companies, in particular, have focused intensely on fulfilling customers' (unexpressed) desires with revolutionary products. They have done this by empathetically observing the behavior of customers as the basis for understanding their most important needs. Sony answered the wish for a small, light, portable music machine with the Walkman. Honda gained market share by including cup holders in its cars. And Yamaha revived the moribund piano market when it promoted electronic keyboards, thereby making a 300-year-old instrument into a fresh and exciting choice for a new generation of teenage musicians.

The trick, in other words, is to know what your customers want before the customers themselves do. "Marketing," Harvard professor John Deighton has said, "is understanding the behavior of customers better than they understand it themselves."

Competitors

In every competitive arena, including business, you must know your enemies in order to defeat them. Athletes, for example, carefully study videotapes and scouting reports to anticipate how their competitors are likely to react under pressure. Armies, politicians, and even restaurateurs do the same kind of research. To win in business, it's important to understand what game your competitors are playing, where their strengths and weaknesses lie, and how you can exploit the situation.

Some guiding questions:

▼ In what distinctive ways are our traditional competitors serving the market? How does their effectiveness compare with ours in the eyes of the customer?

▼ Who are our nontraditional competitors, and what unique benefits are they offering? Who is the most dangerous and why?

▼ What will be the next big breakthrough in serving customer needs? Who is most likely to launch it—us or a competitor—and why?

Never take your eye off the competition, even when they don't seem to pose an immediate threat. It's a principle whose importance the following story illustrates.

Xerox Overlooks the Competition

In 1949 the Haloid Company of Rochester, New York, unveiled a 14-step process by which one could make a copy of text on paper. By 1965, Haloid had become the Xerox Corporation (*xerography* is from the Greek for "dry writing"), a hugely successful company with annual revenues of $500 million. For years, Xerox dominated the American photocopier business. The company's marketing strategy was to emphasize how fast its machines were, and its legendary sales force sold Xerox machines directly to large companies.

In 1975, Canon, a Japanese photocopier maker, was looking for a way to enter the U.S. market. Deciding not to go head-to-head with Xerox on its home turf, Canon emphasized the price and quality of its machines, and sold mostly to individual consumers or small businesses through retail channels. This proved to be a very successful strategy, which built up a lot of goodwill for Canon among consumers (some of whom worked at large companies).

At first Xerox, the behemoth, didn't pay much attention to the upstart Canon. But once Canon had achieved a critical mass in sales, it launched a devastating attack on Xerox's home turf by selling its own fast machines directly to large companies. Soon Canon became a major force in the photocopier market, on all scales. That was the beginning of Xerox's slide—including a disastrous reorganization of its sales force, a shuffle of CEOs, and a free-falling share price—from which the company has yet to recover.

Beware the danger of falling into the same trap as Xerox. It can be tempting to dismiss the threat posed by a seemingly insignificant competitor. Avoid underestimating the full implications of what your competitors are up to by thinking through the competitive game several moves ahead.

In assessing the relative effectiveness of your company in comparison to that of the competition, remember: It's not your opinion about a competitor that is important, it's your *customers'* opinions that matter.

In the thick of the business battle, we tend to view competitors through a distorted lens: Either we dismiss them in an unrealistic way

("They'll never amount to anything") or we invest them with supernatural powers ("We can't possibly compete against them in that market"). These are extreme but common reactions. Ultimately what really matters is that we learn to define our competitors through our customers' eyes. Just looking at market share is not going to tell you enough about the competition. You really need to know what strengths and weaknesses each has, and how you rank in comparison.

Another danger in assessing the competition lies in overlooking your indirect or nontraditional competitors. Convergence is an increasingly important factor in the new economy, and you must be aware of who *all* of your competitors are. This is no longer a simple question. If you are a telephone company, for example, your indirect competitors are not only other telecoms, but also TV, Internet, consumer electronic, and computer companies. To protect market share, you may have to form partnerships or alliances to compete against these indirect competitors, or even go so far as to acquire them.

Convergence isn't only a high-tech phenomenon. Unexpected shifts in more traditional, old-economy industries can pose life-threatening new competitive dangers to companies that appear to be unchallenged market leaders.

Blindsided by the Bagel

In the old days, the debate around the conference table at Kellogg's headquarters in Battle Creek, Michigan, was whether the market would trend toward hot or cold cereal. Back and forth went the debate. Kellogg was a high-performance company, and its cornflakes cereal was a dominant brand. But then, out of left field came a new breakfast phenomenon: the bagel.

Traditionally a food favored by Jewish New Yorkers, fresh bagels require both boiling and baking. They have a short shelf life, and their manufacture formerly required expensive equipment that only large organizations could afford. But in the 1960s, Daniel Thompson invented a small, inexpensive machine for mass-producing high-quality bagels. Slowly at first, mom-and-pop stores selling fresh-baked bagels began appearing, and consumers reacted with enthusiasm to this unusual, chewy treat. The trend accelerated rapidly, and bagels began cutting into Kellogg's market as a quick, tasty, inexpensive breakfast food. Kellogg was caught utterly unprepared for such a shift in taste; the company watched in dismay as sales of cornflakes (and other breakfast cereals) declined.

In 1996, Kellogg attempted to stave off further losses by buying Lender's Bagels, a frozen bagel product sold, like cornflakes, through supermarket channels, for $455 million. But the cereal maker's bet on frozen bagels at a time when freshly made bagels were becoming a national craze turned out to be another disastrous miscalculation. Indeed, frozen bagels were the *only* sector of the bagel market that was declining. Just three years later, Kellogg sold Lender's to Aurora Foods for just $275 million.

But the story doesn't end there. Now the traditional breakfast food market has come under attack from yet another indirect source—the explosive growth of national coffee-shop chains. With stores like Starbucks on virtually every street corner, busy city dwellers are charging themselves up on coffee, bagels, pastries, and muffins as they scurry to the office or relax on weekends. What does this mean for Kellogg? Consider this question: Have you ever tried to order cornflakes in a coffee shop?

The lesson? Indirect competitors can change the playing field in virtually any industry. Sometimes they will operate in areas where it may be hard for you to engage—just as Kellogg is hard-pressed to combat the dual menace of the bagel and the coffee shop. The key for an incumbent company is an early and insightful understanding of the trends and the newly emerging competitors and an incisive assessment of your strategic options—before you are forced into a defensive posture with your room to maneuver severely curtailed.

The final competitor question focuses on breakthroughs in serving customer needs. When coaching executives, I ask them to equate the breakthroughs made in their industry over time with the breakthroughs made by champion high jumpers—from the scissors to the straddle to the Fosbury flop. After they have plotted out these breakthroughs, I ask the second and most crucial question: Who will launch the next big breakthrough, and *why*? The *why* ensures that you avoid too-easy answers and forces you to develop a clear-sighted view of the challenges you face and their potential consequences.

The Firm's Own Realities

When managers look at their own businesses, they have a tendency to fall into the same traps over and over again:

▼ They look at snapshots of their business, rather than the deeper trends.

▼ They don't do a proper variance analysis.

▼ They don't disaggregate their measures of performance.

In light of this, the following are among the questions a company needs to ask itself about the state of its business.

▼ What are the five-year trends on our critical performance measures, and what conclusions can we draw from them?

▼ Where are we making money and where not? (This question requires disaggregation of profit and cash flow by customer, product group, and geography.) Are we addressing our losing propositions?

▼ What are our key strengths that we can leverage for competitive advantage? What are our weaknesses that represent barriers to better performance?

As mentioned before, trends always tell a story, while snapshots never do. You will get what I call a snapshot view of your business by comparing your earnings in this quarter to your estimates, or to your prior year's earnings. But this tells you very little of use. It's much more important to understand the unfolding story—the deeper trends—of your business.

To really understand where your business is headed, track the four to six key elements of your business performance over the past five years. Be selective; don't try to measure everything. Then, when your latest quarterly results are reported, add the key results to the historical trend and look carefully at how the trend is developing.

Executives can become so focused on the current fiscal year

that often the results of this kind of long-term analysis take them by surprise. Countless times I've heard managers say something like: "Wow, I never realized that our gross margin has dropped four percentage points over the past five years—that's \$12 million in profits!" If you don't fully understand the underlying trends in your business, you could be on your way to becoming a boiled frog, as described in Chapter 1.

Beyond Snapshots to Trends

In 1979, I was made the managing director of Van den Berghs UK, a Unilever foods subsidiary that controlled 60 percent of the British margarine market. This large business had achieved success after success over many years, and had become a typical fat cat: proud, profitable, and averse to change. As part of a briefing to me, the chief financial officer, Peter Burnett, did a five-year trend analysis of the key elements in our profit-and-loss (P&L) statement.

What the CFO's graph showed was that Van den Berghs' revenue growth was gradually slowing, gross margin ratios were static, and—most ominously—overhead costs were climbing slowly but relentlessly. In other words, the company was profitable at the moment but its underlying trends were unhealthy.

Peter and I then decided to address the following question: "If nothing changes in our business in the foreseeable future, what will the trends look like?"

A week later, Peter came into my office, looking grim. He had extended Van den Berghs' existing trend lines 10 years ahead, and the conclusions were sobering, to say the least.

"If these trends continue as is, our business will be in loss within seven years," he said. "I never realized it."

At the next executive committee meeting, we pinned the graph to the wall without saying a word. The eight executives stared at it for a while in silence. Finally, the head of operations, a blunt-speaking Yorkshireman, said what was on everyone's mind: "Why the hell aren't we doing something about this?!"

Why, indeed? We got right to work.

Executives are always in search of a useful analytical tool to help them monitor their business, especially one that will tell them where they are making or losing money, and why. In fact, such a tool exists. It is called a *variance analysis*, and it is a form of management accounting that, unlike the statutory accounting format required by law, allows you to delve deeply into the reality of your business and to see the truth in the numbers.

For some reason, many companies are either unaware of this tool or don't know how to use it. When CFOs want to review a company's recent performance, they often dish up a virtual forest of numbers that acts as a barrier to clear thinking. At board meetings, for instance, board members are given a "board book" with every number possible thrown into it—columns upon columns of detailed figures—and it then becomes an intellectual sparring game to see who around the table can make the best sense of it. What a waste of time!

A big mistake is to confuse a variance analysis with a reconciliation statement. When managers are asked to compare today's profit with that of five years ago, the response is often to work their way through the P&L, from the revenue downward, comparing each line item and then showing either a plus or a minus for the five-year period. This is a reconciliation statement, and unfortunately it is nearly useless. All it really does is to provide you with another view of the trees rather than a real map of the forest.

A variance analysis starts at the bottom of the P&L, not the top, and aims to *diagnose the causes of shifts in profit*. For example, just explaining profit decline in terms of revenue drop is meaningless: Revenue can fall for three main reasons—volume, price, or the mix of products sold. To be useful, we need to understand which of these factors led to the decline. Similarly, gross margins can fall because of either price or costs. Again, we need to diagnose the true reasons for the decline.

There is real skill and discipline involved in doing a proper variance analysis. The technique is to examine each potential cause of the profit shift in turn, while holding the other variables constant. This approach cuts through the clutter and tells you simply and clearly what the three to five key factors are that caused your profit to rise or fall. This key diagnostic information should fit on one page—as opposed to the encyclopedias of information with which companies try to manage themselves. As always, the pursuit of clarity and simplicity will lead you to the truth.

When a company does a variance analysis for the first time, there is often a moment of revelation when the people involved say, "I never knew that before."

To show how a variance analysis works in practice, let's take a look at the case of an Italian beverage company (the details of this story have been altered out of respect for confidentiality).

Vanishing Margins at Limonata

The company—let's call it Limonata—had had a lock on its key supplies—fruit juices and teas, mostly—for over a dozen years, and its brand had thrived across Western Europe. By the early 1990s, its business had grown to over a billion dollars. Without significant competition, however, Limonata grew complacent. It failed to innovate, or even to advertise very much. Then a new competitor appeared—let's call it L'Orange—and rapidly gained market share with a trendy new beverage modeled on America's AriZona iced tea. Within three years, Limonata's profits had plunged by $60 million.

The company's many stakeholders began to bicker in search of answers. They decided that price was a major issue and were about to "go to war" with a turnaround plan, when they sought strategic advice.

"Sixty million dollars is a lot of profit to lose in only three years," I said to Marco, Limonata's CEO. "Where did it all go?"

"My estimate is that we lost about half our profit, $30 million, to volume decline," he replied, "and the other half to a margin squeeze—there was an oversupply of juice on the market, which forced down prices and shrank our margins." The CFO offered a similar point of view.

Marco and the CFO seemed confident about their estimate of the reasons for Limonata's losses. But to validate this assessment, we decided to do a variance analysis of the company's profit decline. The comparison of Limonata's numbers in 1997, its last healthy year, to those of 2000 provided an analysis that revealed a very different story than the one Marco and his CFO had believed to be true.

Limonata Variance Analysis

1997 operating profit:	$88 million
2000 operating profit:	28 million
Profit variance:	($60 million)

Sources of Profit Variance

Volume:	($98 million)
Advertising and promotion:	(10 million)
Price:	(11 million)
Cost savings:	59 million
Profit variance:	($60 million)

These figures were the outcome of a root cause analysis designed to isolate those few key things that were causing the decrease in profits. (Decreases are shown in parentheses.) Often the real reasons catch people by surprise—as they did in this case.

The Limonata analysis shows a negative volume variance of a whopping $98 million and a negative price variance of only $11 million. This was a huge revelation, one that showed Limonata didn't really understand the root cause of its problems. And they'd overlooked entirely the positive variance from cost savings, which meant the problem was much worse than they'd imagined. The company's losses were overwhelmingly due to a loss of volume—the result of a collapse in brand performance—and had little to do with margin squeeze.

"It seems we were about to embark on a major turnaround based on a false assumption," Marco said. "That could have been disastrous. To remain competitive, we must focus our energy on turning the brand around."

Let's examine Limonata's volume problem a little further. The stark fact was that if it had simply held its volume constant over those three years, it would have had $98 million more in profit than it actually showed in 2000. But those numbers would still have been unacceptable. Why? Because if volume had remained static in a growing market, Limonata would actually have been losing market share.

If Limonata had simply maintained market share from 1997 to

2000, it would have made an additional $14 million in profits—thus giving a total of $112 million more than the 2000 actual profit.

Within a $60 million adverse profit variance, Limonata's real problem had remained hidden: a brand performance problem that amounted to $112 million, not the $30 million Marco thought. As it turned out, pricing, Limonata's original bogeyman, was an insignificant factor—only $11 million.

This is a dramatic example of how easy it is for companies to misunderstand the trends affecting their businesses. The surprising thing, of course, is that Limonata had not done a variance analysis before. But Limonata's experience is by no means uncommon, and it underscores the importance of using variance analyses to discover the truths hidden in your numbers.

The next story highlights the importance of disaggregation. Most accounting systems tend to measure things in the aggregate. Yet, to understand where your company is making or losing money, it is essential to disaggregate profitability—by customer, products, assets, and/or geography. Such a disaggregation will provide you with a realistic assessment of where the real issues lie.

A Glass House at Tropicana

When I became the CEO of Tropicana in 1990, the company's return on assets (ROA) was just above 20 percent. That wasn't a bad number, but we felt it could be improved. Making and storing not-from-concentrate orange juice is an asset-intensive business, and so we began to look for ways to maximize our ROA. I asked Steve Schechtman, a senior financial planner, to tackle the project. Steve's approach was an object lesson for all of us.

Instead of looking at the total ROA for all of our assets (an average), Steve looked at each major asset separately to see how profitable it was on a stand-alone basis. That is, he treated our major assets as if they were independent entities charging us market prices for their services; in doing this, he enabled us to see clearly the profits and ROA of each asset.

This analysis proved very revealing. Within our huge plant in Bradenton, Florida, we had a large glass plant—the fourth-largest glass plant in the country, in fact—which produced the glass bottles for our juices. The plant was so deeply embedded in our daily business that it was easily overlooked as an independent asset. When we disaggregated the assets, however, we discovered the glass plant was underperforming and dragging down the rest of Tropicana's numbers.

We quickly entered into a joint venture with a third-party glass manufacturer, which substantially raised the ROA of the glass plant. Because the plant was a significant part of the company's total asset base, this provided a substantial improvement in our overall returns.

The important point is that one cannot manage averages. Disaggregation is the key to any profit improvement plan.

Another powerful technique for separating winners from losers in your portfolio of businesses involves applying what is commonly called the 80/20 rule. The chart in Figure 5.2 shows how to apply the rule to your profits.

In the right-hand column, list your most profitable product categories in descending order, while indicating the percentage of profit accounted for. Draw a horizontal line under the list when you have accounted for 80 percent of your total profit. Now, under the line, list the product categories that account for the remaining 20 percent of your profit.

Quite often, you will find that something like 20 percent of your firm's products or customers contribute 80 percent of your profits, and vice versa—hence the 80/20 rule. The 80 percent of products or customers that contribute only 20 percent of profits generally represent a huge misappropriation of resources, and should be addressed aggressively.

The 80/20 analysis gives you the ability to identify and weed out your marginally profitable or loss-making products, customers, or

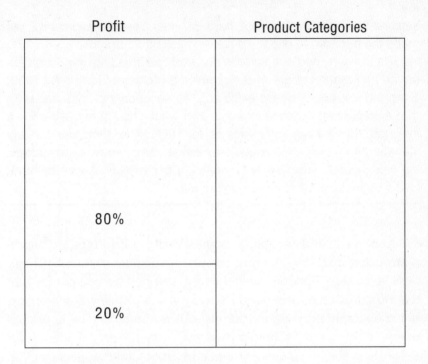

Figure 5.2 Profit Concentration Map

business units, and apply your scarce time and resources to improving the businesses that are most profitable.

Trimming the Seagram's Portfolio

In 1988, when I arrived as the new CEO at Seagram's U.S. spirits business, I learned that the company's profits had been drifting steadily downward over the previous four years. My team did an 80/20 analysis of the company's long list of products. It revealed that a number of underperforming secondary brands were responsible for the decline and were using up a disproportionate amount of time and resources.

This was a difficult moment. Each of those laggardly brands had a history with the company, and their internal champions found every reason under the sun to keep them. But these appeals were based on sentimental attachments, not hard business sense. Ultimately, we made the decision to bite the bullet and sell off 37 brands.

This streamlined our portfolio and had an immediate impact on the profits and market share of our remaining premium brands. By 1992, Seagram's spirits business excluding the secondary brands had realized a 36 percent increase in profits over what it had generated when it included those secondary brands in 1988. The turnaround really stemmed from our 80/20 analysis, which showed where we were making money and where we were spinning our wheels. Above all, it allowed us to focus where it really counted.

Another useful technique is the Portfolio Profitability Map, a matrix that classifies the profitability of various products or business segments. Versions have been developed by companies like the Boston Consulting Group (BCG) and McKinsey & Company, but the simplified version I like to use is similar to the approach of my colleague at Columbia Business School, Larry Selden. It incorporates the language developed by BCG, and it appears in Figure 5.3. (Note that this figure assumes that we are dealing with a

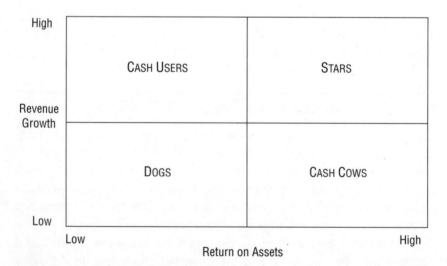

Figure 5.3   Portfolio Profitability Map

manufacturing company. For service companies, I suggest that the horizontal axis show gross margin percentage rather than return on assets.)

Those products that fall into the upper left-hand quadrant (i.e., high revenue growth but low ROA) are typically "cash users." Ideally, you want to move these products or businesses over into the top right-hand quadrant, which is the truly profitable box. These are the "stars" in your company's portfolio. Because of product life cycles and changing consumer tastes, stars shift over time into the bottom right-hand box, where they become steadily earning "cash cows" in their mature years. The aim, of course, should be to use the cash cows to generate new products to replenish the top left quadrant, and to shift those cash users to the top right quadrant, the stars. What often happens, however, is the development of an embarrassingly long list in the bottom left corner, popularly known as "dogs." Think of your dogs as something like the junk most people accumulate in their attics—except that the dogs waste money and other resources, not just storage space.

A good rule of thumb is that products or business units that are stuck in the lower left quadrant—the dog house—for three or more years must be addressed. The options are limited: close, fix, or sell these product lines.

(The rare exception to this rule is when there is a clear and compelling reason to maintain a loss maker, such as when a dog helps to generate profits in other areas of the business. When I was in the liquor business, for example, we didn't make any money on the in-flight sale of liquor on airplanes. Yet all the liquor companies were scrambling to get their brands served on planes because it was a great way to advertise to a captive audience. Occasionally such a loss maker may produce genuine benefits that make it worth retaining. But beware of this slippery slope: It can be very seductive to invent reasons to maintain unhealthy businesses.)

Again, the great value of this exercise is the focus it helps to create. Time after time I've seen companies' performance improve when they have the courage to ruthlessly clean out the attic and concentrate all their resources on those few things that are truly important.

Industry Dynamics

The guiding questions I recommend in this category are:

▼ Which trends in our industry and in the new economy are the most important in shaping our destiny? How will they change the rules of success?

▼ What are we currently doing to exploit these developments so that they produce greater value for our customers?

▼ What barriers must we overcome to take the lead in profitably exploiting these trends? What are the top priorities?

The insurance industry is one that is undergoing radical change in the new economy, but many traditional insurers have been slow to respond. In the meantime, they are facing new competitors every day.

Death by Boiling Threatens the Insurance Industry

"A slow death" is the fate of the traditional insurance industry, according to someone who should know—William H. Donaldson, former chairman of Aetna, America's leading insurer.

For years, insurance companies in the United States were protected from open market competition by Depression-era laws that barred other financial institutions from entering their business. They made money by insuring large, industrial-era businesses with significant bricks-and-mortar assets. Most of these insurance carriers distributed their products through a single channel—either through a direct sales force or through a network of independent agents and brokers. That all began to change in the 1990s, however, with the onset of deregulation, e-commerce, and other shifts.

In response to the new economy, many companies in the conservative insurance industry turned inward and chose to make incremental rather than innovative changes. "Our customers will never buy policies over the Internet," they said. "Commercial insurance is too complex to be sold online." "What do bankers know about insurance?!" As it turns out, plenty of companies *are* using the Internet to purchase insurance; commercial insurance *is* available online; and bankers *have* jumped into the insurance game.

While the big banks like Chase Manhattan and other new players reinvent the game of selling insurance—and grab market share while they are at it—insurance companies are beginning to understand that they are in danger of becoming boiled frogs. Some of them are trying to jump; Metropolitan Life, for example, has announced it will counter-attack by entering the already crowded full-service banking field. The insurance industry's traditional business model is in danger of becoming obsolete. Now insurers must create a bold, fresh approach.

For many companies, e-commerce is simply too big a question to get a firm grip on. Yet the Internet is now a mainstream phenomenon, not a separate business. A useful way to analyze its business significance is to consider it in terms of the River of Business, as shown in Figure 5.4. In this depiction, your company lies midstream. Your suppliers are upstream, and your customers are downstream. Products and services flow from upstream to downstream, and your challenge is to extract the maximum value from this flow.

The usefulness of this diagram lies in its power to help you disaggregate the various roles the Internet can play in your business. For some companies, the primary value of the Internet lies upstream—in the relationship between the firm and its suppliers. These companies

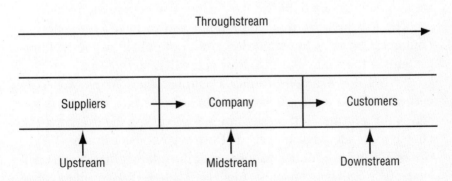

Figure 5.4   The River of Business

will use the Internet to manage their procurement processes more efficiently, thus reducing costs and perhaps creating tightly controlled just-in-time inventory systems that minimize the amount of capital that is tied up in parts and materials.

Other companies will concentrate on the midstream, creating better internal efficiencies—for example, in manufacturing, warehousing, distribution, and invoicing.

For still other companies, the downstream area is most critical. These companies will focus on using the Internet to improve their methods of finding, selling to, and servicing customers. They may concentrate on creating user-friendly web sites where their products can be ordered, or on developing databases of frequently asked questions that will enable customers to quickly and easily resolve most product-use problems without having to speak with a company representative.

Rather than trying to tackle the big question of the Internet as a whole, companies have found it helpful to use the River of Business to break the problem into its component parts and examine each one separately. Which area of the river is most critical to your own economics? Where are the greatest opportunities for new efficiencies concentrated? Where do bottlenecks currently exist that the Internet may help to unclog? The answers to questions like these will help you decide where best to focus your company's Internet initiatives.

Of course, the ultimate advantage is to use the Internet to create a superefficient throughstream covering the entire supply chain. However, it is impractical to achieve this in one fell swoop. It is therefore necessary to tackle the challenge in coordinated stages.

The key point is that you should aim to have an explicit e-commerce strategy, one that describes not only how you will participate in the game, but also how you will take the *lead*.

At GE, for example, former Chairman Jack Welch was concerned that his business units were not aggressively preparing themselves for a future built on the Internet. He asked the executives in charge to create what he called "Destroyyourbusiness.com"—a series of new ways of doing business over the Internet that would challenge GE's existing business models. The executives might have snickered (GE, after all, dominates many categories), but they completed their assignment.

Then Welch startled his executives by telling them to actually implement those strategies. After all, he reasoned, if GE didn't do so, someone else surely would. As a result, GE is one of the leaders among Fortune 500 companies in moving from traditional to Internet-enabled business models.

The Broader Environment

As mentioned in Chapter 3, there's an entire branch of modern science known as complexity theory, which focuses on the seemingly random, discontinuous, and disproportionate nature of change. One of the emblematic metaphors used by the complexity theorists to illustrate the unpredictability of interactions within any complex system is the idea that, given enough time and just the right conditions, a single flap of a butterfly's wings in Peru could eventually produce a cyclone in Japan. Whether or not this is literally true, it's certainly the case that subtle shifts in the broader environment can have an unexpected impact on a business. These days, hardly any industry is immune from the large-scale changes taking place in society. Thus, executives need to focus on a wide array of environmental indicators, launching the discussion by asking:

What is happening around us that will impact our business in regard to the following factors?

▼ Economic trends.

▼ Social habits and attitudes.

▼ Globalization.

▼ Technology.

▼ Demographics.

▼ Government policies.

For example, under the heading of social habits and attitudes, consider the trend toward casual dress in business.

Good-Bye to the Pinstripe?

Casual Fridays—the wearing of casual clothes in lieu of suits to work on Friday—began in the late 1980s as a once-a-week workplace concession. This simple motivational gimmick proved wildly popular, and "casual creep" began to affect workplace dress all week long. In the meantime, the countercultural ethos of Silicon Valley—where creative, highly successful people habitually dress down—began to affect attitudes worldwide. People everywhere are searching for free-flowing "creative synergies" in place of a suit's implied groupthink restrictions.

While many employees applaud this trend toward informality, suit manufacturers are facing a major reversal in business fortunes. Because of a seemingly slight shift in cultural attitudes, their very dependable business is being threatened. In response, large retailers like Brooks Brothers have begun to aggressively market their casual clothing lines to businesspeople. But traditional haberdashers may have a tougher time adapting, and avoiding boiled frogdom.

In the case of demographics, the aging of the baby boomers is going to have a profound effect on many industries.

Those over 80 years of age, the "gray panthers," are the fastest-growing population in the nation. By 2030, over half of all U.S. adults will be age 50 or older. These statistics have tremendous implications for many industries, including:

▼ Healthcare.

▼ Elder care.

▼ Tourism.

▼ Mail order.

▼ Pet care.

▼ Security systems.

Case Study: A Situation Analysis of Med-Surg

In this section, I'll walk you through an actual situation analysis conducted with the large distributor of medical supplies that was introduced in Chapter 1.

As you may recall, Med-Surg was struggling to adapt to the new realities of e-commerce: Thanks to the ruthless efficiency of the Internet, the company was getting squeezed upstream by its suppliers, and downstream by its customers, who are doctors and dentists. The company was desperate not to become a boiled frog.

As always in a situation analysis, the task was to generate winning insights. We did this by asking a series of penetrating questions about the state of the company, its customers, and its environment. The executive team was able to produce a revealing diagnosis.

It was clear from the outset that Med-Surg had fallen into a common trap. While the company's executives were very proud of the services they offered—a first-rate distribution system for medical supplies—Med-Surg had not thought hard enough about what its *customers* wanted. This represents a crucial difference in point of view: They were looking at their customers from the inside out rather than the outside in.

Our first task was to attempt to view the world through the customers' eyes. Just asking about a customer's needs was too big a question. Instead, the Med-Surg executives set out to discover the hierarchy of their customers' needs—to list all the needs they could think of, and then to rank them in order of importance. To identify the most important needs, they asked: "What keeps our customers up at night?" The executives weren't allowed to give the usual rote answers, or to guess. Rather, they had to actually talk to their customers and probe for answers. "Think of yourself as an investigative reporter," I encouraged them. "Keep asking questions until you are satisfied you have reached the truth."

A month later, the managers reported back with a list of their customers' concerns, listed here by priority:

▼ The number one concern of dentists, Med-Surg's primary customers, was that their big equipment—like the X-ray machine, the dentist's chair, and the drill and sink apparatus—work. Their living depends on this.

▼ Both doctors and dentists wanted an efficient way to manage their practices: scheduling of patients, record keeping, billing, insurance claims, and so on.

▼ Finally, they wanted an efficient supply replenishment system (Med-Surg's traditional strength).

This list told us that the company's customers were most concerned about issues of service, not product supply. Med-Surg had all the tools in place to respond to this need. But the company had built its 25-year reputation on selling consumables—the physical products, like cotton swabs and latex gloves, that ranked only third in the customers' wish list. Furthermore, Med-Surg had not yet exploited the Internet, and had not put a strategy in place to do so. The company's challenge became clear: It would not survive for long as a mere supplier of products; a competitor that could provide integrated solutions by supplying both consumables and terrific practice management software would threaten to knock Med-Surg out of the game.

Med-Surg pressed on with the situation analysis. The executives focused on customers, competitors, its own realities, industry economics, and its environment. Here is a brief summary of the insights they unearthed.

Customers

▼ The Internet gives dentists and doctors increased power to:
   Select suppliers and switch between them.
   Drive down procurement costs.
   Buy directly from manufacturers.
   Enhance their practice management effectiveness.

▼ Increasing numbers of our customers are becoming Web-savvy and will therefore use this power.

▼ The hierarchy of needs shows that our customers' most important needs are service-based, where we have yet to make an impact. Pure product supply, our traditional strength, ranks low in our customers' hierarchy of needs.

Competitors

▼ Our traditional competitors are more focused and more profitable than we are. Thus they have more funds to invest in the development of new business models.

▼ New competitors are emerging who are offering Internet-based practice management services to doctors and dentists. Their skills and penetration levels are improving relentlessly. If they are able to acquire product distributors, they would be in a position to preempt us as providers of fully integrated solutions—from product supply to the provision of high-value practice management services.

Our Own Realities

▼ Our profitability is not satisfactory. Our product line is too diverse and fragmented and is burdened by loss makers. We must streamline our offerings and address our losing propositions quickly.

▼ We have the in-house skills to develop an Internet-based service strategy. However, our sales representatives are resisting the move to services. Many of them do not have the competencies to operate in this new world. Unless we can address this problem we will remain stuck where we are.

▼ Our corporate culture is consensus-based, risk-averse, and fraught with internal rivalries. It is a barrier to superior performance.

Industry Dynamics

▼ Our industry is moving to an Internet-enabled model covering both efficient supply chain management and the provision of superior practice management services.

▼ Players who are unable to make a profitable transition to this new model are unlikely to survive.

Environment

▼ The good news is that the aging population will ensure continued growth in the healthcare industry and hence in the demand for our products.

▼ However, the growth of managed care together with Internet-based procurement systems threatens a margin squeeze that must be overcome through a combination of enhanced efficiencies and the provision of value-added services.

Once Med-Surg's executives had discovered and honed these insights, they couldn't simply walk away from them. Indeed, the Strategic Learning process forces you to the next step: to translate your insights into a breakthrough strategy.

Med-Surg is using its insights to transform itself from being simply a supplier of consumables to becoming a provider of knowledge-based services as well. It continues to sell rubber gloves, cotton swabs, and all the other supplies doctors and dentists need. But it is rapidly expanding its offerings to include practice management software, supply management systems that automate the ordering process, and other unique services that make the practice of medicine easier and more profitable for its customers.

Med-Surg is now well on its way to turning around its business. The situation analysis was the springboard for this. Without clear insights into how its environment was changing, Med-Surg would probably have increased its efforts along traditional lines, working (for example) to trim the costs of commodities like paper towels even further. The benefits to be gained from such a strategy would be small and shrinking.

Only by taking a long step back to consider the major trends that are reshaping its industry was Med-Surg able to discover a far more lucrative business arena adjacent to its traditional space, with much greater long-term growth prospects. In today's rapidly changing business world, every company needs to do the same.

6

Defining Your Focus

Having completed the situation analysis, your organization now has a set of key insights about both the external business environment in which you operate and the internal strengths and weaknesses you bring to the competitive arena. You're now ready to embark on the second stage of the Strategic Learning process: defining your strategic choices and the vision that emerges from these insights (see Figure 6.1). Where the situation analysis is a process of divergent learning, this step of defining your focus is a process of convergent learning.

Notice the sequence being recommended here—strategic choices, then vision. Of course, there's nothing wrong with defining a vision as the first step after the situation analysis. However, in my work with executive teams, I've found that, as a practical matter, they often prefer to develop their company's strategic choices and winning proposition first. This then makes the vision easier to articulate.

On reflection, this makes good sense. Vision, after all, is not a thing apart. It is best viewed as an extension of your winning

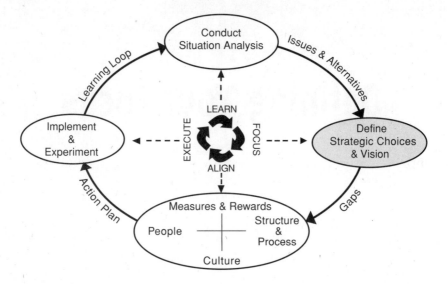

Figure 6.1   Strategic Learning: The Leadership Process—Strategy and Vision

proposition—an aspirational statement of where your winning strategy can take you in the future.

This chapter, therefore, begins with an explanation of strategic choices; it concludes with a discussion of vision.

While in the throes of the strategy process, many executives like to remark, with a knowing air, that "At the end of the day, it's all about execution." It's a comment that generally provokes nods of agreement around the table. Yet my experience suggests otherwise. I've often seen companies wrestling with what they view as the difficulties of implementation. Yet on closer analysis, in the majority of these cases, the real problem is not implementation. It is the lack of a clear and compelling strategic focus. The rush to discuss execution ducks the most crucial issue.

Is execution of the plan important? Of course, and we'll discuss that stage of the process in detail in the proper place. But effective execution is impossible unless you start with a clear focus. Seneca, the Roman statesman and philosopher, said it well: "Our plans miscarry because they have no aim. When a man does not know what harbor he is making for, *no* wind is the right wind." The truth is that developing a clear focus is something most companies find extremely hard to do. Thus, developing focus is in itself one of your greatest implementation challenges.

Dan Denison, formerly a professor at the University of Michigan Business School and now at the International Institute of Management Development (IMD) in Lausanne, Switzerland, has conducted extensive research examining the various components of corporate culture to determine which factors contribute most directly to outstanding financial performance. The results are astonishingly unambiguous. Clarity of purpose—what Denison calls "mission"—is the single factor that most strongly correlates with superior financial performance, while lack of such clarity correlates most strongly with poor financial performance. Thus, it isn't only our gut instincts that attest to the importance of focus. Hard evidence points to the same conclusion.

A Winning Focus Begins with Insight

As we've seen, the challenge of the strategist is to make the most intelligent choices about the best use of scarce resources. And the quality of the insights you generate in the situation analysis will have a direct impact on the quality of the strategic choices you make.

When Commander Noel Evans made his choice between planting peaches and plums, he literally bet the farm. His choice of peaches was not based on luck; it was based on the insight that all of his neighbors were planting plums, and that he had a ripe opportunity for success with peaches. He made a winning choice.

In the same way, the most successful strategic choices made by companies can virtually always be traced back to a clear insight—some truth that the company saw first or better than the competition and was able to transform into a plan for winning.

55 Broad Street: Location, Location, Bandwidth

Nestled in the heart of New York City's bustling "Silicon Alley," 55 Broad Street, the world's first "smart building," provides an excellent illustration of strategic innovation within a traditional industry—commercial real estate—that has been around as long as civilization itself.

The 1960s-era office tower at 55 Broad had been the headquarters of the now-defunct financial giant Drexel Burnham Lambert. After 1990 it was vacant, a victim both of Drexel's collapse and of the flight by many financial firms from downtown Manhattan into New York's suburbs.

The property appeared to be a white elephant, a hard asset in a soft market that had become a significant drag on earnings. Conventional real estate wisdom offered the building's owners, Rudin Management, a familiar set of options: Sell the building; reduce the rent to fill space; modernize the building and increase the rent; or convert the space into some other use, such as residential housing. None of these was financially attractive.

Instead, the Rudins hired John Gilbert III, a young real estate executive and tech visionary who created an entirely new business model. Gilbert's idea took advantage of several interlocking trends—telecom deregulation, the emergence of a tech-oriented new economy, and the fact that a number of high-tech communications and media firms were considering relocating in lower Manhattan. But most important was his insight into the *social* needs of the people who work at the forefront of new technologies—specifically, their desire to interact, exchange ideas, and learn from each other. From this understanding arose the concept of providing not just desirable rental space, but also the unique value of membership in an exciting learning community.

To realize Gilbert's strategic vision, Rudin Management gutted the building and renovated it as a digital on/off-ramp featuring a state-of-the-art telecommunications platform. Seven separate telecom systems connect everyone both inside and outside the building, providing tenants with plug-in access to high-speed voice, video, and data transmission.

While the infrastructure gives the building its "smarts," the building's true genius lies in the social architecture that makes it into a learning community. Rudin marketed 55 Broad as the watercooler for cyberspace, a place where serendipitous meetings among entrepreneurs from many tech-related industries could take place. Set-aside spaces within the building were dedicated to social interactions: For example, the Community Sandbox provided room for parties, exhibits, and special events, while the Hearth was a common lounge for relaxing, chatting, and playing pool. The concept exploded. The building was fully leased within 18 months under the worst possible market conditions and was soon being heralded by the global business press as the heart of New York's Silicon Alley.

Today the building houses a *Who's Who* of new-technology firms ranging from smaller start-ups to tech mainstays such as Sun Microsystems, IBM, Ericsson, Silicon Graphics, Inc. (SGI), and Nokia. Through its experience at 55 Broad, Rudin Management has reinvented itself as a new-economy firm. Rudin is expanding its "smart-ready," community-based real estate concept to several other buildings in New York City and London, the first nodes in a projected network of smart buildings around the world.

John Gilbert explains, "Nothing is more brick-and-mortar than real estate. Our strategic innovation lies in how we were able to reposition our physical assets into a twenty-first-century product that integrates quality real estate, global connectivity, and a learning community under a single roof."

The same essential ingredient—a superior insight—has been at the heart of one of the most celebrated turnarounds of recent business history, involving one of the world's largest companies in one of the most competitive industries.

IBM's About-Face

When Lou Gerstner took over the leadership of IBM in 1993, Big Blue had suffered $18 billion in losses over the previous three years. Clearly, drastic action was needed. Gerstner had to make a stark choice: Either decentralize the businesses or integrate IBM's many disparate parts more tightly than ever before.

At the time, IBM was poised to spin off many of its units in a massive decentralization effort. When Gerstner took over from his predecessor, John Akers, he put a temporary hold on the plan, and then spent three months canvassing IBM's customers about their needs. (The fact that Gerstner himself had been an IBM customer during his years at RJR Nabisco may have made him more sensitive to customer interests than the typical promoted-from-within CEO.)

What he discovered was that the greatest need facing customers was, quite simply, sense making for the new world of information technology (IT). They were being bombarded, not only by IBM but also by IBM's competitors, with a confusing array of new IT products and services—everything from hardware, software, installation, and process design to systems integration and training and technical support. Overwhelmed by the choices they faced, their overriding questions were, "What do we really need, and how do we make it all work together?"

In this environment, the big opportunity for IBM's people was not to approach customers in separate teams, selling lots of different things. It was for a unified IBM to provide *integrated* solutions to its customers—something IBM, with its preeminent history and its unmatched breadth of expertise, was uniquely positioned to offer.

This was a crucial insight that has helped shape the destiny of IBM. What it meant, of course, was that if IBM were to split itself into many smaller companies, as planned, it would be unable to provide such integrated solutions, the very thing its customers were clamoring for.

In a now-famous moment, Gerstner canceled the spin-offs and instead began an aggressive push to provide integrated solutions. "Our customers are not in the technology business," he explained in 1997, "and they don't have time to go door-to-door around IBM's product groups to build their own solutions. They want someone to do that for them. This is what we mean when we talk about solutions. . . . It all begins with an intimate understanding of what the customer is trying to accomplish."

Gerstner's choice was a huge bet and not without risk, but it was based on a penetrating insight into what was most important to customers. It eventually turned IBM's faltering Global Services division into the largest computer services company in the world—and quite possibly saved Big Blue.

The Meaning of Focus

Remember that the ultimate job of strategy is to define how you will win. What does this mean? It doesn't necessarily mean being the biggest and most profitable company in the world—after all, there can be only one of those—or even in your industry. Not everyone can aspire to overtake GE or Microsoft. Winning means creating greater value for your customers and superior profits for your company in a defined arena—the specific business or businesses you've chosen as your target market.

Positioning is sacrifice, as the saying goes. Trying to be all things to all people is a recipe for failure. Instead, pick a place to play where you have a shot at being the best, where it's possible to know your customers and the market superlatively well. Then focus intensely on this segment. The longer and smarter you work at it, the better you'll become at serving these customers and the harder it will be for competitors to emulate your strategy.

Making the Strategic Choices

Now let's consider the process of making choices and defining the winning strategy for your company.

The insights gained in the situation analysis will help illuminate the key issues and alternatives facing your business. You'll now need to turn these insights into winning strategic choices. Executives often ask for a process to help them do this. I've found the following approach to be fruitful.

▼ Summarize your key insights by consolidating the main points from each of the five categories used in the situation analysis into a single list of the most important findings.

▼ List the major threats and opportunities that these insights bring to light.

▼ Identify your strategic alternatives—the major alternative courses from which you have to choose.

▼ Consider the pros and cons of each alternative as the basis for making your final choices.

Going through this bridging process, starting with the insights and analyzing the issues they raise, should help the strategic alternatives emerge quite naturally and assist you in making the right choices.

As illustrated in Figure 6.2, the strategic choices involve three main elements—customer focus, the winning proposition, and your five key priorities.

1. *Customer focus* defines which customers your firm will serve and which it will not. It identifies what is most important to those customers (their hierarchy of needs). Finally, it defines what products and/or services your firm will offer to its customers.

2. *The winning proposition* is the heart of your firm's strategy. It defines what your firm will do differently or better than its competitors to achieve greater value for its customers and superior profits for itself—and hence greater value for its shareholders.

3. *The five key priorities* ensure that your firm's key resources will be concentrated behind your strategy. They define the most important things the firm will do to achieve its winning proposition—those few things that will make the biggest difference.

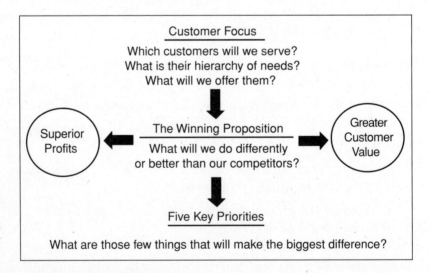

Figure 6.2   The Strategic Choices

As you can see, the emphasis in all three elements is on focus. The challenge is to select a particular set of customers, a particular set of product or service offerings, a particular winning proposition, and a limited number of priorities. Every time you fail to choose, you're choosing to spend a percentage of your scarce resources on the wrong things. Your resources will be dissipated and wasted in a futile attempt to do everything at once, and you'll likely end up achieving nothing. Thus, one crucial litmus test of a good strategy is that the firm has decided not only what it *will* do, but also what it will *not* do.

Making strategic choices and sticking to them is difficult. It takes courage to choose one course of action over another and fortitude to stick to your decision when the pressures of daily business tempt you to blur your focus. As Roger Enrico, ex-chairman of PepsiCo, puts it, "The best decision is the right one. The second best decision is the wrong one. And the worst decision is *no* decision."

I recently walked past a church in my New York City neighborhood. It bore a sign reading, "I don't know the secret of success, but I know how we fail—when we try to please everybody." It's true in life, and it's certainly true in business.

Cleaning the Attic at Med-Surg

Having decided to transform Med-Surg from its exclusive focus on product distribution into a management services company for the medical industry, the company's leaders realized that they first needed to clean up their base business. They had too many vendors, too many lines of business, too many customer segments, and too many products, taxing the warehouses, invoicing and delivery systems, and other customer service systems required to maintain their plethora of businesses.

They did an 80/20 analysis and used their findings to "clean the attic" by spinning off, closing, or selling most of their small or underperforming businesses, and by greatly increasing their focus on their high-margin products. The result was a healthy upturn in Med-Surg's business.

Let's now examine in more detail what's involved in making your company's strategic choices.

Customer Focus

The starting point is always the customer. And the first step here is to ask yourself: *Which customers will we serve, and which will we not serve?*

Every great strategy clearly defines its target market. Consider the auto industry. BMW appeals to affluent customers in search of a thrilling driving experience; Mercedes aims at upscale drivers who value luxury and the best engineering; and Volvo focuses on those for whom safety is most important. At one time, General Motors was known for its clearly delineated "ladder of brands" that customers climbed as they grew more affluent (and conservative), culminating in the high-end Cadillac. In recent years, however, General Motors has suffered from "brand blur"—overlapping brands and look-alike cars. This loss of clear customer segmentation has undoubtedly contributed to its steady decline in market share (one exception: GM's Saturn brand, which has successfully focused on appealing to women drivers). To maximize its future success, GM will have to relearn the segmentation genius of its legendary CEO, Alfred P. Sloan, and find fresh ways of defining the distinct customer benefits of its Pontiac, Chevrolet, Cadillac, and other brands.

But it's not enough to decide which customers to serve. The key to success is to understand their needs, and more particularly their *hierarchy of needs*.

Determining the relative importance of your customers' various needs is vital if you are to develop winning strategies for serving them. For example, we saw that the doctors and dentists served by Med-Surg were far more concerned about managing the business elements of their practices on a day-to-day basis than they were with getting quick, cheap, reliable deliveries of basic supplies. The latter business had been Med-Surg's specialty. As soon as the company understood its customers' priorities, it was clear that Med-Surg had to redefine its business or risk becoming fundamentally irrelevant to its customers.

Defining your customers' hierarchy of needs, then, is a fundamental tool for determining which specific customer benefits your company will offer through its products and services. The better job you do at meeting your customers' most important needs, the stronger and more profitable will be the bond you'll develop with them.

GE Appliances

In 1998, GE Appliances decided to set up an Internet-based system for arranging delivery of appliances to Home Depot customers. One benefit that GE considered offering through this system was next-day delivery. After all, it was reasoned, a homeowner whose washing machine or refrigerator needed replacing would surely put a high premium on getting a new appliance as quickly as possible.

However, before finalizing these plans, GE managers decided to check their intuitive sense of customer priorities by using focus groups, what-if scenarios, and other surveying tools. The results surprised them. GE discovered that customers actually placed little or no value on 24-hour deliveries. According to Michael P. Delain, GE Appliances' quality manager for local delivery service, the GE customer studies "eliminated any perceived need for evening deliveries, next-day deliveries, Sunday deliveries, all sorts of costly things that we had wrongly thought would be important to customers."

Instead, GE found that customers were more concerned about having deliveries done when promised, and about having the installations handled in a soothing and professional manner. If the delivery person's demeanor was caring, GE discovered, customers were quite happy to wait a few days for the delivery itself. By focusing on these concerns, GE addressed its customers' real wishes while saving the huge sums they would otherwise have spent on 24-hour deliveries.

The moral? Don't assume that you know what your customers value most—study them instead.

The Winning Proposition

Once you are clear about which customers you will focus on and what products and services you intend to offer them, you are now in a position to define your company's winning proposition. Remember, the challenge is to define a *winning* proposition, not just a value proposition; the latter is often nothing more than a me-too concept.

A winning proposition does two things: It defines how you'll win the competitive battle, and it provides an internal rallying cry. A compelling winning proposition helps you to compete externally, helps to keep the troops inside your company focused and motivated, and also helps to draw the best and brightest to your cause.

To develop a winning proposition, you must answer this question: *What will we do differently or better than our competitors to create greater value for our customers and superior profits for ourselves?*

Greater value for customers can take many forms. As the 55 Broad Street, IBM, and GE Appliances examples illustrate, choosing the right form of customer value to focus on depends on the accuracy with which you've analyzed your customers' needs. In business after business, the company that identifies the most important customer needs and moves massively to satisfy them better than anyone else is the one that outperforms its competitors.

But a winning proposition is one that creates both greater value for your customers and superior profits for your firm. It is not enough simply to delight customers. Sometimes this is easy to do. You can keep adding wonderful features to your products or provide the ultimate in customized service. But all this is to no avail if you can't figure out how to generate superior profits from these customer benefits.

Let's take Amazon.com as an example. Up to this writing, it has provided terrific customer value. Millions of customers enjoy the convenience of buying books, CDs, and other products online at competitive prices with quick, reliable delivery. But so far the company has not turned a profit, and the support of investors is gradually drying up, putting increasing pressure on the company and its founder, Jeff Bezos. It remains an open question whether Amazon has found a true winning proposition—that is, one which will create a sustainably profitable retailing business on the Internet.

There are those who say when asked for a winning proposition that there can be only one answer: "The purpose of our business is to create shareholder value." This is not so much wrong as simply unhelpful. It's true that the creation of shareholder wealth is the *ultimate* scorecard by which a company's management is judged. But the reason "to create shareholder value" is unhelpful as a winning proposition is that it gives no indication of what choices management must make—that is, what they will actually *do*—to achieve this desirable outcome.

It's a bit like saying that the purpose of baseball is to score the most runs. The real question is *how* you intend to do that. A great baseball coach doesn't simply run up and down the sidelines shouting, "Score runs! Score runs!" but instead offers some specific how-to strategies that make effective use of the talents of the team: "Lenny, I want you to lay a bunt down the third base line. Then, Wally, your job will be to hit to the opposite field and move Lenny down to second base so Keith can drive him home with a base hit." *That's* what a winning proposition is like.

In any case, I would argue that shareholder value is too narrow a goal. For one thing, a business must serve stakeholders beyond those who own its stock, including customers, employees, suppliers, and the larger community; if any of these are seriously alienated, the long-term success of the company will sooner or later be threatened.

Furthermore, purely financial results can be generated—especially in the short term—through various techniques of financial engineering: stock buybacks, divestitures and acquisitions, spin-offs, special dividends, and so on. While these tactics may be necessary and beneficial in specific circumstances, they don't define good corporate health any more than a successful surgery defines good physical condition. Unless your company is doing a superior job of creating value for customers, there's no basis for building long-term growth, no matter how rosy your results may look for a quarter or two.

Don't misunderstand: Over the long term, one of the primary duties of management, as a steward of shareholder assets, is to protect the value of those assets and work to ensure their growth. But merely repeating the mantra of "shareholder value" is not a sufficient definition of your business's winning proposition.

Five Key Priorities

The final step in forming your strategic choices is to make a list of the top priorities that will help your firm effectively concentrate its scarce resources to achieve its winning proposition. Your priorities are those few things that make the biggest difference, on which you must focus relentlessly to be successful.

The key to this step is to make a list of all the important things you need to do to achieve your winning proposition, and then to pick only the top *five* as your priorities. The great danger here is to produce a laundry list of 10, 12, or 15 priorities. If you set any more than five priorities, the clarity of your message begins to get blurred, and its effectiveness becomes compromised.

"Why pick five?" people sometimes ask. George A. Miller's classic research on memory showed that most people can carry no more than five to seven ideas in their minds at once. Miller may have been right, but I say: If you can keep seven goals for your company clearly in mind, you should join Mensa, the club for geniuses. Experience suggests that for most of us five is the maximum number. And Pietersen's Corollary to Miller's Rule is this: When the rule of five is violated, and the number of ideas swells past six toward 10, the result isn't merely diminishing returns—it's a total wipeout. Chances are good that people presented with 10 priorities will remember *none of them*.

Here's an easy way to make sure you follow Miller's Rule: When you get up before an audience to describe your company's top priorities, tick them off with the fingers of one hand—and keep the other hand buried in your pocket. That'll help you resist the temptation to throw in two or three more priorities. Count to five—then stop.

Simplicity Is Not a Shortcut

There are two vital reasons for striving to state your strategic choices as clearly, specifically, and simply as possible. First, the effort to do so will force you to clarify your own thinking—to focus not vaguely but precisely on the customers you will serve, the winning proposition you will offer, and the priorities that will make it possible. Second, achieving simplicity is crucial to your success in communicating the strategy to everyone inside (and outside) your organization. No one responds to a complex message; it paralyzes an organization. In fact, one of the most important tasks of leadership is to simplify complexity.

Make no mistake—simplicity is hard work. Blaise Pascal, the French mathematician and philosopher, is said to have written to a friend, "I am sorry to send you this long letter, but I didn't have time to write you a short one." Don't fall back on Pascal's excuse. Invest the time needed to state your strategic choices in clear, succinct terms.

One approach sometimes used is called the Little Old Lady Test: If you can't explain your strategy in terms that anyone's grandma can understand, you probably haven't *got* a strategy. Perhaps that's a bit extreme. But your strategy must take a form that you can communicate to your employees with clarity and confidence. Imagine standing before your employees to explain the strategy for your company or for one of its divisions. They look up at you hopefully, wondering, "Where are we going? And how does our leader intend to get us there?" As you speak, one of three possible reactions will appear on their faces: the glazed stare of incomprehension; the downcast glance of doubt; or the bright, eager look of belief and enthusiasm.

The words in which you formulate your strategic choices *must* be crafted with the simplicity, clarity, and directness needed to elicit that third response. If they don't, it's highly unlikely that you will energize your organization to achieve your strategy.

A great winning proposition is as much about leadership as about strategy. It's a call to action that suggests to your people what they must do—and will do—when they go to work on Monday morning. Indeed, the clearer your focus, the more powerful its effect will be. I have seen the power of focus in operation at many companies, but the most dramatic example was the story of Sony Media Solutions.

The Magic of Focus

The Sony Media Solutions Company (MSC) is a subsidiary of the $19 billion Sony Corporation of America. MSC manufactures and markets a variety of media products, including audiotape, videotape, CD-ROMs, and, increasingly, network-based digital memory. MSC is a company of firsts with a rich history of innovation: The videocassette, the 3.5-inch floppy disk, the CD-ROM, the MiniDisc, and the Memory Stick were all Sony innovations.

In 1999, when my colleague at Columbia Business School, Bill Klepper, and I first began to work with MSC, the division had fallen on hard times. Profit and volume targets had been missed consistently for several years, overhead had risen steadily, and margins were shrinking. While doing the situation analysis, the small group working on the division's own realities was asked to capture these trends in a story or metaphor. After some deliberation, they concluded that the business was in a "death spiral," and they explained in chilling terms why this was true. The company had to take action fast. My Columbia colleagues and I worked with cross-functional teams to define the business's winning proposition and key strategic priorities, which included cost reductions, improved efficiencies, and better focus on the most important customer needs.

As a follow-up, we met with the division's 120 top managers in Orlando, Florida, six weeks later to discuss the gaps that needed to be closed, the milestones to be achieved, and the steps to be taken to achieve their strategic priorities. One by one, the team champions around the room stood up to discuss their assignments.

"I don't really know why this is happening," said the first executive, "but since we defined our priorities, the major performance gap on which we were focused seems to be closing on its own, even though we haven't begun doing any work on it yet." An executive from another team stood up and said that the same thing was happening in his group. A third executive said he'd had the same experience. People began to laugh, it seemed so absurd.

At this point, the division's CEO, Marty Homlish, turned to me and said, "You're guiding this process. What's going on here?"

"I don't know," I replied. "I last saw you six weeks ago. You're the people who did it. *You* tell *me*—what's happening? What's moving this forward?"

We held an impromptu discussion with the group and quickly agreed on an explanation. Once the people at Sony Media Solutions understood the company's focus and what they had to do to improve, they'd begun to take the necessary steps on their own. It was as if the entire workforce was saying, "Now that we see what's expected of us, we know what to do when we go to work."

"That's the answer," we concluded. "This is the magic of focus."

Indeed, Sony Media Solutions' clearly defined focus turbocharged the company's turnaround. Within 10 months, the company was back in the black and making some of the best returns in the corporation. It was a huge lesson for all of us.

The Arithmetic of Business

During strategy workshops, executives sometimes ask whether simply having the lowest costs can be their winning proposition. I believe that the short answer to this question is no. But let's explore the issue a little further.

As shown in Figure 6.3, a simple equation called the Arithmetic of Business provides a useful way to consider the strategic choices your business faces. The equation illustrates the basic truth that

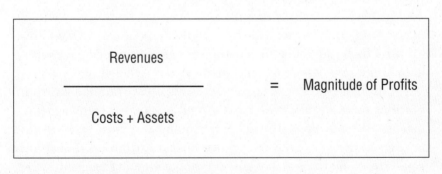

$$\frac{\text{Revenues}}{\text{Costs} + \text{Assets}} = \text{Magnitude of Profits}$$

Figure 6.3   The Arithmetic of Business

operationally there are just three key moving parts in a business enterprise: revenues, costs, and assets.

The profitability of a business is essentially the quotient that results from dividing total revenues (the numerator in the equation) by the costs and assets employed (the denominator). The task of management is to make that quotient as large as possible.

The obvious corollary is that there are two possible ways of increasing profitability: by increasing revenues or by decreasing costs and assets. Both approaches are necessary, but it's important to understand the differences between them. When you focus on reducing costs and assets, you're engaged in denominator management. The evidence shows that this is about staying in the game rather than winning the game. Nowadays, thanks to the Internet and other technologies, the tools for superb efficiency are widely understood and generally available. Thus, it's crucial for most businesses to reduce costs as much possible—to operate at maximum possible efficiency—simply to avoid being squeezed out of the market by leaner, tougher competitors.

However, denominator management isn't enough. For one thing, as all the companies in a given market adopt efficiency measures, customers are sure to demand that the cost savings be passed along to them in the form of lower prices—and if you aren't willing to meet this demand, someone else will. Thus, the positive effect of denominator management on your profits is likely to be temporary at best. As the saying goes, you can never save your way to success—or shrink your way to greatness.

Furthermore, merely running an efficient operation isn't enough to give your company an edge over your competitors when it comes to attracting and retaining customers. As a customer, I want to know *what you can do for me*—not just how efficiently you'll do it.

Thus, denominator management is necessary but not sufficient. For long-term success, you need strong numerator management—that is, an innovative strategy for building revenues by attracting new customers or generating more business from each customer you have. Numerator management is about winning the game.

Let's look at the strategic choices of a company that has mastered the art of denominator management—but wisely recognizes that numerator management is the most important part of a winning strategy.

Strategic Focus at Southwest Airlines

The key to Southwest Airlines' success (which is unparalleled in the industry) is that it has focused all of its energy and resources intensely on its strategic choices. These choices are so specific and followed so rigorously that no competitor has yet managed to copy the Southwest blueprint—though many have tried. Here's how they might be outlined.

Southwest Airlines' Strategic Choices

Customer focus: Budget-conscious travelers.

Winning proposition: To operate at the lowest costs in the industry while providing fun-filled air travel that competes with the cost of car travel.

Five key priorities:
1. Have fun.
2. Focus on the needs of the customer.
3. Ensure that every employee helps out.
4. Maintain superior operational efficiency.
5. Apply tight cost controls.

Because this list of strategic choices is so clear and focused, everyone at Southwest knows exactly what the company's strategy is and what the airline will and will not do. For example, Southwest serves no meals on its flights. Suppose one of Southwest's competitors introduces fancy new meals on a route served by Southwest. Does Southwest try to match this customer perk? No—that would violate the focus on lowest-cost operation. If Airbus introduces an exciting new jet model, is Southwest going to buy it? No—Southwest has a strict policy of flying *only* Boeing 737s, which drastically simplifies maintenance procedures, eliminates dealing with the bugs every new aircraft has, and maximizes employee flexibility (since every pilot, flight attendant, and engineer gets to know the peculiarities of the 737 inside out).

How this intensity of focus works in practice is remarkable. While it takes most airlines an average of 55 minutes to turn around a flight on the ground, Southwest manages to do so in only 15 minutes, which saves money, improves on-time arrival rates, and makes more flights possible. While most airlines have a rigid and hierarchical culture, Southwest *requires* that everyone have fun and help everyone else succeed: Captains move luggage; flight attendants help the check-in process; and even founder and CEO Herb Kelleher has been known to dress up in costume to hand out bags of peanuts.

Kelleher and his top team constantly communicate the essence of this strategy to their employees in simple and compelling ways. Even more important, they unfailingly set an example by modeling the behavior that lies at the heart of Southwest's success.

Vision

As I mentioned at the start of this chapter, you should think about creating a vision for your company *after* you have nailed down your strategic choices. This will ensure that your vision becomes an extension of your company's strategy, not a thing apart. Interestingly enough, often a company finds that, if it has done a great job defining its winning proposition, that proposition alone is a sufficiently strong call to action.

However, there's no doubt that a vivid and compelling vision statement can have a galvanizing effect on an organization. But it's equally true that a bland, one-size-fits-all vision—such as "We shall strive for excellence in all that we do"—can be a terrible waste of time and energy; indeed, such meaningless statements can actually create confusion and cynicism.

A powerful vision is a concise word picture that describes what an organization aspires to become, giving employees at all levels of the company a clear direction to follow. An effective vision is simple, motivational, and realistic. Martin Luther King Jr.'s famous "I Have a Dream" speech is a great example of a powerful vision statement. It inspired a movement and, ultimately, a nation, with its clear, vivid image of an America in which all citizens would be accepted on their own merits rather than being judged by the color of their skin.

Other noteworthy examples of powerful vision statements include:

▼ President John F. Kennedy's vision for the NASA space program: "By the end of this decade, to land a man on the moon and return him safely to earth." So clear and exciting was this challenge that the goal was fully achieved by 1969, within Kennedy's timetable, which many scientists had considered hopelessly optimistic at the time he proposed it.

▼ Ogilvy & Mather, the advertising agency: "To be the agency most valued by those who most value brands." The emphasis on brand building here sets a single long-term benchmark for the success of all the efforts Ogilvy manages on behalf of its clients, whether in advertising, marketing, public relations, or other areas.

▼ Walt Disney: "We use our imagination to bring happiness to millions." This vision is broad enough to include Disney's work in motion pictures, theme parks, television, and many other media, while it is specific enough to define Disney as a particular *type* of media company, quite distinct from such rivals as AOL Time Warner, Rupert Murdoch's News Corporation, or Viacom.

▼ Marriott Hotels: "Every guest leaves satisfied." Notice how this Marriott vision creates a specific objective against which every daily action by each employee can be measured: "What must I do *now* to make certain that *this* guest will leave satisfied?"

A great vision should involve stretch, encouraging transformational behavior rather than incrementalism. The test of whether your vision is, indeed, transformational will be if the reaction from your people is: "That's great! It's exactly where we want to go—only we can't get there by doing what we're doing today." Which is exactly the point.

In 1999, I attended a conference addressed by Carly Fiorina, now CEO of Hewlett-Packard and then a group president at Lucent Technologies. Fiorina summed up the role of the leader in an organization like this: "To define a clear vision and inspire your people to invent their way there." It's an excellent formulation, one that effectively summarizes the role of your vision statement.

Aligning the Organization

Having defined the winning proposition and the key priorities, we now turn to step three of the Strategic Learning process—creating alignment behind your new strategy (see Figure 7.1).

Bluntly put, the question implementation raises is: How do I get my organization to do what I want it to do?

Implementing strategy is a daunting task for any organization, and for many executives it is the highest hurdle of all. It would be great if we could simply flip a switch to automatically align every person and process in our organization behind our new strategy. In a sense, this can happen at a start-up company: If an entrepreneur has a brain flash in the shower one morning, everyone in the organization can hear about it and begin acting upon it by lunchtime. But for large, complex organizations with ongoing businesses and complicated, carefully planned processes, implementation is a major challenge—particularly if the strategy requires a major shift in the company's mind-set, skills, and practices.

The hard truth is that many new strategies fail because leaders are simply unable to mobilize their organizations to implement them.

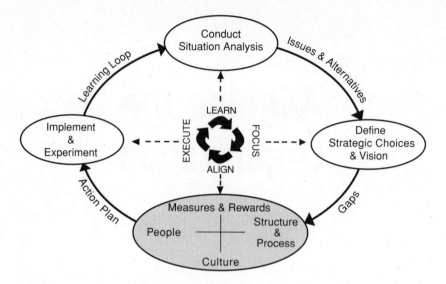

Figure 7.1   Strategic Learning: The Leadership Process—Creating Alignment

Fortunately, as with the rest of the Strategic Learning cycle, having a tested process to follow will greatly increase your chances of success. I offer here a set of principles developed over the years that research and experience have shown can help your company succeed in strategy implementation. These time-tested rules form an integrated, practical process that can help you get beyond the all-too-common situation in which many managers find themselves—having to throw mud against the wall and hope it sticks. Of course, there can never be a guarantee of success. But when you apply these principles conscientiously, your chances will substantially improve.

Four elements are crucial to success in strategy implementation:

1. A clear, overarching focus.
2. Identification of systemwide gaps and accountabilities proceeding from this focus.
3. Alignment of the key levers of the business system to drive the new strategy.
4. An action plan to overcome resistance to change and inspire your people to achieve exceptional performance.

In the pages that follow, we'll discuss all four.

Clarity of Focus

Chapter 6 stressed the need to define your company's strategic focus through a clear articulation of your winning proposition and key priorities. I now return to this theme to emphasize this crucial point: Clarity of focus is not just a good idea; it is the essential precondition for successful implementation.

Remember that strategy creation and implementation are mutually interdependent. The one can only be as good as the other. In fact, when I'm called in to help companies with an implementation problem, more than half the time I find that the real problem is a lack of focus. As mentioned before, executives are naturally biased toward taking action, and in the rush to get things done often ignore the importance of focus. This is one of the major sources of failure. Indeed, I'd go so far as to say that until you have a *crystal-clear* focus that is fully understood by your entire organization, don't even bother to start the implementation process.

Identification of Systemwide Gaps

Once clarity of focus has been achieved, the big challenge is to operationalize the focus so that it is rapidly translated into results. As a first step in doing this, an effective practice is to look at each of your strategic priorities and ask yourself what performance gaps must be closed in order to accomplish each one. In other words, you need to convert your strategic priorities into *gap statements*, defining the difference between the current state of your business and the desired state for each priority. Your task, then, is to bridge the difference—to close the gap.

Don't forget, your strategy is your plan to win; and to win, you must aim to be the best. Set the bar high. When creating a gap statement, you should strive for worldwide best practices, not simply to be the best in your local market or industry segment. Remember, local competition is extinct; today, the competition for the best ideas is global. Ask yourself: Will closing this gap give us worldwide best practices and put us ahead of our competitors? If the answer is no, then go back to the drawing board and try again.

In looking for worldwide best practices against which to measure your own performance, don't consider only those companies against which you compete. Look at anyone who excels in the area that is crucial to you. When Cemex, an innovative manufacturer and distributor of cement and other building supplies, wanted to create a computerized information network to speed up its deliveries to builders and contractors, it didn't study other cement makers. Instead, it examined how 911 emergency-call systems managed to dispatch large fleets of vehicles quickly and accurately in response to calls from fire and accident victims. In time, the company developed ways of performing up to the same world-class standards of speed, accuracy, and reliability within its own industry.

Your gap statements should be expressed in concrete, measurable terms. For example:

▼ To improve customer satisfaction rates from 70 percent to 90 percent.

▼ To raise sales from products introduced in the past three years from 20 percent to 40 percent of total revenues.

▼ To reduce average new-product time to market from seven years to four years.

In coaching companies on gap statements, I recommend organizing people into teams and naming individual gap champions—executives who will be held accountable for specific gaps, diagnosing obstacles, and generating solutions to overcome them. The champion-led teams then meet regularly to review progress, promote cross-fertilization and healthy competition, and renew their focus on closing the gaps.

To overcome inertia, it is vital that follow-through be relentless. Keep returning to the same themes over and over again. Put your strategic priorities and gaps at the top of the agenda at all of your key meetings. Support the initiatives with clear measurement and reward systems. Jump in immediately to help clear away obstacles, and celebrate victories publicly.

Aligning the Levers of Your Organization

The closing of performance gaps is a matter of good, hard-nosed project management. At the same time, this investment of time and energy is deeply strategic, because it is based on the five key strategic priorities necessary to achieve your winning proposition. This is all to the good, but on its own it is not enough.

For any strategy to succeed, it is essential that *all* of the key elements of a company's business system be effectively aligned in support of that strategy. Without such comprehensive alignment, no amount of project work can carry you to success.

The key supporting elements of a company's business system are shown in Figure 7.2: measures and rewards, structure and

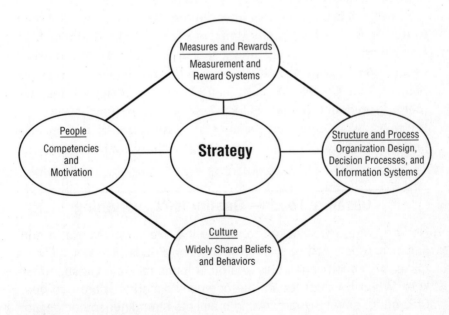

Figure 7.2 Aligning the Organization

process, culture, and people. To successfully implement your new strategy, it is essential that each of these elements:

▼ Directly support the new strategy.

▼ Directly support each of the other elements.

Don't forget that your present system of alignment, which was probably developed over a period of years, was designed to support yesterday's strategy. The task now is to redirect it, as a total system, so that it supports today's strategy.

Companies frequently overlook this crucial principle of total alignment. They pick only *one* aspect of their business—such as the organizational structure (a favorite target)—and go on a crusade, believing that if they change just that one thing they'll achieve success. The company sets out to reorganize its way to success; when it doesn't work, they simply do it again. Before long, they have become serial reorganizers. Bitter jokes begin to circulate in the corporate halls: "Say, if you run into my new boss, could you ask him his name?" The time and resources devoted to reorganizing end up dissipating rather than focusing the company's energies.

The truth is that selective interventions hardly ever work. I refer to this danger as the trap of Managing Things in Isolation, or MTI. Companies are especially likely to fall into the MTI trap when caught up in a popular management fad or movement, such as Six Sigma, Total Quality Management (TQM), or reengineering. Let there be no doubt: Initiatives like these can be extremely powerful. But they'll work only if they support the firm's strategy and are supported in turn by all the elements of the business system.

Ultrafine Foods—Quality Isn't Everything

Not long ago, I was asked to advise the executive team at a consumer products company I'll call Ultrafine Foods. It's a well-known maker of canned vegetables and other foods marketed in supermarkets. When I was called in, the company's market share had been eroding for several years, owing mainly to strengthened competition from other food companies.

Ultrafine's profits are driven by the success of its core brand (as is true for all branded goods companies), which is measured largely by market share. This requires a primary focus on growth strategies. But Ultrafine's executives had never in fact prepared any true strategy. These managers were brilliant at operations, and were nearly fanatical about manufacturing processes. They could tell you all about how to handle the procurement of fresh vegetables, how to slice and dice them with minimal wastage, and how to can them so as to preserve great flavor. But they were uncomfortable dealing with the larger issues of strategy.

A bad case of MTI set in three years ago when Ultrafine became enamored of a Total Quality Management initiative. The company began applying TQM diagnostic and analytic processes for ensuring quality in every aspect of the firm's operations, from the flow of paper in the headquarters to the flow of products through the company's enormous canning operations. Unfortunately, they managed the TQM process in isolation, without linking it to strategy or to the other elements of the business system, as if quality by itself could magically solve all their problems. In time, TQM became a substitute for a strategy. Ultrafine was more focused on saving 35 cents a day by restricting office paper flow than on driving the growth of its brand.

While it's important to create efficiencies, of course, Ultrafine's use of TQM was neither focused nor strategic: It was at best a distraction that kept the firm absorbed with "doing things right" instead of "doing the right things."

Only after the entire company was mobilized behind a clear strategic focus on building the Ultrafine brand (with first-rate product quality as an important supporting element) did Ultrafine's fortunes surge.

Think of your organization as an ecosystem—like a rain forest, a desert oasis, or a stand of trees in a North American pine forest—which functions successfully only when all of its interdependent parts support one another. If any single element is unable to play its supporting role, or when the elements start to work against each other, then the system breaks down. And so it is with a business enterprise.

In order for a company to be successful, all of its interdependent parts must be operating in sync with one another and with the firm's strategy. Success comes not from isolated actions, but from orchestrating the right *inter*actions. A symphony orchestra is led by a conductor because its success is not based on the actions of any one individual but rather on the *inter*action of the entire group. When this interaction is well coordinated, the orchestra will produce wonderful music.

When coaching executive teams on these principles of interdependence, I like to tell the story of the giraffe and the acacia tree.

Several years ago, my family and I went on safari to South Africa's Mala Mala Game Park. Our guide was a keen student of nature named Alan Yeowart, who was a fount of insightful, fascinating stories about African flora and fauna. The animals, we discovered, were so accustomed to visitors that Alan was able to drive his open Land Rover filled with tourists within a few feet of the grazing herds and shut off the car's engine, affording remarkable close-up lessons in animal behavior.

On one occasion, Alan pointed out a nearby giraffe, quietly browsing on the sweet leaves growing at the top of one of the abundant acacia trees. "That's a favorite treat for giraffes," he explained. And then he added, as if struck by a sudden thought, "You know, I'd be willing to wager that this giraffe will stop munching on that tree and move on to another, inside of—oh, say, six minutes." He pulled a coin from his pocket—a South African rand—and tossed it on the car seat beside him. "What do you say? Do I have any takers?"

Naturally, we were puzzled. But several of us were game. One of our party bet a rand that Alan was wrong—that the giraffe would go on eating at the same tree for longer than six minutes. Another said, "I've got a rand that says he'll shift in eight minutes." A third bet on 10. Soon we all found ourselves—rather absurdly—staring at our watches, timing the dining habits of a randomly chosen giraffe.

Three minutes passed, then four. A few seconds after four minutes had elapsed, the giraffe stopped chewing and deliberately walked some 30 feet to its left, where another acacia tree stood. Soon it began to nibble at a clump of seemingly identical leaves atop the second tree.

Alan laughed and collected his winnings. "What's this all about?" we demanded. "How did you know when the giraffe would switch trees?" One Texan in our group jokingly accused Alan of having trained a pet giraffe as a way of fleecing the tourists.

"It's really very simple," Alan explained. "The acacia tree gives the giraffe its marching orders. You see, after the giraffe eats a certain number of leaves, the tree, in self-defense, begins to produce bitter-tasting chemicals called tannins. The tannins spread through every limb and leaf, and soon the giraffe is repelled by the nasty taste. When that happens, the animal moves along to the next tree, and the whole process starts again."

"Isn't that remarkable!" someone exclaimed, and we all nodded.

"The facts are more remarkable still," Alan went on. "The acacia isn't merely protecting itself from overbrowsing. In fact, acacias rely heavily on browsing animals like giraffe and kudu for the process of cross-pollination. The fact that the browsing animal spends so little time on each individual tree means a high degree of cross-pollination while the plant is in flower. And as a result, the kingdom of acacias expands its territory. The animals benefit, and so do the trees." Alan laughed. "Talk about a win-win situation!"

More than merely a striking anecdote, the story of the giraffe and the acacia tree is a lesson in mutual interdependence. The acacia tree provides the giraffe with food while being careful not to endanger itself by permitting overgrazing. In so doing, it guarantees its own survival while also assuring the giraffe of a long-term food supply. The use of tannins to repel the giraffes after a few minutes of eating encourages the broadest possible range of cross-pollination. Examined closely, a seemingly random act by a browsing giraffe reveals an intricate web of finely tuned relationships that helps an entire ecosystem to survive and thrive.

The elements of your business system are similarly interdependent. The key to success is orchestrating the many interrelated actions rather than performing isolated actions.

Getting the Business System to Work in Sync

Here's a well-tested four-step process for aligning your business system:

1. *Describe each element of the present business system.* We're not always conscious and clear about the real status of the current business system. Consider each of the four items shown in Figure 7.2: measures and rewards, structure and process, culture, and people. Then ask yourself: What activities do we currently measure? On what basis do we distribute rewards? What does our organizational structure look like? and so on. For each element, a baseline measure is needed, defining the starting point of the alignment process. Take the time needed to talk through these issues and make certain you understand exactly where your company system stands at present.

2. *Recap the new winning proposition and strategic priorities.* Here, you can simply refer back to the strategic choices you developed in the previous step of the Strategic Learning process. The alignment of the business system must be single-mindedly dedicated to making this strategy work. Therefore, it's necessary to hold this strategic focus vividly before you as you proceed with the alignment process.

3. *Define the future business system needed to support the new strategy.* The best approach to this crucial step is what might be called *reverse visioning.* Imagine that your business system has already been realigned in support of your new strategy. The business is operating in total harmony, creating brilliant success and winning decisively on the competitive battlefield. Now imagine that you are a journalist charged with describing this wonderful success. Ask yourself, "What does the business system that created such success look like?" Write down your answer for each element of the business system, and you've defined the system your new strategy needs.

Don't worry yet about the mechanics of creating such a system or the obstacles you're sure to encounter in doing so. Ignore the small internal voice that says, "Oh, that's impractical. How can we hope to transform our existing organization into the well-oiled machine we're imagining?" There's time enough to deal with those issues later, and you will. For now, the key is to liberate your thinking by focusing on where you'd like to be in a perfect world.

4. *Define the early actions and next steps to be taken to reach this successful state.* For each element in the new system that you've imagined in step 3, define the *first* things you need to do in order to create the new alignment. It's important to be able to say, "Here are some things we're going to do right away in pursuit of our goals—starting first thing Monday morning." Then go on to list the next steps that will follow these, so that a pathway from here to there is mapped.

It's crucial not to "backload" your strategy, with all the key actions planned for 12 months out or later. This has a way of turning into a permanent stall. Make some early moves in at least one area directly in support of the new strategy, to establish momentum. Then begin hammering away relentlessly at each of the four elements. Don't stop until the total system is in alignment behind the new strategy.

Your Organization as a Unique Ecosystem

As I've emphasized, an organization must be considered as an integrated whole, all of its parts working together in support of the chosen strategy. I've used the analogy of an ecosystem to clarify this idea. But of course no two ecosystems are quite the same. The community of plants, animals, insects, birds, and microorganisms that develops around a water hole in New Mexico's Sonoran Desert will differ dramatically from the ecosystem in a similar-sized bit of rain forest in the Amazon River valley. And the differences will be reflected in the evolutionary "choices" made by the creatures in every conceivable niche in each ecosystem. In much the same way, the specific strategy you've developed—the proposition by which you plan to win—should be uniquely reflected in every element of your business system.

To fully explain what I mean, let's compare two hypothetical examples—an organization whose strategy focuses mainly on *high efficiency* in its operations versus an organization whose strategy is directed mainly by *product innovation* (see Table 7.1). We might imagine that the former is a coal mining company, while the latter is a producer of snack foods. Notice how the difference in core

Table 7.1   Organization as Ecosystem: Efficiency versus Innovation

	ABC Coal Mining (Efficiency Organization)	*XYZ Snack Foods (Innovation Organization)*
Measures and Rewards	Focused mainly on operational excellence and safety.	Focused mainly on customer generation and retention and the creation of new products.
Structure and Process	More formal structures, strict protocols, and centralized controls; often organized by function.	Fewer controls, decentralized structures, venturing units; often organized by customer grouping.
Culture	Emphasis on continuous improvement and replicating what works.	Emphasis on risk taking, experimentation, and challenging the status quo.
People	Emphasis on professional/functional rigor; greater continuity of job tenure.	More freethinkers and mavericks; greater job rotation.

strategy dictates differences in every aspect of their respective business systems.

As the chart suggests, an efficiency organization is designed to *reduce* variation, while an innovation organization is designed to *increase* variation. Of course, these don't represent the only kinds of organizations that exist; a similar list of elements could be created for almost any conceivable business strategy. Moreover, these represent two polarized extremes. There are few, if any, organizations that fit exclusively into any single framework; a coal mining company will probably have an R&D division focused on innovation, while a snack food company will need to emphasize efficiency on its production lines.

The real point of this comparison is simply that there's no such thing as a one-size-fits-all approach to any element of the business system. For example, it's impossible to define one ideal set of measures and rewards that would be suitable for all strategies. Instead, every piece of your business system must be custom-tailored to fit the organization's strategy. It's another good reason to resist the allure of management fads, which often pretend to offer plug-and-play solutions that can fix the problems of *any* business. That's simply not how business works in the real world.

Measures and Rewards

A good place to start your examination of the business system is with measures and rewards, an element that people in your organization are sure to be aware of. "What gets measured gets done. What gets rewarded gets done repeatedly," the old saying goes. This aphorism expresses an eternal truth, yet one that's often ignored or overlooked through familiarity. It applies not only to business but to almost any field of human endeavor.

Take law enforcement, for example. New York's former mayor Rudolph Giuliani attributed the city's sharp decline in crime during the 1990s to the so-called CompStat program, which applies a classic measures and rewards strategy to crime fighting. Short for "computer comparison statistics," CompStat allows police to track crime incidents as they occur. Previously, the main measure was the number of arrests. The new measurements also include information on the crime, the victim, the time of day the crime took place, and other details that enable officials to spot emerging crime patterns.

At weekly CompStat meetings, trends are reviewed using state-of-the-art computer-mapping techniques able to pinpoint crimes down to the block level. Precinct commanders are called upon to account for crime activity and provide detailed strategies to attack crime outbreaks in their precincts.

The results are powerful. Overall crime in New York is down 57 percent and has reached its lowest level in 30 years, leading to increased tourism and economic revival in many parts of the city. Once infamous around the world for its dangerous streets, New York has now been recognized by the F.B.I. as the safest large city in America for the past five years.

Does the idea of tracking crime statistics and holding local police leadership accountable for improving them seem obvious? Maybe so. But until 1994, New York City had no such program. Similarly, many businesses fail to develop and implement the same kind of powerful techniques for measuring and rewarding the behaviors they want.

Remember, when you measure anything—cash flow or market share, for example—you are actually doing two things. You are *gauging progress*, and you are telling your people *this is important*. Conversely, when you don't measure something, it sends an equally strong message—*this is not important*. Thus, it is crucial that the measurement and reward system mirror the strategic aims of the firm.

It is surprising how often a firm will try to introduce a new strategy while continuing to measure and reward the behaviors that supported the old strategy. If this happens, your new strategy will be dead in the water. You will need to make deliberate shifts in your measurement and reward system to reflect the crucial priorities of your new strategy.

Measures and rewards are yet another example of choice making in strategy. A firm cannot measure everything; if you try to do so, you will end up measuring nothing. Therefore, you must select the critical measures—those that tell you most clearly whether your strategy is on track—and focus on them.

One key tactic for effective measures and rewards: Try to measure not only *outcomes*, which are the results you seek, but also *drivers*, which produce those results. Because drivers show up on the radar screen before outcomes, measuring drivers gives you the opportunity to take corrective steps before the outcomes appear, while there's still a chance to influence them.

Thus, if improved cash flow is one of the outcomes you seek, you should also measure and reward the business drivers that influence cash flow, such as inventory levels, accounts receivable and payable, speed of order fulfillment, and forecasting accuracy. These numbers are the early warning signs that tell you what cash flow will look like next month or next quarter; if you focus on these, you'll have a shot at fixing cash flow problems (or seizing cash flow opportunities) in a timely fashion.

Similarly, if market share is a crucial outcome for your business, you should consider measuring such drivers of market share as customer complaints, customer satisfaction levels, product returns, repeat purchasing patterns, and distribution levels.

The distinction between outcomes and drivers reveals a major weakness in the approach of the so-called hard-nosed manager who impatiently demands, "Just show me the bottom line—that's all that matters!" Of course the bottom line is vitally important. But it's history. Instead of focusing backward, the manager must be a diagnostician, studying the drivers that forecast next quarter's bottom line, while there is still a chance to improve them.

This also explains why it's dangerous to allow your management accounting system—which is, in effect, your decision support system—to be designed purely in accordance with statutory reporting requirements. By definition, these are focused backward, on historical results. The smart manager is focused forward, on the company's future.

Structure and Process

A new strategy often requires important changes in the way a firm is organized and how its decisions get made. Therefore, it's necessary to ask such questions as:

▼ To best support the new strategy, should the firm be organized by product line, customer grouping, function, geography, or some other principle?

▼ Should we introduce some form of matrix system to ensure that the proper linking mechanisms are in place?

▼ What should be the level of centralization or decentralization for each activity in the value chain?

As your strategy changes, it's likely that your answers to these questions need to change, too.

Suppose, for example, that your company is in a once-stable industry that has recently been shaken by dramatic technological innovations. As a result, you've determined that it's important to shift your strategy from one that concentrates on production efficiencies to one that focuses on pioneering new technical ideas that provide superior solutions for the customers in your market. Moving to a more innovative mode will probably require significant changes in the way your firm is organized and how its decisions get made. For example:

▼ It might be best to reorganize according to customer group or market sector rather than by function or product category, so as to encourage greater awareness of customer needs and readiness to respond to them in proactive fashion.

▼ You may want to do far more market research and scanning of customer preferences than you've ever done before. Increased budgets and staffing for the relevant departments may be in order.

▼ There would probably need to be a greater level of decentralization to push decisions out as close to the customer as possible.

▼ The corporate structure might need to become flatter to speed decision making and encourage more innovative thinking.

▼ Staff departments like human resources and finance may need to evolve from being "yes/no police" into being facilitators and providers of expertise and resources in support of the decision makers on the front line.

Culture

Culture is very different from the other organizational levers. It's much harder to wrap your arms around—harder to define, harder to explain, harder to change. As a result, dealing with your corporate culture is a challenge you never complete—a journey without any final destination. Yet you ignore culture at your peril. If your strategy shifts, so must your culture.

Hard-nosed managers are often intolerant of the "soft stuff," of which culture is the ultimate embodiment. They feel more comfortable with the hard stuff—financial measures, competitive analysis, market research, product specifications. But the so-called soft stuff is more likely to undermine your strategy and so defeat it than the hard stuff is. As it turns out, the soft stuff is really the hard part of leadership, as IBM's Lou Gerstner has pointed out, while the hard stuff is the easier part. And yet the macho managers are inclined to walk away from cultural issues—in part because they scorn them, in part perhaps because, deep inside, they feel unsure about how to deal with them.

So tackling the culture of your company—making it work in support of your strategy alongside the other organizational levers— is one of the most important and difficult challenges faced by any business leader. It's so important, in fact, that we'll devote the entire next chapter to it.

People

An organization is not a machine. Success will be achieved only if its people are *focused*, *skilled*, and *motivated*.

A firm that defines and communicates its strategic choices with clarity and simplicity will create the necessary focus. It then needs to build the competencies required to support the new strategy. This often involves recruitment, training, and job rotation. Sometimes, hard decisions must be made about the need for layoffs. And if the competency overhaul is radical, a firm may need to acquire or partner with an organization that has the required skills.

Let's return to the example of a company that is aiming to increase its focus on innovation. Such a company might need to consider the following moves:

▼ Recruitment of employees with greater creative and marketing skills.
▼ Partnership with or acquisition of a firm with employees who possess the needed skills.
▼ Training and development programs to enhance the skills of the existing workforce.

▼ In hiring, emphasis on greater diversity (in gender, age, culture, experience) so as to bring in more outsiders with new perspectives to shake up the thinking.

▼ More job rotation and creation of cross-functional teams so as to stimulate cross-fertilization of ideas between departments.

Motivation is of course a pivotal factor. The evidence shows clearly that high-commitment organizations outperform those where employees exhibit lower levels of motivation. Yet human beings by nature resist change. People do not easily leave their comfort zones to embrace the uncertainties brought by change.

We need to address this psychology of resistance with specific actions designed to overcome the resistance and convert it into active support for the new strategy. Simple exhortation will not be enough. We have to address the underlying causes of resistance. This is, perhaps, the most difficult of all leadership challenges—one focused on in greater depth in Chapter 9.

Let's look at some examples of effective organizational alignment.

Alignment in Action at 3M

As is well known, Minnesota Mining and Manufacturing (3M) is an example of a highly successful company whose strategy is built around excellence at product innovation. Less widely understood is how well it has aligned its organizational levers specifically to encourage a continual stream of strong new-product ideas. For example:

▼ Divisions are required to generate at least 30 percent of their revenues from products introduced within the past four years (measures).

▼ Prestigious corporate awards are given for the best technical and commercial innovations (rewards).

▼ A corporate venture capital fund is devoted to the support of promising new ventures (structure and process).

▼ The company is organized into over a hundred small business units to foster flexibility and creativity (structure).

▼ Scientists are permitted and encouraged to spend 15 percent of their time working on any project that interests them, regardless of its commercial potential (people and culture).

Alignment in Action at Southwest Airlines

Southwest Airlines is a company that has superbly aligned all of its organizational elements behind its strategy.

The effectiveness of Southwest's strategy begins with the stunning clarity of its winning proposition: "We will operate at lowest industry costs, and provide fun-filled air travel that competes with the cost of car travel." Note that the airline states very clearly that its customers are budget-conscious travelers, not business travelers subsidized by deep corporate pockets. This decision, and Southwest's intense self-discipline, keeps the airline focused on efficiency and on providing an enjoyable travel experience for its customers above all else.

Here is how Southwest keeps all of the key elements of its business system working in concert.

Measures and Rewards

▼ Tight cost controls.

▼ Key efficiencies constantly measured.

▼ CEO approval required for all expenses over $1,000 ("Herb is watching").

▼ Profit sharing for all employees.

▼ High recognition for employees who embody Southwest goals.

▼ Career advancement aligned with all company practices and values.

Structure and Process

▼ Emphasis on fast, efficient, on-time service.

▼ Point-to-point travel only (no connecting flights through crowded hubs).

▼ Use of only smaller, less congested airports.

▼ No interline baggage service.

▼ No seat assignments.

▼ No in-flight meals.

▼ Only 737s flown, simplifying maintenance and ensuring that every employee knows every plane.

Culture

▼ Have fun.

▼ Employees have broad latitude to make decisions that benefit customers.

▼ Everyone helps out, creating a sense of community.

People

▼ "Hire for attitude, train for skills."

▼ Training focused on team building.

▼ Peer hiring—referrals so as to replicate the DNA of Southwest's already successful employees.

▼ Eighty percent of promotions internal.

Of course, these supporting elements must be applied consistently to be effective—and they are. Southwest has resisted the temptation to violate its business principles "just a little" by serving meals on certain flights or making exceptions to the no-hub policy. So tightly are all of Southwest's organizational elements aligned behind its strategy that it has proven impossible for competitors to emulate its success—although a number have tried.

As Michael Porter of the Harvard Business School has pointed out, there is a powerful arithmetic behind the difficulty of emulating a company that is relentless about aligning every element of its business system behind its strategy. Here's a way of looking at it. Suppose the chance of a competitor successfully imitating any one element of your business design is 80 percent. If there are two elements that must be imitated, the chance of achieving this would be 64 percent (80% × 80% = 64%). Add a third element, and the chance falls to 51 percent; a fourth, and it falls to 41 percent. Once the number of elements to be imitated reaches 10, the chance of a competitor imitating them *all* drops to just over 10 percent.

The lesson is clear: Even if each single element in your business system is fairly easy to imitate, having a large number of tightly interlocking elements makes the whole system extremely difficult to copy.

Creating an operation as finely tuned as Southwest's takes tremendous dedication and hard work. But it pays off handsomely. For more than a decade, Southwest has been by far the fastest-growing and most profitable airline in the United States, making money even in the bad years when the rest of the industry was floundering. It is impressive testimony to the power of alignment.

The success of Southwest's tightly aligned organization raises another question. What is the relationship between alignment and adaptiveness? Isn't an organization consisting of many tightly interlocked elements more difficult to change in response to shifts in the business environment and the marketplace? And if so, doesn't this mean that, when adaptation is demanded, strong alignment may become a dangerous form of rigidity?

The answer is yes, it can be. The conflict between alignment and adaptiveness may sometimes exacerbate the second curve dilemma—the difficulty most companies experience in trying to change while they are successful. The solution, however, is *not* to abandon alignment. Instead, organizations that sustain their success over time are able to combine seemingly contradictory skills—that is, they are able to tightly align their business systems behind their current strategy, but when conditions change, they are also capable of quickly and effectively refocusing to develop a new strategy and realigning their systems behind that new strategy.

8

Transforming the Culture

As mentioned before, culture is probably the most misunderstood and mismanaged part of the business system, yet it is also one of the most powerful success factors—or causes of failure. It's so difficult to manage and so different from the other levers of the business system (as depicted in Figure 8.1) that it warrants a chapter of its own.

What Is Culture?

In a broad sense, *culture* refers to the learned and shared assumptions of a group that produce predictable behavior and decisions. These behaviors persist because they are rewarded and because failure to practice them is penalized. A society's culture develops as a way of solving the problems it faces, including economic problems (How will we distribute resources among the members of our society?), political problems (How will important decisions affecting the members of our society be made?), and social problems (How will conflicts between groups in our society be resolved?).

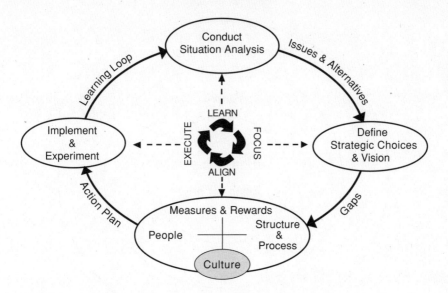

Figure 8.1 Strategic Learning: The Leadership Process—Culture

Thus, culture is above all a problem-solving mechanism—a means to an end rather than an end in itself.

The so-called onion model of culture, as depicted in Figure 8.2, shows the various elements that go to make up any culture. At its core we find *underlying assumptions* about life, death, the origin and destiny of the world, and other fundamental issues. These are usually unstated and in fact rarely need to be articulated because they are broadly, tacitly shared within the culture.

Built around this core and based on these assumptions we find *values*—beliefs as to what is important and what is not, what is right and what is wrong, what makes for a good life, success, and so on.

Finally, built around these values, we reach the outer layer of the onion—the only part of culture that is visible to the naked eye. These are *behaviors* and *artifacts*.

Behaviors, of course, are ways of acting. Artifacts are physical signs—for example, the art and architecture, styles of dress, preferred foods, and everyday products typical of a society. Both reflect the values and underlying assumptions of the people who share a particular culture.

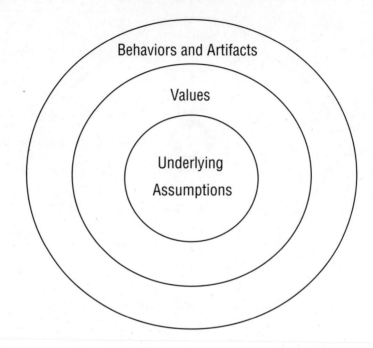

Figure 8.2   The Onion Model of Culture

When we grow up in a society, its underlying assumptions and values which we learn from birth are so deeply ingrained in our unconscious that we are rarely aware of them. An encounter with a foreign culture may be necessary to make us recognize how these assumptions and values shape our daily behaviors.

While serving as president of the Seagram Beverage group, I had occasion to visit Japan with a colleague to discuss a potential joint venture with the Kirin Brewing Company, Ltd., a Japanese beverage firm. When we arrived at the company's headquarters, we were greeted in the lobby by senior executives of Kirin and invited upstairs to begin our conversations. The elevator held, in addition to us two Westerners and the (all-male) Japanese executives with whom we'd be meeting, several other employees of Kirin, including some (female) secretaries and clerks.

When the elevator arrived at our sixth-floor destination, the doors slid open, and I automatically followed my usual custom: I leaned over and held the door open with one hand, and with the other gestured toward the secretaries and clerks, urging them to step out ahead of me. Meanwhile, my executive hosts were beckoning *me* to leave first. No one budged. Several long, awkward moments passed as each side beckoned with increasing urgency, while the young women just as tenaciously held back. Finally, the elevator doors closed again, and we were whisked toward the higher floors.

What had happened? The explanation is simple: a clash of different cultures. For me, the Westerner, courtesy demands that I let women precede me through an elevator door, regardless of their level of seniority. Japanese culture prescribes a very different rule of etiquette. Precedence in Japan is determined by status, regardless of gender, and guests are always given the highest status. As the honored guest, I was expected to leave the elevator first, taking precedence over all my fellow passengers. I would be followed by my more junior Seagram colleague, and the Japanese passengers would then leave in strict order of seniority, with the female secretaries exiting last. My inflexible attempt at politeness—Western style—was actually a mild affront to my Japanese hosts.

As our elevator approached the sixth floor for the second time, the tension was palpable. My colleague, Catherine, leaned over toward me and commented wryly, "May I suggest you *not* try to reform Japanese culture while riding the elevator?" I took her suggestion. This time, when we reached our destination, I stepped past the ladies and led the way out of the elevator.

Cultural Persistence and Change

As we've noted, culturally determined behaviors tend to persist over time because they are rewarded, while failure to engage in these behaviors is penalized. These rewards and penalties may be explicit and obvious, or they may be implicit and subtle. American culture, for example, emphasizes (among other values) the importance of respecting individual ownership of property. (This is not a universal human value. Among many African, Native American, and Pacific tribes, land was traditionally felt to be owned by no one, which helped produce predictable but tragic clashes when the indigenous peoples came into contact with land-hungry Western colonists.) Those who violate the socially prescribed norm are subject to various kinds of sanctions. If the violation is serious—building a house on someone else's property, for example—legal penalties will probably be invoked. If the violation is minor—bicycling across a neighbor's front yard, for example—the sanctions will be much more subtle, perhaps confined to a glare of annoyance or an angry remark. Most members of the society readily understand the messages these kinds of subtle responses convey, and they generally react by reverting to the culturally approved behaviors. Through such mechanisms—as well as through formal and informal education by parents, teachers, and social institutions—cultures tend to perpetuate themselves over time.

A culture, then, consists of learned behaviors that have been reinforced in groups of individuals through a lifetime of explicit and implicit lessons. As a result, cultures are relatively difficult to change. Think how hard it is to learn to pronounce a foreign language with no trace of an accent: Not only must you master an array of new and unfamiliar sound combinations, but you must first unlearn (at least temporarily) all the familiar linguistic habits you've practiced since infancy. In much the same way, cultural change requires unlearning hundreds of (often unconscious) behaviors and replacing them with new ones that often seem strange at first. No wonder cultural change tends to be slow and difficult.

Yet cultures do change over time, often in response to changes in the environment, demographic pressures, economic and political shifts, and other social forces. For an example, simply consider how greatly the culture of Victorian England (strictly hierarchical, sexually repressive, intensely pious, strongly family-oriented) differs from the culture of contemporary England (more socially fluid, sexually permissive, tolerant of religious variation, relatively individualistic). It would be a complex and subtle challenge to identify all the reasons for this evolution, but it seems clear that technological, political, economic, and environmental changes have all played a role.

Behavioral psychologist B. F. Skinner has pointed out that there are remarkable similarities between the Darwinian process of natural selection and the evolution of cultures. Remember that culture is a means to an end, a set of behaviors used by a society to solve the internal and external challenges it faces. According to Skinner, new cultural practices arise as "mutations," comparable to the biological variations that develop due to random mutations in the genetic code of living things. While most of these new cultural practices will disappear quickly under the pressure of societal disapproval, a few will prove to be beneficial, in that they help the society to solve its problems more effectively. These beneficial cultural mutations will be selected and reinforced, just as beneficial genetic mutations are reinforced by the process of natural selection, and gradually they may come to displace the traditional cultural norms. Over time, such small cultural changes accumulate, eventually producing large-scale shifts in the culture as a whole.

Culture at the Corporate Level

To this point, we've been talking about culture at the societal level, as studied by anthropologists and sociologists. But smaller units of human organization also have their own cultures—collections of learned and shared behaviors that are characteristic of a particular group of people and serve the group as a more or less effective means for solving its internal and external problems. These cultures will usually have much in common with the culture of the society as a whole, but they will also have distinctive qualities of their own. Thus, social groups such as the U.S. Marines, the Amish, the avant-garde artists living in New York's SoHo district, the members of the football team at Notre Dame University, and the motorcycle-loving members of HOG (the Harley-Davidson Owners' Group) all have their own unique cultures that set them apart to some degree from the surrounding society.

Business organizations, too, have their own cultures. Over time, any organization tends to develop assumptions and shared values that deeply influence its members' behavior. And just like culture at the societal level, a company's culture can be viewed as essentially a way of solving its internal and external problems. Organizational culture is a way of answering such questions as: "How do decisions get made here?" "How is information shared among our people?" "What kind of employee tends to get raises and promotions?" and so on. In short, a company's culture defines "the way we do things around here."

The behaviors that define a corporate culture tend to persist because they are rewarded, while noncompliance is penalized. Again, the rewards and penalties may be quite subtle. For example, in a company that highly values hierarchy, seniority, and protocol, improper behavior may be discouraged through small, almost imperceptible acts, such as a few seconds of chilly silence when a junior employee dares to disagree with his boss during a staff meeting. Even subtle cues like these are generally sufficient to send powerful messages throughout the organization about what kinds of behavior are and are not acceptable, ensuring that the desired behaviors are reinforced and the disfavored behaviors are extinguished.

Thus, corporate culture, like societal culture, tends to perpetuate itself over time. When the culture is beneficial to the company—that is, when the behaviors it encourages are supportive of the company's strategy—this self-reinforcing quality is a positive force. But when the culture is counterproductive because it conflicts with the company's strategy, it can create huge problems for the organization. The company then faces one of the greatest leadership challenges: the need to change an ingrained corporate culture in response to a changed strategy.

Don't misunderstand. In speaking about changing corporate culture in response to strategic changes, I don't mean to imply that culture is infinitely malleable. Some principles, especially ethical ones like honesty, integrity, and respect for others, may never change and *should* never change. But there's a layer of principles that are closer to the surface of the onion and therefore closer to daily business activities that often *must* change if a company is going to adapt successfully to changes in its environment. I'm referring to cultural changes like these:

▼ From a conservative culture to a risk-taking and experimental one.

▼ From a consensus-driven culture to individual accountability.

▼ From efficiency to innovation.

▼ From a product-focused to a customer-focused culture.

▼ From knowledge hoarding to knowledge sharing.

▼ From silos and fiefdoms to integration and unity.

These are cultural values that do not involve issues of morality. And they have enormous power. The assumptions and values your employees share in these areas will largely determine their day-to-day behaviors—and ultimately the success or failure of your company's strategy.

Remember: Culture is a means to an end, a way of solving the problems your organization faces. To serve this purpose effectively, your culture must be in sync with your strategy. Therefore, when your strategy changes, your culture needs to change as well. As Edgar H. Schein puts it in his book *The Corporate Culture Survival Guide*:

> A given organization's culture is "right" so long as the organization succeeds in its primary task. If the organization begins to fail, this implies that elements of the culture have become dysfunctional and must change. But the criterion of a right culture is the pragmatic one of what enables the organization to succeed in its primary task.

Cultural change, then, is an inevitable corollary to strategic change. And cultural change is a difficult, even painful process.

Here's the bad news: Something like 80 percent of attempts by companies to change their corporate cultures end in failure.

Here's the good news: It's possible to explain why this happens, and therefore to improve the odds of success.

Six Myths about Corporate Culture

The poor management of culture usually stems from six myths—false assumptions about culture that managers often believe to be true. Here they are.

1. Culture is vague and mysterious.
2. Culture and strategy are separate and distinct things.
3. The first step in redirecting our company should be defining our values.
4. Culture can't be measured and rewarded.
5. Our leaders must communicate what our culture is.
6. Our culture is the one constant that never changes.

Let's begin our consideration of corporate culture by debunking these myths point by point.

Myth 1: Culture is vague and mysterious. Culture is the "soft stuff," many people say. "It's unmanageable." Many business leaders feel there's nothing hard, definable, and concrete to manage about culture. It's true that culture is more elusive and complex than, say, cash flow or profit margin—and much harder to change. Yet culture expresses itself through specific, observable everyday behaviors that are every bit as tangible as cash flow and have as profound an effect on organizational success.

Those who take the macho, real-men-don't-give-a-damn-about-culture approach are unconsciously consenting to become victims of circumstance. As IBM's Lou Gerstner notes, the soft stuff is actually the hard part—the area of business that is the most difficult to manage. And if you don't make it your business to manage your company's culture, the culture will end up managing *you*.

Myth 2: Culture and strategy are separate and distinct things—and should be kept that way, like the separation of church and state. This notion is also badly flawed. As already pointed out, the culture of a society is based on what works best in coping with its external challenges and the relationships between its members.

In the same way, the performance of a business organization and the specifics of its culture are interdependent.

One version of this myth is the belief that there's something sacred about a company's culture, or that it represents an end in itself. This attitude is sometimes seen at companies with a long, proud tradition and history, and in practice it often leads to complacency or rigidity, with the culture treated as a kind of holy relic that mustn't be tampered with: "We can't change [whatever]—our founders would roll over in their graves!"

When taken to this kind of extreme, the treatment of culture as an end in itself can be highly destructive. A strong culture can be a powerful advantage, but the key is to understand that it is a means to an end. Culture, as we've established, is expressed through everyday behaviors. When those behaviors support your strategic aims, then your culture can be one of the most powerful drivers of success. But when your inherited culture is a barrier to the successful implementation of your new strategy, it needs to be changed.

Myth 3:   The first step in redirecting our company should be defining our values. As I discussed in Chapter 5, many of the companies I coach assume that they ought to define their values before creating their strategies. But as we've seen, this is a mistake. Defining corporate values in a vacuum is a meaningless exercise. Companies should *first* make their strategic choices. Only then will they be able to define those values and the attendant behaviors that will help them achieve success in pursuit of their strategies. The more clearly they define their winning propositions, the easier it will be to describe what those behaviors need to be.

Myth 4:   Culture can't be measured and rewarded. This myth arises from the first myth, that culture is something vague and mysterious. Because culture is expressed through specific behaviors, it can certainly be measured and rewarded—just as you would measure and reward any other aspect of your business practice.

The point is that if you don't assess your culture and reward the desired behaviors, you will have little chance of changing your culture and getting the behaviors you want. The golden rule is: What gets measured gets done; what gets rewarded gets done repeatedly.

Myth 5:   Our leaders must communicate what our culture is. We frequently hear this from the leaders of companies in the midst of a major change: "Now that we're striving to become more agile, innovative, and risk-taking, we need a plan to communicate the new culture to our employees." It's true that the leader must consciously and deliberately transmit culture to the employees. But it's not so much about *communicating* culture as it is about *living* it. Leaders must behave in accordance with the culture they profess. If they do, the message will be transmitted clearly with minimal use of words. If they don't, it doesn't matter what they say. As Ralph Waldo Emerson put it, "What you do speaks so loudly that I cannot hear what you say."

Myth 6:   Our culture is the one constant that never changes. It's true that some companies have cultures that are remarkably stable over time. But as we've seen, a close examination of the culture of almost any society or organization will reveal historic changes, sometimes subtle, sometimes profound. This is natural and proper. After all, the business environment constantly shifts in unexpected ways, and a company that refuses to adjust its values and behaviors in response to these changes will soon become dysfunctional.

Thus, when there is a major change in the challenges you face, you must be prepared to shift both your strategy and your culture in response. If you shift your strategy but not your culture, and this causes a misalignment between the two, then your new strategy is very likely to fail.

The Importance of Starting with Strategy

There are those who maintain that the starting point for truly great companies is with a set of core values, or culture: Strategy, they say, will follow naturally from there. To make this argument, they point to companies like Sony or 3M, which were built by leaders who first defined a set of corporate values, then built a strategy in alignment with these. (As early as May 1946, 10 months after founding Sony amid the ruins of a defeated Japan, Masaru Ibuka had drafted a lengthy values statement for the company filled with such idealistic principles as "We shall eliminate any unfair profit-seeking, persistently emphasize substantial and essential work, and not merely pursue growth.")

Building on this concept, Charles A. O'Reilly III and Jeffrey Pfeffer write in their 2000 book *Hidden Value*:

> [Such firms] have turned the typical logic of strategic management on its head. Instead of beginning with a business strategy, aligning the organization with this strategy, and hiring people to fit the organization, they have begun by being absolutely clear about their values and how these values will define their organizations and determine how they are run. . . . Values come first. Only then do the companies ensure that the strategy is consistent with people's values. This logic violates the "business first" mentality so common in today's organizations. But by doing things this way, these companies have been able to align the company's purpose with the spirit of their employees, capturing their emotional as well as intellectual energies.

The process as described here may be an accurate description of what happened when these companies were originally founded. Starting from a set of core values, they then created a strategy that was in alignment with those values and with the other elements of the organization. It was this alignment that made the strategy work. But the question is: What happens later when the environment shifts and the company must shift its strategy in response?

The answer is this: To reestablish alignment between the culture and the strategy, the culture must be altered to fit the new strategy. And in this situation, the new culture cannot be created in advance of the new strategy. For established companies making a strategy change, this is the only practical sequence: strategy first, then culture. In other words, first be clear on how you will win; then define the values and behaviors that will make your new strategy successful.

Gerstner's Guerrillas

In 1993, when Lou Gerstner joined IBM as the first CEO brought in from the outside, he faced both strategic and cultural challenges. When he took the helm, he inherited a plan to break up IBM into myriad "Baby Blues." Recognizing that his first order of business was to determine the most effective strategy for IBM, Gerstner and his team studied and ultimately rejected this plan in favor of an "integrated solutions" strategy. But it was clear that this would remain only an idea unless Gerstner could transform the company's culture in support of the new strategy. IBM had to be remade into a single, integrated, "silo-free" system that would bring a total solution to bear for customers.

"We can't share knowledge, we can't reach out to customers, if we continue to operate in silos inside IBM," he said. "We've got to work as a team. We can't be part of a division or a product; we've got to be part of IBM—coming together, delivering solutions." This transformation required a heroic effort.

The proud, patrician culture created by IBM founder Thomas Watson Sr. had proven highly effective for years, but by 1993 it had mutated into a rigid, complacent, self-absorbed culture. "Our culture was . . . so congenial you never knew where you stood," one senior IBM executive recalled. "Meetings would always go fine. You'd go in, and everything would be very proper and well dressed, and a bunch of people would sit around and have a nice chat. The results might be good, and people would say, 'Thank you very much.' Or the results might be awful, and it would still be, 'Thank you very much; we know you tried your best.' "

Gerstner understood that this culture was in conflict with the new strategy, and he worked on two fronts to transform it. He simultaneously rooted out the existing ethos and created a new culture based on "restless self-renewal."

Gerstner also understood retooling IBM's culture was the duty of the commander in chief, a responsibility that required him to be the beacon of cultural change at Big Blue. "If the CEO isn't living and preaching the culture and isn't doing it consistently, then it just doesn't happen," he said.

Moving at a blitzkrieg pace, he immediately eliminated the no-layoff policy, the most sacred of IBM's cows. Next, he instituted a casual dress code in place of IBM's famous navy blue suit—a highly symbolic gesture that sent the message, "Things are different here now."

Then he called for 5,000 volunteers—known as "Gerstner's Guerrillas"—to help him lead the change effort in all levels of the organization. These change agents, he wrote to the staff, should be:

- ▼ Committed to the long-term success of *all* IBM in a fast-changing, intensely competitive global business environment. Commitment to your career and to your business unit are not enough.
- ▼ Zealous in making things work for the customer, especially when the customer's needs require the involvement of several different parts of IBM. Turf barons and baronesses need not apply.
- ▼ Undeterred by bureaucracy, obstacles, and this-is-the-way-we've-always-done-things thinking. I can assure you, there are some in the company who will fight you at every turn. I'm looking for people with the guts to go above, below, around, or through internal hurdles.
- ▼ Willing to take risks in the face of conventional wisdom and practice.
- ▼ Constantly looking at everything we do with a critical eye, finding new ways to do things better and more productively. I need people who spend company money and use IBM resources as prudently as they spend their own money and resources.
- ▼ Aware that the race goes to the swift, and willing to set the pace in an already breathless environment.
- ▼ Looking to the future with confidence. (No handwringers!)

Gerstner understood the proper sequence for redirecting a company: First, make the right strategic choices; then remake the corporate culture so that it is squarely aligned behind the new strategy.

Gerstner also understood that the CEO is the leader of a company's culture. It's a role that cannot be delegated. His efforts to transform the culture of Big Blue have been wrenching but necessary. When he talks about that change effort today, he says: "Fixing the culture is the most critical—and most difficult—part of a corporate transformation."

Again, Edgar H. Schein has summarized the key insight succinctly: "Never start with the idea of changing culture. Always start with the issues the organization faces; only when those business issues are clear should you ask yourself whether the culture aids or hinders resolving the issues."

When Culture Fights Strategy

Changing the culture of your company will not happen overnight. In that sense, culture is very different from the other levers in the business system. If you want to change your company's compensation structure, you can do it at a stroke. If you want to change your company's organizational structure, the same applies. But if you want to change your company's *culture*, then understand that you are embarking on a long and arduous journey. In fact, it is a journey that never stops.

A cultural change is harder to accomplish than almost any operational project. It requires an unwavering commitment, strong leadership, and continuous reinforcement. This is a challenge that many CEOs have difficulty with, and it is a process that many companies bungle. I learned just how difficult it can be to change an entrenched culture when I served as the nonexecutive chairman of a Polish company a few years ago.

Sabotaging Change at Brzeg

In the mid-1990s I was hired by an American investment group to coach N.Z.P.T. Brzeg, a newly privatized company and the leading producer of margarine in Poland, in the ways of the free enterprise system. I saw this as an exciting challenge, a great opportunity to lead an enormous transition effort—but it also helped to reinforce some important leadership lessons.

Privately, I worried that Brzeg's executives, most of whom were holdovers from the state-run system, would not be suited to the task of competing in a free enterprise system. In the old Socialist central-planning system, waste, protectionism, and corruption were the norm.

The people who thrived in that system were inward-looking, hierarchical, and risk-averse. In order to win medals, they had only to meet production quotas, adhere to cost budgets, and comply with (low) quality standards. They had never had to deal with customers, competitors, brands, or trade channels, and they had little understanding of profit. They were supreme bureaucrats: very well educated, but with absolutely no experience in running a business in a competitive environment.

I tried to explain to Brzeg's managers that they were now playing a totally new game, and that their traditional ways of doing things would be no match for international competitors that could draw on their successes around the world. The *only* way for them to compete, I said, was to build their brand, Kama, by focusing relentlessly on satisfying customer needs. This would require a cultural revolution. Much like Polish society in general, they had to go from inward-looking (bureaucratic, quota-oriented) to outward-looking (customer-focused, risk-taking, competitive).

But the holdovers from the old state-run system just shrugged. They viewed any change to their way of doing things as a threat. I tried everything from politeness to exhortation to tough talk, but I couldn't get them to change their ways.

The primary roadblock was Brzeg's CEO, a swaggering power broker who had enjoyed the perks of his job for many years and was not about to give them up. He was cunning. When I flew to Poland, he "yessed" me in person, and assured me he was researching global best practices and implementing our aggressive brand-building strategy. But once I left, he snickered, told his managers to ignore our initiatives, and actively undermined our entire program. "We're Poles, they're Americans, and they don't understand how we do things," he said to his lieutenants. "I'm in charge, and we'll continue to do things my way. If you follow the Americans, I'll fire you." As a result, they remained inward-looking, bureaucratic, and risk-averse.

In retrospect, I see that beneath his swagger he must have been terrified. Although he used all the right words, he probably felt doubt about his ability to compete in the free market system, and he didn't know how to manage a change of this magnitude. Instead of rising to the challenge, he stuck to the safe, known path. And Brzeg margarine paid the price.

As expected, international competitors soon applied worldwide best practices to distribution and marketing, built their brands, focused relentlessly on the customer, and overtook Brzeg. Our brand, Kama, began to flounder.

Of course, when I realized the destructive role being played by the CEO, I knew we had to act. He had been given every opportunity to commit himself to a new culture. Shortly thereafter, we fired the CEO and brought in a new management team headed by a Canadian, and the implementation of free market practices began in earnest.

The younger people in the company responded enthusiastically, and the difficult process of change was underway. Pockets of resistance remained in place, and it was necessary to replace more key people before real progress was possible. But we persevered, and slowly reversed Brzeg's volume losses. Ultimately, Kama once again became Poland's number one margarine brand.

This painful story illustrates a crucial truth. When culture resists strategy, culture wins and strategy loses. Under circumstances like these, drastic action—such as firing the person most responsible for the obstruction—may be unavoidable.

When Culture Supports Strategy

By contrast, a stunning example of the power of culture as a competitive weapon is the Toyota Production System (TPS).

The Toyota Production System

Widely acclaimed as the global standard of manufacturing efficiency and product quality, the Toyota Production System has long been regarded as a primary source of Toyota's success in the auto industry.

TPS has been studied extensively by academics and practitioners alike. Yet its exact genetic code remains an enigma to the scores of companies that have tried to adopt its practices and philosophy.

Each year, Toyota opens its doors to thousands of executives from a variety of industries—competitors and noncompetitors alike—seeking a deeper understanding of what makes the company tick. They conduct tours of their manufacturing plants, describe TPS in detail, and point out many of the specific techniques and practices that make it work. It's a bit like Coke inviting Pepsi over to watch batches of its secret formula being prepared.

To the uninitiated, TPS is deceptively simple. The procedures used by Toyota workers are surprisingly straightforward and clear. Yet most folks that visit the plants simply don't get it. One has to look under the surface to fully comprehend the brilliance of TPS. From Toyota's perspective, its well-known *kanban* cards, *andon* cords, and quality circles are merely physical manifestations of deeper cultural values that have been fostered over many years. On the one hand, each and every task is refined to absolute perfection, or *kaizen*. Yet at the same time, Toyota's processes are evolving continuously through learning and are highly adaptable to changing circumstances.

Professor Takahiro Fujimoto of Tokyo University explains: "Toyota's real strength resides in its ability to learn. Its employees are problem-conscious and customer-oriented. . . . The company's practices are constantly changing, even though its basic principles are unchanged."

This culture drives a ceaseless set of experiments, over time creating a built-in ability to study its mistakes, learn from them, and improve itself on an ongoing basis—the cornerstone of an adaptive culture.

Competitors have tried to emulate Toyota by copying the practices that the company freely demonstrates on its factory tours. But by and large, they have failed, simply because they have neglected to emulate the underlying culture that is the real driver of success.

What It Takes to Create a Cultural Change

I've been stressing the point that when a company's strategy changes materially, its culture needs to change as well so as to support the new strategy. How do we make this happen?

The high rates of failure in attempts to change corporate culture are usually based on the six myths described earlier. And because culture is so personal and deeply felt, these failures have an especially negative effect on employees, building cynicism and killing motivation. It is crucial that we demolish the myths about culture and harness the drivers of success. There are two essential factors for success in changing a corporate culture: *the right starting point* and *a sustaining process*.

The Right Starting Point

There are four basic rules of success for creating the right starting point:

1. Your company's values should directly support your strategic priorities.
2. They should be described as behaviors.
3. They should be simple and specific.
4. They should be arrived at through a process of enrollment.

Let's consider each rule in turn.

Your Values Should Directly Support Your Strategic Priorities

First, define how your corporate culture looks today. What are the values and behaviors that define "how things work around here"? Second, review your company's winning proposition and strategic priorities. Then define the values and behaviors needed to support your new strategy.

How AGL Realigned Its Values and Behaviors behind a New Strategy

The Atlanta Gas Light Company (now a subsidiary of AGL Resources) provides a good illustration of how culture must respond to strategic change. Here's an excerpt from the company's 1993 annual report. The gas industry had been deregulated, and AGL was forced to make a massive shift in its strategy; without a concurrent shift in culture, the company's change effort could easily have failed.

First, the company defined its new vision:

Atlanta Gas Light Company will become America's leading natural gas and energy services company by being the provider of choice for customers, employees, and investors.

Next, it defined the values and behaviors essential to the success of this new vision:

To be the provider of choice . . . Atlanta Gas Light Company must change . . .

For Customers

▼ From . . . emphasis on regulation . . . to emphasis on competition.

▼ From . . . offering what we think customers want . . . to providing what customers value.

For Employees

▼ From . . . being "good enough" . . . to being the best.

▼ From . . . rewarding for longevity . . . to rewarding for performance.

For Investors

▼ From . . . "We have always done it this way" . . . to "How can it be done better?"

▼ From . . . business as usual . . . to increasing shareholder value.

Guided by the principles on this list, which were directly linked to its new strategy, AGL was able to succeed in its do-or-die transition.

Your Values Must Be Described as Behaviors

The onion model is a useful way for us to understand the various layers that make up an organization's culture. However, it can also lead us to a false conclusion. We tend to feel, intuitively, that if we want to change our company's culture, then it is logical to start at the core, with the underlying assumptions, and then work progressively outward, to the behaviors. In theory, this sounds convincing, but in practice, this is not the most effective process, particularly for a large company. It would certainly take a very long time—more time than most companies have for dealing with the competitive challenges they face. (Refer back to Gerstner's statement of the new values needed at IBM earlier in this chapter. They were described very specifically as behaviors, one crucial reason for the effectiveness of Gerstner's initiative.)

The best approach, then, is to start at the outside of the onion, with a clear definition of the necessary *behaviors*, not at the core. Of course, these behaviors should always be linked to the new strategy so that their logic is clear, and this will help to influence the underlying assumptions. However, the wrong question is: How do we change the *thinking* around here? The right question is: How do we change the *behaviors* around here?

Organizations that are devoted to fostering fundamental change in people's lives were among the first to discover this principle. Alcoholics Anonymous begins freeing people from the grip of addiction *not* by exhorting them to alter their beliefs but by providing them with practical help to stay sober, one day at a time. Weight Watchers operates in a similar fashion, starting with specific eating and exercise habits rather than with underlying values. And these organizations have found that if you work from the outside in a curious thing happens: As behaviors change, people's thinking gradually begins to change as well. It's as if the onion begins to change from the outside in.

"The real task," as management scholar Richard Pascale has written, "is to behave your way into a new way of thinking, rather than to think your way into a new way of behaving."

Your Value Statement Should Be Simple and Specific

Long, rambling statements don't work. GE, a huge, $131 billion conglomerate, has repeatedly stressed four simple concepts in its internal and external communications: "boundarylessness, speed, simplicity, and self-confidence." These four ideas have become an important part of the company culture, helping to drive GE to heights few companies have ever matched.

Follow GE's example. When describing your company's values, limit yourself to the five most important behaviors. No one will respond to long lists and complex statements. Harley-Davidson, for instance, uses a value statement that includes the following five simple behaviors, which everyone can easily remember:

▼ Tell the truth.

▼ Keep your promises.

▼ Be fair.

▼ Respect the individual.

▼ Encourage intellectual curiosity.

Your Values Should Be Arrived At through a Process of Enrollment

In order for a set of values to take hold and work, you cannot simply impose them on your employees. It is essential to *enroll* people. That is, get them motivated, build belief in the new culture, and get them to "sign up" for it. There is, after all, a huge difference between commitment and compliance.

Building commitment is not something that can be done at a weekend retreat, by publishing a document, by handing out laminated cards, or by hanging gold-leafed plaques on your walls. Nor can it be done by simply issuing exhortations from the top, no matter how eloquent and heartfelt. These empty gestures build cynicism rather than motivation, and cynicism is the acid that eats away at a company's foundations. The point to understand is that what you are creating is not a document but a way of life. This can require extraordinary efforts.

Creating Commitment at Sterling Winthrop

When Sterling Winthrop set out to devise a clear set of values for itself, meetings and workshops were held around the world, describing the company's strategy and getting input and agreement to the values and behaviors necessary to make that strategy succeed. The resulting sense of ownership in the outcome was both wide and deep. The values statement that was developed—carefully designed to describe the company's values in terms of behaviors—was as follows:

Sterling Winthrop's Values
1. Our behavior toward one another will unfailingly show mutual respect, candor, and trust.
2. Market needs will drive our choice of products and services and the way we deliver them.
3. We encourage a healthy dissatisfaction with the status quo, openness to change, and vigorous experimentation in our ceaseless quest for a better way.
4. Speed of action will be the hallmark of how we get things done.
5. We believe that integrity is an essential asset. We will always do the right thing.

To show how committed he was to doing things right, my predecessor as president of Sterling Health, Herb McKenzie, took a blown-up version of this values statement on a worldwide tour of Sterling Winthrop subsidiaries. He asked our people from the various operating companies around the world to sign the huge document as a symbol of collective commitment. Of course it would have been a lot easier for him not to go on that trip—a trip that cynics might interpret as a mere publicity stunt. But this tour had an enormous internal effect and helped to energize and unify Sterling Winthrop's people behind a clear set of values.

Most important, they then ensured that those values were constantly nourished, modeled, measured, and rewarded. Building culture is a journey without end. Hence the importance of the second factor for success: a sustaining process.

A Sustaining Process

By itself, the right starting point is not enough. Without a sustaining process your culture change initiative will probably be no more than a seven-day wonder, producing the cynicism we've spoken about. Here are the key elements of a sustaining process that can help to ensure that your new culture takes hold, develops roots throughout your organization, and is continuously reinforced.

1. Align your culture with all the other key levers in your business system.
2. Measure and reward the desired behaviors.
3. Unfailingly set the example by your actions.

Align Your Culture with All the Other Key Levers

Remember the lesson of the giraffe and the acacia tree. Your business system is an ecosystem, and your organization's culture must work in harmony not only with your strategy but also with the other key supporting elements of your business system—that is, with your measurement and reward system, your organizational structure and decision processes, and your people policies.

If you need creativity and personal accountability as part of your culture, then this won't work if your organizational structure is rigid and hierarchical. Furthermore, your people policies—job rotation, recruitment, training, and development—have to be aligned with creativity and accountability. And, of course, your measurement and reward system must also reinforce these behaviors. Without such alignment, the ecosystem will not function effectively.

Measure and Reward the Desired Behaviors

While alignment with *all* the other levers of the business system is crucial, I want to stress the importance of measurements and rewards. Somehow, this vital requirement gets systematically overlooked when it comes to culture.

Think about it: What do companies measure and reward? Only the most important things, such as sales revenues, product quality, profit margins, and cash flow. As I've mentioned, when you measure something, you are sending a strong message: "This is important." If you fail to measure culture, you will be unable to gauge your progress. And you will be sending an equally strong message, "This is *not* important—no matter what we may say."

Far too often companies say they are determined to create a high-performance culture but fail to create the measurement systems that are vital for success. It should be as routine as the measurement of cash flow: If you want to improve cash flow but don't take the trouble to measure progress and reward performance, then it is very unlikely you will see improvement. The same rules apply to culture.

There are various ways to measure culture. Let's consider the most important.

First, your organization's cultural values and behaviors can be measured through periodic surveys. There are many assessment tools offered by various consultants. In my view, most are too complicated. When the Institute for the Future performed its own cultural analysis, it used a simple measurement tool with just a dozen items. To be focused and effective, you need a measurement instrument customized for your particular company and carefully administered. It's best to have an independent expert design and administer the survey, in order to minimize bias and make it easy for employees to feel confident about giving frank answers. Be sure that all employees are included.

A simple way of doing this is to use a five-point rating scale as illustrated in Figure 8.3. The sample items shown are taken from a company I have worked with, here called ABC for confidentiality.

Such surveys can give you useful readings on key beliefs and behaviors. You can then break these readings down in various ways—by geography, by function, or by headquarters versus field operations, for example. This allows you to identify gaps and enables the various teams in the company to take actions to close them. If, for example, your European operation scores a two out of five on the risk-taking scale, and the company is at a four over-

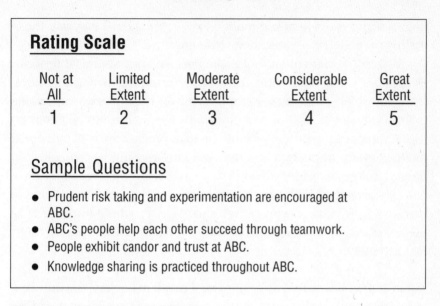

Rating Scale

Not at All	Limited Extent	Moderate Extent	Considerable Extent	Great Extent
1	2	3	4	5

Sample Questions

- Prudent risk taking and experimentation are encouraged at ABC.
- ABC's people help each other succeed through teamwork.
- People exhibit candor and trust at ABC.
- Knowledge sharing is practiced throughout ABC.

Figure 8.3   Measurement of Culture

all, this gives the European leadership a measurable gap to close, and the head of Europe should be held accountable for doing just that.

Of course, simply measuring once is not enough. Like any good measurement system, these surveys should be repeated at regular intervals so that trends can be measured and managers can see— and be rewarded for—the results of their efforts.

A second way of measuring your company's culture is through 360-degree feedback. This process entails getting confidential feedback on how well you and the company's other leaders live the company's values, anonymously from people at all levels of the hierarchy—those above you, on the same level, and below you. We all have strengths and weaknesses, and a rating scale will help determine where your gaps are. Once you know where you need to improve, form a personal action plan and work on closing those gaps. This is a sensitive exercise, one that occasionally creates resistance. It can be somewhat painful at first, but is ultimately a rewarding experience of self-discovery. My recommendation is that the senior team undergo the 360-degree survey first, to demonstrate their willingness and provide a role model. Only then should they ask those below them in the organization to do so.

A third measurement tool is the performance appraisal process. Most companies have some form of performance management system, in which managers are appraised by their bosses on results measured against established objectives. For culture to be taken seriously, part of the process should be to appraise how well individual managers are actually living the company's values and inculcating them into the teams they lead.

An important part of implementing these measurements is the *follow-up*. Just measuring is not enough. The whole purpose is to define goals, act on what you learn, and reward people for their achievements.

Measuring the desired behaviors is only half the battle. The other half is rewarding them. As you'll recall in society, the only reason that a culture persists is that adherence is recognized and rewarded, while noncompliance is penalized. The same is true in corporate culture. Making certain that your corporate system of rewards reinforces the desired behaviors is crucial when you are mounting a cultural change effort.

The chief executive of a firm I was working with recently looked at me in amazement and said, "But Willie, how do you reward something like *culture*?!" He was, of course, a victim of Myth 1—the belief that culture is vague and mysterious. But as I've pointed out, culture is expressed through concrete behaviors. As a result, there are a number of ways to reward culture, both financial and nonfinancial, just as you reward things like cash flow. Here are a few suggestions.

First, let's consider financial rewards. Making compensation dependent on how well your people live the values of the company can be done through:

▼ Incentive compensation.

▼ Base pay increases.

▼ Ad hoc cash bonuses.

▼ Stock options.

Using bonuses is an especially visible and symbolic way to reward people's adherence to company culture. Peter Heinze, the president of International Specialty Products (ISP), a New Jersey–based chemical company, demonstrated this in a stunning way.

ISP Puts Its Money Where Its Mouth Is

It was the late 1990s, and ISP was working its way through a difficult transformation from a product-focused to a customer-focused business. At an executive workshop, we developed the new strategy, and then defined the supporting behaviors the company would need. Everyone saw the importance of aligning culture and strategy, acknowledging, "It's essential that we bring about a radical shift in behavior."

Later, at a coffee break, Peter Heinze asked my advice on how to bring this about.

"Perhaps you should demonstrate your seriousness by rearranging the bonus system to make a significant percentage of your people's bonuses dependent on their living the new values and encouraging the values within their teams," I suggested.

"What percentage do you recommend?" he asked.

"At least 25 percent."

Heinze surprised me when he said, "That's a good idea, but I don't want to interfere with the bonus system we already have in place. I'd like to add *another* 25 percent to people's bonuses, based on how well they embody our culture."

"You sound very committed, Peter," I replied. "If that's what you plan to do, why don't you announce it *right now?*"

Heinze did just that. I can't think of a better example of leading through meaningful—and dramatic—action.

Nonfinancial methods of rewarding the right behaviors can be as powerful an incentive as money—or, in the case of job promotions, can be even *more* motivating than money. Indeed, career advancement may be the ultimate reward. The decision about whom you promote sends a loud message about what you consider important. Whenever you promote someone who lives the values of the company, you are telling your people that this is important; when you promote a person who doesn't embody company values, this promotion makes an equally loud statement to the contrary, and one that your people will immediately internalize.

The nonfinancial incentives may include:

▼ Promotions.

▼ Annual values awards.

▼ Mention in company newsletters.

▼ Public praise.

▼ Recognition letters.

Here is a crucial question: What do you do about a person who produces outstanding financial results, yet doesn't live the company's values? If you mean what you say about your values, and if you want your employees—present and future—to take those values seriously, then you must impose some kind of serious sanction on those who violate them. It's important that you be clear on this point, announce your policy in advance, and then have the resolve to act on it. In some cases, demotion or even dismissal may be necessary. This will require a good deal of courage, but it will send a very clear message about what is important to the organization. People will notice and remember.

You won't change a company's culture overnight. It takes hard, conscientious work. But if you systematically measure and reward the values you seek and relentlessly follow up on the gaps, it will substantially help your efforts.

Unfailingly Set the Example by Your Actions

As a leader, it is vital that you continuously communicate the values and unfailingly set an example through your own behavior.

The CEO is the organization's cultural leader. It's a role that cannot be delegated. If the CEO doesn't live the corporate values, any efforts to instill them in the company will be dead on arrival.

A prime example of this danger is the chairman of a company I recently worked with. I'll call it A-One Technologies.

The Reluctant CEO

A-One produces high-tech equipment. Despite its cutting-edge product, however, the company's decision-making process is consensus-driven and agonizingly slow. At the invitation of A-One's chairman, "Ben," I worked with the company on developing a new strategy based on speed, and on aligning the culture behind the strategy. The executive team was committed and was ready to run with the ball, but, ironically, the real source of the problem turned out to be the chairman himself. Ben is a brilliant man, but he gets mired in details and endless deliberation. He expected everyone else to become more agile, but he remained stuck in his consensus-driven mode.

The dilemma was clear. If Ben didn't change his behavior, then his executive team wouldn't either, and the failure would cascade down throughout the organization. The attitude of the leader infects everyone else—for better and for worse. In the end, A-One would rise or fall based on whether one person, the chairman and CEO, could shift his behavior.

I had the delicate task of dealing with this dilemma. I suggested to Ben that A-One's big shift in strategy also called for a reevaluation of his own leadership style, and I recommended that he consider hiring a personal coach. Ben readily agreed, and he is now working on his own personal development plan. It's a fine example of a leader showing by his own behavior that culture is important and must be taken seriously if the organization is to reach its full potential.

The Adaptive Culture

I'm often asked what values characterize the adaptive organization. My answer is to offer the following list of key behaviors:

▼ Teamwork.

▼ Risk taking and experimentation.

▼ Continuous learning.

▼ Knowledge sharing.

▼ Candor and trust.

Competitive skiers like to say that if you don't fall down once in a while, you aren't pushing yourself hard enough. The same could be said for any kind of risk-based pursuit, including business. Risk taking is a process of exploration and discovery. But an inescapable consequence of risk taking is making mistakes. They are two sides of the same coin. To be risk averse and afraid of making mistakes is to shut down your learning. If you don't make any mistakes, then, like the skier who never falls, you aren't pushing your company hard enough.

James Joyce, the Irish writer, made an acute observation when he said, "Mistakes are the portals of discovery." In other words, don't be afraid to make mistakes, but make sure you *learn* from them.

There is a famous corporate legend, possibly apocryphal, about Thomas Watson Sr., the founder of IBM, who heard that one of his managers had made a mistake that cost the company $10 million. He summoned the manager to a meeting. The night before, the manager said to his wife, "I really blew it this time. Tomorrow I'll be fired." The next day, he went before Watson and explained what had happened, noted the important things he had learned in the process, and then admitted that he expected to lose his job for such a costly mistake. "You've got to be kidding," Watson supposedly said. "We've just spent $10 million on your education!"

Many companies would indeed have fired that executive. But Tom Watson had the wisdom to see the value hidden in a mistake.

The question, then, is: How do we develop a tolerance for mistake making?

When I mention this in my workshops, managers sometimes look at me in surprise. "You want us to *reward* mistakes?" they ask. "You want us to say, 'Hey, Fred, that was a real mess-up; here's a big bonus'?" Of course not. Companies don't function like that.

I like the approach of my friend Bob Dewar, a professor at

Northwestern University's Kellogg School of Business, who says the real issue is to distinguish "smart" mistakes from "dumb" ones. Dumb mistakes should be defined in advance and appropriately discouraged or penalized. They include:

▼ Repeating your own mistake.

▼ Repeating someone else's mistake.

▼ Risking more than you can afford to lose.

▼ Acting impulsively, without thought.

▼ Doing something illegal or unethical.

All other mistakes are smart mistakes, *provided* the learning from them is made explicit and then shared across the entire company. These kinds of mistakes should be encouraged.

The best approach to risk taking is to try many different things on a small scale, test them in practice, and see what works or doesn't before ramping up to the next level of magnitude. That's the way learning works in scientific discovery: By conducting experiments, we learn from numerous small-scale failures. As the 3M company philosophy says, "Try a lot of things and keep what works."

This is also the approach that venture capitalists use when they fund start-up companies: Nine out of 10 bets may fail or be only moderately successful; the gamble is that one or two investments will pay off so handsomely that they cover all of the venture capitalist's losses and generate a profit besides.

It would be nice if life were so neat and tidy that we make only small, safe mistakes. But real life doesn't always work that way. If you're pushing the envelope, every now and again you'll make a big mistake. This can become a major moment of truth for a company. Do you make an example of the mistake maker and risk traumatizing the company, or do you accept the damage and move on?

Business is all about the management of risk, says Niall FitzGerald, my former colleague and now chairman of Unilever. FitzGerald is no stranger to risk and failure himself.

Risk Taking at Unilever

In 1994, Niall FitzGerald was head of Unilever's detergents division—and the CEO heir apparent—when he spearheaded the ill-fated launch of Persil Power, a laundry detergent that tended to destroy rather than clean people's clothing.

At the time, Unilever and Procter & Gamble were in the midst of a long-running battle for the European detergent market. Unilever's Persil Power had been put on a fast-track development cycle to beat P&G's Ariel Future to market. One of Persil's ingredients was a manganese-based accelerator.

In advance of Persil's launch, P&G learned that the product would contain manganese. Their scientists had evidence that, while manganese had excellent cleaning properties, it could also damage colored fabrics. They expressed their concerns about Persil's formula to Unilever's top brass. While this was a generous gesture, it was not entirely altruistic—P&G was concerned about the impact of a botched product release on the worldwide detergents industry. But the warning apparently fell on deaf ears; Unilever's scientists clearly believed otherwise. Legend has it that the P&G delegation was politely shown the door.

FitzGerald, a brilliant and tough executive, launched Persil Power with a massive ad campaign that cost more than the development of the product. Within weeks of Persil Power hitting the shelves, P&G counterattacked with an aggressive ad campaign deriding Persil Power's ingredients and featuring pictures of boxer shorts filled with holes. Unilever cried foul and denied there was any problem with its new product. But there was. The miracle manganese did indeed put holes in people's boxer shorts. It was a public relations nightmare, and the British press had a field day with it. Eventually, Unilever withdrew its new detergent from the market, and Persil Power joined the Ford Edsel and New Coke in the ranks of embarrassing product failures.

As head of Unilever's detergent division, FitzGerald was in the hot seat. Yet he was also slated to become chairman of the company. The question was: How would Unilever react to this huge, costly, and very public mistake?

After an internal review clarified what had happened and a modification of practices ensured that it would never happen again, Unilever's senior executives decided it made no sense to derail FitzGerald's promotion. Had they done so, the message to the entire company would have been: Don't take risks, don't be aggressive, don't try your hardest. As things turned out, FitzGerald—bruised, but wiser—dusted himself off and has since proven himself a very capable chairman. The message *that* sends is: Mistakes happen; don't be terrified of them; learn from them—and keep taking risks.

Knowledge Sharing as a Crucial Value

One of the hallmarks of an adaptive organization is the ability to share knowledge. As we've seen, global competitiveness demands global best practices everywhere, all the time. This requires that organizations become outstanding at knowledge sharing. The problem is that there is often a reluctance to share knowledge with others, especially at the senior level. This is a result of our natural competitiveness and insecurity, and it is particularly a problem in highly political organizations characterized by fiefdoms and power struggles. In such a setting, knowledge is power, and sharing one's knowledge is a kind of unilateral disarmament. The natural inclination is to hoard it. But the truth is that knowledge hoarding can severely limit, or even cripple, the effectiveness and growth of a company.

Creating an atmosphere of candor and trust is the foundation on which to build an adaptive enterprise. Such an environment—what the Institute for the Future calls the "culture of giving"—fosters teamwork, experimentation, learning, and knowledge sharing. All genuine learning organizations have developed a culture of giving.

Buckman Labs, a specialty chemical business based in Memphis, Tennessee, with operations in 21 countries and customers in 90, is an excellent example of a learning company whose adaptive corporate culture is specifically designed to encourage and reward knowledge sharing.

Knowledge Sharing at Buckman Labs

Buckman Labs has been a learning organization since the day of ro-
tary phones, propeller planes, and battered leather briefcases. Today, the company's extensive computer network simply enhances a
knowledge-sharing system that has been in place for years.

Since the late 1940s, the company has been sending teams of
Ph.D.'s to job sites around the world to fix problems for customers.
They stay on-site until the problem is fixed, then share what they've
learned, often via visits to other Buckman facilities everywhere—thus
creating a deepening well of knowledge that all Buckman personnel
can access.

Today much of this knowledge sharing is done via the Internet. Indeed, everyone at the company is *required* to contribute to this propri-
etary knowledge management system. An employee who fails to
contribute sufficiently will get an e-mail from Robert Buckman, the
company's founder, reminding him or her to do so: "Dear Associate,
You haven't been sharing knowledge recently. How can we help you?
All the best. Bob." This is the kind of human attention required to keep
the culture of knowledge sharing alive.

Furthermore, it's generally known within the company that
choice assignments and promotions are most likely to go to those
who have done the most to produce knowledge *and* share it. At
Buckman Labs, power comes not from hoarding knowledge but from
sharing it.

The result is that Buckman Labs is the archetype of a highly adaptive, and therefore highly competitive, organization.

Notice that Buckman entrenched its culture of knowledge sharing long before the era of the personal computer, let alone the Internet. Today it is merely using technology to facilitate what it has
always done. A mere database or intranet is an empty vessel. It will
be filled and drunk from only if there is a preexisting culture of
knowledge sharing.

Buckman's system provides customers with superior solutions,
and is based on a conscious decision to learn and adapt on an ongoing basis—one of the core principles of Strategic Learning.

Many companies fall into the technology trap: They know they must share knowledge to be competitive, and they assume that building an intranet will automatically solve the problem. But technology alone won't spark a new set of learning behaviors. As Buckman Labs has demonstrated, knowledge sharing is 90 percent sociology and only 10 percent technology. After all, it's not computers that share knowledge—it's people.

9

Overcoming
Resistance to Change

You know, I'm all for progress. It's change I object to.

—Mark Twain

We've been discussing the third step in the Strategic Learning cycle—aligning the company behind your strategic choices. As we've seen, adaptive organizations are continuously able to modify their strategies in response to changes in the environment. Sometimes these changes will be small, incremental adjustments; at other times, radical change is called for (as when Richard Fosbury reinvented the high jump, or when Nicolas Hayek revolutionized the watch industry). This chapter focuses on the people challenges of successfully leading *large-scale* change.

Managing large-scale change calls for people skills of the highest order (see Figure 9.1). Thus, the creation of an adaptive organization requires that strategy and leadership interact seamlessly. As I've emphasized, strategy is a central part of leadership, and leadership a crucial part of strategy; you will achieve sustained success only when you fully integrate the two.

As we've seen, a great leader offers an inspiring vision of the future and a practical method for getting there. But difficult as this is, it's not enough. If the organization is to achieve its goals, the leader

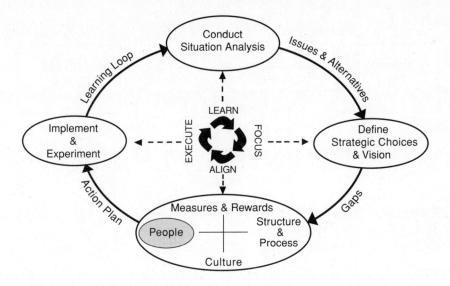

Figure 9.1 Strategic Learning: The Leadership Process—People

must also help his or her people overcome the natural opposition to change nearly all humans instinctually feel.

Because of this deep-rooted resistance to change, there is no greater leadership challenge than leading an organization through large-scale change. The key is to transform people's resistance to change (a negative) into active support of change (a positive). This requires strong, inspiring leadership.

As you may recall from our discussion of the sigmoid curve in Chapter 2, success contains the seeds of its own destruction. The key to long-term survival is to change while you are still successful—but this is also the most difficult time to change. "If it ain't broke," resisters will say, "why fix it?" But that is a self-defeating mind-set. Once things have started to go bad, support for change will grow, but the probability of success will diminish. As we've seen, this is one of the painful paradoxes of business: A change effort enjoys the highest chance of success when support for change is at its lowest, while the lowest chance of success exists when support for change is at its highest. One of the leader's greatest challenges, then, is to find ways to motivate people to embrace change

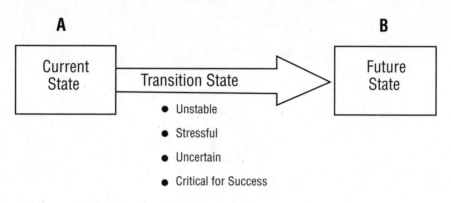

A

B

Current State

Transition State

Future State

- Unstable
- Stressful
- Uncertain
- Critical for Success

Figure 9.2 Change Leadership: Getting from A to B
Source: D. Nadler and M. Tushman.

at times when the need for change is not apparent—to foster adaptation and innovation in an atmosphere more naturally conducive to pride, self-satisfaction, and complacency.

Think of change leadership as the challenge of successfully leading the organization on a journey from point A to point B (see Figure 9.2). An adaptive organization is constantly undergoing a series of A-to-B changes; each is a journey that must be skillfully managed. It's a series of point-to-point shifts that add up to a cumulative, ongoing process of evolution.

Getting from A to B

The dilemma of change leadership came home to me in a big way when, in 1997, I was leading a workshop for a group of Polish executives—the group from Brzeg margarine that I mentioned in Chapter 8—at Columbia Business School.

Change Leadership—or Change *the* Leadership?

With Brzeg margarine having recently been privatized, the leaders of this Polish company (of which I was the nonexecutive chairman) had to learn how to manage the company in an environment that was completely new to them—the competitive world of free enterprise, in which success and even survival depended not on government fiats but on the judgments of customers and the actions of competitors in an open marketplace.

To tackle this challenge, we brought the senior managers from the Polish company to Columbia Business School for a week and had members of our expert faculty deliver an educational program on the keys to success in a free enterprise economy. We covered topics like brand building, the basics of finance, how to create winning strategies, and so on. We had them work in groups to define point A, the old Socialist way, and then later to define point B, the keys to success in the new free enterprise system.

We soon found that the Polish managers were able to define the rules of the new game with great clarity. In fact, there was absolutely nothing wrong with their understanding of what success in the free market would look like. Suddenly I was struck by a fresh insight: The executives of Brzeg could define point A and define point B, but they had no idea how to undertake the journey from A to B.

We sometimes make the mistake of assuming that once people understand what point B looks like, the process of getting there should be obvious. We therefore simply concentrate on "selling" the future state. That's a serious blunder. In reality, the journey from A to B is highly uncertain and fraught with difficulty—a messy, frustrating, arduous task full of pitfalls and opportunities for failure.

Most of the Polish managers attending the program at Columbia spoke little English. Accordingly, we had set up a booth in the back of the classroom occupied by two interpreters who translated between Polish and English as we spoke. Of course, this took time and made our communication a bit of a shared struggle. However, the system worked reasonably well until the moment when I realized that the key missing element was a road map for the journey from point A to point B. Addressing the class, I shared this insight and added, "This is the key challenge we'll need to focus on together— what we call *change leadership*."

I paused as the translator conveyed my ideas in Polish, and was startled to observe the reactions on the faces of the participants. The junior managers exchanged amazed glances among themselves, and some were snickering gleefully, while the senior leaders wore expressions of thunderstruck dismay and indignation. I was puzzled—what could this mean? Suddenly the door to the translation booth burst open, and the young translator came running up to me.

"I think I made a mistake with your last sentence," she said. "You referred to 'change leadership,' didn't you?"

"That's right."

"Well, I'm afraid I mistranslated you. Rather than 'change leadership,' I said instead that they must 'change *the* leadership.'"

In other words, the Poles thought I'd recommended that all their top executives be sacked! And it was clear that, while the younger folks thought this was a fine idea, the senior executives didn't care for it at all.

Naturally, we halted the discussion and explained the error (which provoked gales of laughter from the younger managers), took a little break, regrouped, and started again. Ironically enough, in the end, it *was* necessary to change the top leadership of Brzeg margarine. But our classroom was neither the time nor the place to propose that idea!

Of course, the story reveals some of the perils of cross-cultural business education. But on a deeper level, it illustrates the range of intense emotions (pride, defensiveness, fear) that the prospect of serious change evokes. If "change leadership" is seen as a daunting personal challenge by many leaders, one reason is that change always carries the possibility that the leader's own secure role may be threatened—that change leadership may ultimately mean changing the leadership.

It's not enough for your people to understand the company's current state (point A) and to be able to envision its future state (point B). The move from A to B always creates an unstable, stressful, uncertain situation, involving pain and discomfort. This is simply the nature of change, and it's the leader's role to help the organization effectively negotiate the journey.

Pitfalls of Change Leadership

It's a common misconception that other people see the world in the same way you do—that everyone thinks rationally and will understand the logic of your well-thought-out strategy. And so it can be a rude surprise when you discover that your coworkers are resisting your strategic initiatives or are actively trying to subvert them (and you).

The specter of change produces what's sometimes called the FUD factor—fear, uncertainty, and doubt. And if you can't devise ways to overcome people's resistance, then your change efforts will fail. To overcome this resistance, we need to understand why people dislike change. Here we enter the realm of human psychology. I don't mean deep Freudian analysis, but rather the psychology of everyday human interaction.

We can map the psychology of change like this:

▼ To change is to suffer loss—loss of several kinds. We lose certainty, the comfort of the known and the familiar. We lose the sense of competency, financial security, and status that goes along with the existing order of things. And when change is being imposed upon us (as is often the case in a corporate setting), we lose the sense of control and personal choice.

▼ Because change involves loss, people must be convinced that the gains will be greater than the losses if they are to embrace change.

▼ To succeed, therefore, the driving forces in support of change must be greater than the restraining forces of fear, uncertainty, and doubt.

The challenge of motivating people at all levels of your organization to embrace change is one of the major stumbling blocks for many companies. The research of Warner Burke, a professor of organizational psychology at Teachers College, Columbia University, shows that most companies are reasonably good at managing the organizational aspects of change, but earn only a grade of C when it comes to managing the people aspects of change.

Indeed, research shows that executives leading change efforts frequently miscalculate the following factors:

▼ The amount of resistance to change they will encounter.

▼ The time needed to shape, sell, and execute the change.

▼ The resources, support, and sponsorship required.

▼ The need to model the change personally.

▼ The emotional impact that the change will have on employees (the FUD factor).

When planning a major change, therefore, we need to be conscious of the risk of making these kinds of miscalculations and deliberately manage all the key factors that influence the success of the change effort.

The process of change thus moves people out of their comfort zones, forcing them to exchange certainty for a sense of uncertainty and danger. It is a natural instinct to resist this. But your comfort zone can also be an even more dangerous place. In coaching executives, I often use the sport of bullfighting to explain what I mean by this.

When most people watch a bullfight they get caught up in the external action—the mortal, ritualized face-off between matador and bull. But aficionados of the sport are attuned to a subtle psychological contest being played out beneath the surface. Bullfighting is an intuitive, interpretive activity. The temperament of every bull is different, and the matador uses the first few flourishes of his red cape to establish the bull's pattern of behavior. After a bull has been repeatedly challenged, it will begin to retreat to its comfort zone—that is, to a familiar pattern of behavior. This familiar pattern or tendency is known as the bull's *carencia* (pronounced "carenthia").

A great matador will identify the bull's *carencia* faster than a lesser matador, and once he has done so the contest is essentially over. The next time a bull retreats to this pattern, the matador will plunge the sword into its shoulder blades.

The moral of the story is that when we are threatened, just like the bull, we tend to retreat to our comfort zone for safety and cling to it more fiercely than ever. But your comfort zone can actually be the most dangerous place of all.

Think of yourself as the bull and your competitors as matadors. To take a risk and change your routine will be unsettling; but to play it safe and retreat to your *carencia* is far riskier.

An Equation for Successful Change

At Columbia Business School, we use a simple equation—involving dissatisfaction, vision, process, and cost (D, V, P, C)—to show how successful change is brought about. It takes basic rules of psychology and converts them into a practical business method for leading change (see Figure 9.3).

What the equation tells us is that for change to be successful, there needs to be dissatisfaction with the current state, a clear vision of the future state, and a practical process for getting there. These three factors in combination must be greater than the cost of change.

Notice that the first three elements in the equation are *multiplied* by one another. In mathematical terms, this means that if any of the boxes equals zero, the product of all three will equal zero. In other words, if any of the first three elements—dissatisfaction, vision, and process—is completely lacking, the change effort will be unsuccessful (see Figure 9.4). Thus:

▼ When D (dissatisfaction with one's current state) is missing, there is no felt need for change. People refuse to support any change effort because the overwhelming mood is one of

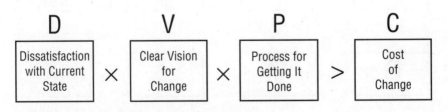

Figure 9.3 Equation for Successful Change
Source: M. Beer, adapted from R. Beckhard and R. T. Harris.

complacency and smugness. The prevailing sentiment is: "Why should we give up what we know?"

▼ When V (a clear vision for change) is missing, people recognize the need for change but can't envision the end state. The result is a mood of anxiety and confusion as people struggle to understand where the organization ought to be heading. The prevailing sentiment is: "We're being asked to give this up, but for what?"

▼ When P (a process for getting it done) is missing, people accept the need for change and know where the company wants to go, but they don't understand how they will get there. The mood is one of frustration and ultimately of rejection of the change effort due to lack of confidence in the organizational leadership. The prevailing sentiment is: "We don't know how to get there."

To make the workings of this equation clear, I like to draw an analogy portraying change at a personal level—namely, the psycho-

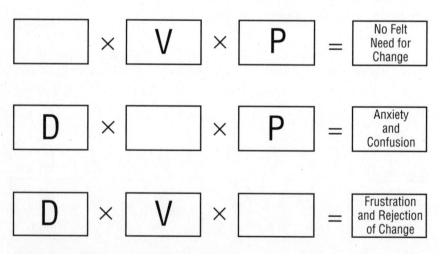

Figure 9.4   How the Tools Work Together
Source: M. Beer, adapted from R. Beckhard and R. T. Harris.

logical process typically involved in losing weight. Here's how the equation of successful change applies.

Dissatisfaction with Current State

Does the following scenario sound familiar? When the cold and dark of winter give way to the warmth and light of spring, you look at yourself in the mirror and are dismayed to see that you have put on weight. You try on your lightweight clothes and are shocked to discover that they no longer fit. You go for a jog, and are embarrassed to find that a spare tire judders and shakes around your midsection. You walk by a shop window, and while glancing at your reflection you are appalled by the unsightly bulge of your stomach. You are now dissatisfied with your physical state. You begin to feel an overwhelming need for change.

Clear Vision for Change

Having become thoroughly dissatisfied with your current state, you find yourself noticing pictures of remarkably lean and fit bodies in magazines. You run into an old friend who is exactly your age but looks 10 years younger than you do. In a family photo album, you spot an old photo of yourself looking trim, youthful, and energetic. All of these images combine to create a picture of what you *wish* you looked like today. You now have a clear vision of the change you want to achieve.

Process for Getting It Done

You know you want to lose weight and can picture how you want to look, but how will you go about it? You read articles about a few of the popular diet plans, but they sound unappetizing and impractical. You decide they aren't for you. A friend mentions his success with a personal trainer, but you don't have the time to invest in such a rigorous plan. Then your doctor reminds you of something she has said before: Simple, regular exercise and a low-fat, high-fiber diet are the best ways of trimming down your gut and toning up your muscles. *That* makes good sense to you. It's a new way of life, not a temporary fad. You sketch out a simple regimen: Take a brisk walk on the treadmill for half an hour four times a week, and change your eating habits to reduce meats and sweets and increase fruits and vegetables. You now have a clear and sustainable plan of action.

Cost of Change

Here's where the pain begins. It's Monday morning, the day you promised to start your new life. But you don't really want to go to the fitness center—wouldn't an extra half an hour in bed be more pleasant?—and a scoop or two of ice cream for dessert looks awfully attractive. But then you spot yet another jowly reflection of yourself, and you think, "Oh, no! Get me to the gym!" You've reached the point were the potential benefits of your fitness program outweigh the discipline and self-sacrifice involved. You take action.

This personal example involves the same factors as a change initiative in a company. You must create dissatisfaction with the current state in your firm, give your people a clear vision of a better future, and offer them an effective way to get there. And the benefits of the projected end state must be seen as outweighing the costs of getting there.

In both the weight-loss and business scenarios, the most difficult step is the first one: creating such dissatisfaction that it overwhelms the natural resistance to change. This is particularly true of mature, successful organizations—those that suffer from the curse of success.

GM, IBM, and the Curse of Success

Think about General Motors and IBM, two of the great icons of American business in the postwar period. Although they have many obvious differences as companies, both dominated their industries for decades until they encountered unprecedented and unexpectedly tenacious competition, lost market share, suffered huge financial losses, and came to the brink of outright failure.

But what else did GM and IBM have in common? Prior to their near-death experiences, both were subjected to lengthy antitrust investigations by the federal government. What's the significance? In both cases, the government was sending a clear message to the management of these companies: "You are *too* successful, so successful that we suspect you may be guilty of unfair competitive practices." The emotional reaction of management—unspoken, unacknowledged, but inevitable—must surely have been, "Too successful? My God, we must be *good*. After all, the U.S. government has told us so!"

It would be simplistic to attribute the complacency, even arrogance that both GM and IBM subsequently exhibited in the face of changes in their marketplaces solely to this reaction. Still, the facts are clear. For too long, the leaders of GM and IBM "believed their own press releases," as the saying goes; overconfident about their strategic prowess, they ignored the competitive warning signs that should have alerted them to the need for change. Element D in the change equation—dissatisfaction with one's current state—was missing. Thus, it was impossible to mount an effective change campaign at either company until years later, when the seriousness of their financial woes became too great to overlook.

Question: In the wake of recent antitrust action against Microsoft, will Bill Gates and his leadership team fall prey to the same complacency that almost destroyed GM and IBM?

How to Lead Change: Six Golden Rules

Mountains of books have been written on the leadership of change, to the point of creating confusion. If we distill all of this information down to the essentials, the result is six golden rules for successful change leadership. The great leaders of change are those who are able to harness these key rules of success.

1. Create a simple, compelling statement of the case for change.

2. Communicate constantly and honestly throughout the process.

3. Maximize participation.

4. If all else fails, remove those who resist.

5. Generate short-term wins.

6. Set a shining example.

Let's examine these rules one by one.

Create a Simple, Compelling Statement of the Case for Change

This brings us back to the question of strategy. If you've done your work well, your winning proposition will be based on clear, cogent logic and represent a compelling case for change. To do its job, the case for change should contain the following elements:

▼ Explain *what* the change will be. This comes from the winning proposition that was generated in your strategy creation work in the Strategic Learning cycle.

▼ Explain *why* the change is necessary. This is where the work from the situation analysis (Chapter 5) comes into play. Summarize the key insights that were generated and provide the underlying logic for the strategy.

Your challenge is to combine these two elements in such a way that you create a simple and compelling story that creates dissatisfaction with the current state and represents a call to action. Martin Luther King Jr., Mohandas K. Gandhi, and Winston Churchill were all great leaders who articulated the *what* and the *why*, and so brought about momentous change against great odds.

Brzeg Margarine and the Compelling Call to Action

In Poland, when I was coaching the Brzeg margarine company, the firm's Socialist-bred executives had to learn about such unfamiliar business concepts as profit and loss, return on assets, and cash flow. In addition, I explained the importance of building a strong brand. We talked about brand strategy, marketing and advertising, pricing and promotion—a complex picture with many variables. In other words, we were communicating some fairly complex ideas to the Brzeg people, all through translators.

It soon became clear that, although the Brzeg managers understood each individual element of the message we sought to convey, they were struggling to tie all the elements together in a way they could readily grasp and use as a guide to their daily business decisions. The trick was to find a unifying theme to convey a message that was absolutely clear, compelling, and concise. We came up with this formula: "A great brand equals a great company." In other words, the destiny of the company would depend on the strength of the brand.

When they heard this, the faces of the Brzeg executives lit up. *Here*, finally, was something they could understand. This maxim facilitated our discussions in many ways. A hundred corollaries tied into it, each opening up an important topic for exploration: "A great brand generates great profits for shareholders." "A great brand represents a promise of product quality." "A great brand is supported by first-rate employees." And the slogan provoked excellent questions: "What makes a brand great?" "What do customers expect from a great brand?"

Our simple maxim turned into a compelling call to action—a single shining light that the Brzeg executives could follow, rather than a confusing laundry list. Using it, we were able to communicate the whole story: Brand building means attracting and retaining the right customers, offering superior benefits, advertising strongly, operating efficiently, and so on.

Although the managers of Brzeg margarine faced unique challenges as members of the first generation of free-market corporate executives in post-Communist Poland, the communication challenges are really no different when dealing with seasoned business people in the West. A successful change effort requires a clear and compelling statement of the case for change around which everyone in the organization can rally.

While doing a situation analysis, Sony Media Solutions discovered it was in a financial hole, which they labeled the "death spiral." The phrase raised the alarm, rallied the troops, and ultimately helped mobilize SMS to become a top performer again. The concept of the "death spiral" became the galvanizing idea around which an entire change effort was focused.

In these examples, clear, compelling statements distilled the business case for change in a memorable way, and helped transmit a sense of focus, action, and urgency throughout the entire organization.

Communicate Constantly and Honestly throughout the Process

Your statement of the logic for change should be repeated over and over, in many different ways and at every opportunity. In fact, your goal should be to try to *overcommunicate*. In actuality, this is impossible. The more you communicate the message, the more firmly it will become lodged in the consciousness (and even the unconscious awareness) of your people.

Repetition doesn't mean you should be boring. To help motivate and direct your people, tell them stories and make surprising connections, but always bring them back to the central message. Recruit allies to spread the gospel. Encourage many voices to communicate the same message using their own words, stories, examples, metaphors, analogies, and anecdotes.

Storytelling is a vital part of this communication process. Nothing is more expressive, vivid, and memorable than a simple anecdote or image that encapsulates your idea. The world's most dynamic leaders have all understood this. Think of Abraham Lincoln, who read Aesop's *Fables* as a boy and went on to use his own homespun stories as a powerful leadership tool. Or think of Jack Welch, who used pithy metaphors to convey business strategies in unforgettable fashion: "Get inside the winner's circle. Be number one or number two in your industry, or you'll be closed, fixed, or sold."

It's crucial to keep hammering away at your central theme whenever you can. During our work with the executives from Brzeg margarine, for instance, they would ask questions like, "Isn't it important for us to have an efficient production system?" Because our mission was to get them to think in terms of the brand, we would answer: "Yes, efficient production is important because it will generate more money that you can invest in strengthening your *brand*." Or they would ask, "I work in a lab where we are focused on improving the quality of our products. Isn't that important?" "Of course," we would answer. "Your quality needs to be better than your competitors', because nothing wrecks a *brand* faster than poor quality."

In addition to being consistent and focused, your communication about the issues of change must be genuine, meaningful, and, above all, honest. Dishonesty and lack of communication only heighten the FUD factor (fear, uncertainty, and doubt). If your people believe that their leaders are trying to hide or disguise the truth, they will invent their own versions of events to fill in the knowledge gaps.

During World War II, my father traveled on a troop ship. For reasons of security, the troops themselves were not told where they were going or what their mission was until after they'd arrived at their destination. At night no lights were allowed, and the darkness compounded the sense of anxiety and uncertainty suffered by the soldiers. As a result, wild rumors abounded. "We're going into battle tomorrow," people said. "We're on a suicide mission." "The ship is infected with smallpox, and the officers are secretly dropping bodies overboard at night. . . ."

This is an extreme example, under wartime conditions, but the same kind of behaviors take place in the workplace. People cannot function in an information vacuum, particularly in times of stress, so they manufacture their own reality. Once rumors flare up, it's very hard to regain control and get people to accept the facts as they are. By contrast, honesty and open communication build trust and are crucial to getting the people aligned behind a new strategy.

It may not always be possible—for legal or other reasons—to tell everyone in the company about every aspect of a change effort as it is unfolding. But instead of glossing over the need for confidentiality, explain it. Say, for example, "I am telling you as much as I can at this point." Be forthright about the things you can talk about, and explain why the other things must remain confidential. Promise your people that you will tell them what is going on as soon as you can, and then keep your promise. The point is to never lose touch with your crewmates during the journey.

The most powerful demonstration of the benefits of honesty I've ever witnessed came at a time when I least expected it—a time when I had to lay off hundreds of employees.

Truth Telling in a Time of Crisis

In 1980, I was named president of Lever Brothers' Foods Division in the United States, at a time when the company was losing a lot of money in its margarine business. Our production and distribution systems were a hopeless mess, and the company was drifting into a crisis. We had noticed a small competitor, Shedd's Food Products, which had a superefficient "make-to-order" production and distribution system. If we could capture its economics, it was clear we could turn Lever Foods around.

We entered into a contract with Shedd's (a company we later bought), under which it agreed to produce and distribute our margarine direct to our retail customers. This eliminated our 13 costly distribution centers spread around the country. It also meant, however, that we had to take the painful step of closing our margarine plant in Hammond, Indiana. This move was considered radical at the time, but it was the only way for us to move forward.

The logistics of adopting Shedd's production and distribution system required a six-month transition period. The Hammond plant was located in a gritty and somewhat depressed community southeast of Chicago. I was warned that closing our plant there was going to be difficult. There was much debate at company headquarters in New York over how to handle the closing. "Don't tell the workers anything until four weeks before we close the plant," some advised. "It's a rough crowd out there. If we tell them now, they'll be furious, our efficiencies will drop through the floor, and our losses will get even worse."

After debating all the points and counterpoints, we decided that this advice ignored a crucial point. There was only one certainty, after all: The workers in Hammond *would* hear about our plan to close their plant. The only question was, who would they hear it from? If they heard about it from someone other than us in the leadership team, our credibility would be shot. Even worse, the story would probably spread in garbled form, which would encourage rumors and deepen the mistrust. After that, it would be terribly difficult to set the record straight. Thus, we concluded, it would be far better—however painful—for us to deliver the news ourselves, and to do it right away. That way we could tell the Hammond workers exactly what we were doing and why, and try to gain their understanding.

With this decision in place, we immediately set about preparing the groundwork for the closure. We created plans for outplacement, retraining, and personal counseling, and crafted a bonus system for maintaining productivity. Within a week, we were ready to explain what we were doing.

Accompanied by Maarten Van Buren, the head of operations, I flew out to Hammond to deliver the news in person. At the plant I was given a hard hat to wear: "These guys have been known to throw things when they don't like what you're saying," Maarten said. When some 350 workers were assembled, I stood up and told them that I was there to speak as honestly as I could about the state of the business. I explained the losses we were incurring and the reasons for them.

"We need to close this plant in six months' time," I said. I admitted that I was nervous and hated telling them this, and that I wished it were otherwise. "But," I said, "we can't see any other way of saving the company." I outlined the severance package and bonus system, and I appealed to them to maintain productivity until the plant closure. Then I promised I'd return to Hammond once a month to discuss their progress and have a constructive dialogue about their issues and concerns.

To my surprise, there was applause after I had finished. I turned to Maarten and said, "What the hell is going on? This is the first time I've ever heard people applauding the news that they're out of a job!"

"I think they're applauding our honesty," he replied.

But here was the really big surprise: I was afraid that productivity at the plant would drop, which could potentially cost us millions of dollars. But in the next six months productivity at Hammond actually *increased* to its highest levels in five years. On one of my visits to Hammond, I asked a union leader to explain the reason for this. He raised his chin, and answered with one word: "Pride."

It was a defining moment for me. I've never experienced anything like it before or since.

Maximize Participation

Leading change is not a one-person job. To be effective, you must recruit allies to your cause. The more people who will help you tell the story, manage the change, and motivate the troops, the better.

As I've said before, people will support that which they help to build. The academic research on this is clear, and I've seen it over and over again in the course of my career.

Globalizing Panadol

In 1992, as president of Sterling Winthrop's Consumer Health Group, I faced an interesting challenge. Our main product outside the United States was Panadol, the headache remedy, which was sold in 64 countries in almost as many different kinds of packages. I wanted to turn this hodgepodge into a single, global brand. But there was stiff resistance from our regional managers around the world, a group of strong-willed lions who considered their autonomy from headquarters a virtual right and viewed any attempt to change their ways as a threat.

My predecessors, I was warned, had failed in their attempts to standardize the Panadol brand. Nevertheless, I felt it was imperative. The challenge was to overcome the resistance to change, and to motivate these regional managers to support the single-brand initiative.

At a meeting of our worldwide team, I gave a talk about the power of global branding. I projected a slide of the familiar Coca-Cola logo—but instead of using Coke's familiar red and white colors and rolling script, I used a random selection of different colors and fonts. "Imagine if Coke's packaging looked like this around the world," I said. "Would you recognize this patchwork of labels as one brand?" My audience laughed.

I did the same for Kodak: Instead of yellow and black, the Kodak logo was done in many different shades and sizes. Again I got a laugh.

Then I put up a slide of Panadol's actual packaging from around the world. It looked like a collage of 20 different designs done by 20 different ad agencies—which is exactly what it was. This time there was an awkward silence. "This isn't a brand," I said. "This looks like a collection of different products sharing the same name." I was taking a risk, of course, hoping that these shock tactics would persuade my audience of the need for change.

"To remain competitive in an increasingly unified world," I concluded, "Panadol needs to become a truly global brand." We broke up the large meeting into several smaller groups, each charged with discussing how best to go about harmonizing Panadol's many images into a single global brand. Managers from our human resources department were assigned to facilitate the discussion in each of these breakout sessions.

After about an hour, I was urgently called to one of the groups. "We have a problem here," I was told. "People are very upset. In fact, the atmosphere is explosive." Sure enough, when I walked in, the tension was palpable. Some in the group were red-faced with anger and frustration. Others were clearly on the defensive, sitting stiff-legged with their arms crossed and their eyes averted.

I sat down and listened to the conversation for several minutes. What I heard surprised me. There was no reference to the challenge of harmonizing Panadol's global image. Instead, the sole theme was the traditional power of the company's regional managers, and the fact that this power was now—apparently—to be stripped away in favor of centralized control. The only idea that the regional managers had taken away from my presentation was the notion that they would be losing their authority. And they were using the breakout session to berate the staffers from the New York home office, who had no idea how to respond.

I briefly visited each of the other breakout groups, and found the same dynamic at work there. It was clear that a fast adjustment was needed to keep the entire effort from dying. I huddled with our human resources team, and together we diagnosed what was happening. It was now crystal clear why previous attempts to globalize Panadol had foundered. The source of resistance was not the business logic behind the concept of globalization. It was the perceived loss of autonomy. We quickly developed a strategy that we hoped would turn the tide, and reassembled the entire group.

I took the podium. "I've heard the kinds of discussions you've been having, and I sense resistance to the idea of globalizing Panadol." (That was putting it mildly.) "I understand your feelings. You assume that this concept means stripping you of your powers and making all the harmonization decisions in New York. If I were a regional manager, I wouldn't like the idea myself.

"But the assumption is false. I'm asking *you* to come up with a globalization strategy. We'll appoint a team of regional managers to tackle the job. There'll be just one head-office person in the group, whose job will be to coordinate the overall effort. Otherwise, the task of recommending the way forward will be in your hands. We'll need to select a single global ad agency and package-design firm, but guiding their work will be your responsibility."

A sense of relief flooded the room. The regional managers willingly undertook the task. We selected Batten, Barton, Durstine & Osborn (BBDO) as the global ad agency and Landor Associates as the package-design firm. Within four months, the regional manager team came up with a several-stage recommendation for creating and implementing a global Panadol brand image.

The lesson is clear. If you develop a program for change and simply hand it to your people, saying, "Here, implement this," it's unlikely to work. But when people help to build something themselves, they will support it and *make* it work.

If All Else Fails, Remove Those Who Resist

It is crucial to get the entire organization behind a change initiative, but you'll inevitably meet some resistance. Occasionally, you will encounter one or more highly tenacious resisters; some will resist openly on principle, while others will maneuver more secretly in pursuit of their own political agendas. I refer to the latter as "smiling assassins."

Dealing with unyielding resisters is a delicate leadership challenge, but it must be addressed. Don't forget: Everyone in the company is watching what happens; they want to see who will win—you or the resister. Your actions have great symbolic significance, and how you deal with resisters can determine the success of the entire change effort.

If you remove resisters the wrong way (especially if they are popular), you can do real damage to the organization. You should never simply descend from the sky and chop someone's head off. This can seem arbitrary and brutal, and there can be real collateral damage—your people may become afraid and risk-averse, which will ultimately hurt your business.

Before taking action, make sure that you *know* the person is a resister. Don't rely on hearsay; it's possible that you've misinterpreted someone's words, or someone has misinterpreted yours. Sit down and have an honest conversation with this person.

Once you've determined the facts and uncovered a true case of an unrepentant resister, you need to show a combination of courage and compassion. Be firm, but fair. My rule of thumb is that if you encounter a true resister who threatens to undermine your change effort, give the person a reasonable warning, define your expectations, make sure there is a clear understanding between you, and set a timetable for change. I suggest no longer than three months. If after that time the person continues to resist, then you are justified in moving him or her to another job within the organization, or, in the most serious cases, in removing the individual from the company altogether. This will clearly indicate to the organization that you are serious about the change effort, but that everyone will be given a chance to get on board or leave. The key is not to let it drag on.

Generate Short-Term Wins

This is a much-overlooked but extremely important rule for managing change. Large-scale change can be a long, formidable undertaking, and so it is important to create short-term wins. A number of early victories, even if they are small, create self-confidence and the belief that bigger successes are possible. This belief builds a psychological momentum that sustains the effort needed for large-scale, long-term change.

The key is to actually plan some early successes. Don't backload your change effort, with everything happening 18 months or two years down the road. Plan some visible progress for one month, three months, six months, and 12 months hence, so that good things begin to happen soon.

It is hard to overestimate the importance of psychological

motivation when undertaking any difficult task, as the story of Roger Bannister's record-breaking mile demonstrates.

In 1954, Bannister ran the mile in 3 minutes, 59.4 seconds, in Oxford, England, thus becoming the first person ever to break the four-minute barrier. In the following two years, 50 runners equaled or bettered his time for the mile. How could this be explained?

Simply put, because Bannister had done it, others came to believe that they could do it, too. Henry Ford put it this way: "Whether you believe you can, or can't, you are right."

The Lever Foods Turnaround

When Lever Foods began its turnaround (shortly after the acquisition of Shedd's), our list of priorities was:

▼ Install Shedd's make-to-order system throughout Lever's American margarine operation.

▼ Improve product quality.

▼ Institute brand-building strategies.

As we expected, using Shedd's make-to-order system immediately improved our financial situation. Then we noticed a strange thing happening: All of the other aspects of our business system—R&D, selling, merchandising, advertising, and so on—began to improve as well. Before we knew it, the entire company was beginning to improve on all fronts. It was startling.

I called a meeting of my executive team. "There's something going on here I don't fully understand," I said. "We've scored some important successes in selected areas. But now, seemingly on its own, the business is firing on all cylinders. All of our key metrics are improving. What's going on here?"

The only answer we could come up with was that, spurred by our early victories, a collective belief that we could succeed had begun to emerge. And so we did.

Set a Shining Example

This rule is the essence of leadership. Above all, it is what leaders *do*, not what they *say*, that communicates their true intent.

The first lesson officers learn at military school is that your troops will always follow your example. In his autobiography, General Norman Schwarzkopf of Gulf War fame describes a harrowing incident during his tour of duty in Vietnam that illustrates the unmatched power of a leader's example. A company of soldiers had become trapped in the midst of a minefield. Searching for a way out, they were wandering through the field, trying desperately to avoid the mines. But one by one, they began detonating the mines, losing limbs in the process.

Alerted by radio, Schwarzkopf arrived on the scene by helicopter. One man, his leg badly injured, was apparently bleeding to death. He was thrashing on the ground and screaming for help, and his cries were helping to spread panic among the other soldiers. Schwarzkopf knew that if the men broke and ran, they'd all be sure to set off mines. No one would make it out alive.

Schwarzkopf had several options. He could have ordered one of his men to brave the minefield in an effort to rescue the wounded man. He could have asked for a volunteer. Instead, Schwarzkopf took responsibility himself. He ordered the soldiers to stay where they were lest they set off more mines. Then he began picking his way, inch by inch, through the minefield, studying the ground as he walked, gripping each leg to steady a trembling knee before taking a step. Schwarzkopf managed to make it to the injured soldier. He used the man's belt to lash his damaged leg in place, and he waited with him until a medical evacuation helicopter arrived and lifted him to safety. (The soldier survived.) Calmed by the leader's poise, the other soldiers remained in place until a unit of engineers with metal detectors could arrive and mark safe paths through the minefield.

Schwarzkopf kept his head and demonstrated, by his personal example, the kind of calm, deliberate action needed to survive a situation of profound danger. As a result, an entire company of soldiers was infused with the same spirit. Although business leadership doesn't call for the same kind of physical heroism, it does demand a similar willingness to lead by example, even at risk to oneself.

A leader's words and actions must be seamlessly integrated to be effective. This is at the root of what we mean when we say that leadership is about integrity. Your words and deeds must be utterly consistent. The moment they diverge, your leadership is compromised.

Equality of Sacrifice, True and False

In 1979, when the Chrysler Corporation was struggling with $4.75 billion in debt and facing almost certain bankruptcy, CEO Lee Iacocca managed to secure a controversial $1.5 billion loan from the U.S. government with which to resuscitate the troubled organization. But a more notable act of leadership was Iacocca's move to reduce his own salary to one dollar a year until Chrysler returned to profitability.

Iacocca called this "equality of sacrifice," noting that individuals will endure hardships willingly if everyone is suffering together. Iacocca commented in his 1984 autobiography, "Leadership means setting an example. When you find yourself in a position of leadership, people follow your every move." Thus, at a time when Chrysler's rank-and-file workers were being asked to tighten their belts to ensure the company's survival, Iacocca felt it was important to him to make an equivalent sacrifice.

Meanwhile, at rival General Motors, the United Auto Workers (UAW) had just agreed to freeze their annual cost-of-living pay increases in favor of a profit-sharing arrangement tied to GM's profitability. Attempting his own symbolic act of leadership, CEO Roger Smith cut his own seven-figure compensation by $135 per month, which matched the average cost-of-living sacrifice of the UAW employees. Smith even had GM's public relations department issue a national press release to publicize the gesture.

The public outcry was intense, to say the least. Iacocca sardonically commented, "Now there's a company that doesn't understand equality of sacrifice."

Finally, during a change effort, a leader must set an example by demonstrating relentless determination. Every change effort encounters roadblocks and barriers. You'll encounter criticism and resistance; you'll make mistakes and suffer setbacks. But like a champion athlete, you must pull yourself up and try again. As the Japanese say, "Fall down seven times, get up eight."

It is easy to get discouraged when things go wrong. And negative thinking is a virulent bug. As a leader, you must overwhelm negativity with the equally infectious bug of enthusiasm. I don't mean the kind of blustering enthusiasm that just generates heat; I mean genuine enthusiasm that generates light—the kind of enthusiasm that is based on a clear strategic focus and the confidence that your people can execute it.

10

Implementing and Experimenting

The final stage of the Strategic Learning cycle is implementation and experimentation (see Figure 10.1). Of course, this is both the final stage of one cycle and the first step into the next cycle. As you work your way around the learning cycle again and again, your firm continues to update its insights, learn, and adapt to new conditions. The Strategic Learning process never ends.

Furthermore, to refer to this step alone as *implementation* is a bit of a misnomer. After all, the *entire* Strategic Learning process— learn, focus, align, and execute—is a challenge of implementation. Each stage of the process has its own set of hurdles and rewards, and, when done effectively, each stage builds on the previous stage to create a powerful momentum behind your strategy. If all of the components are in place, then this cohesion will help you to execute your plan rapidly and successfully. But the implementation of your strategy will only be as effective as your insight, focus, and alignment are. If you've constructed your strategy in a piecemeal fashion, failed to build it on solid insights, or neglected to consider how you will align the levers of your organization behind it, then

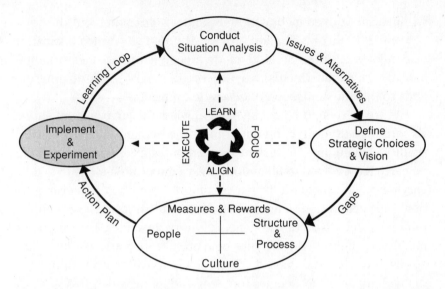

Figure 10.1   Strategic Learning: The Leadership Process—Implementing and Experimenting

your chances of success are slender. Thus, implementation should be seen as part of the continuum of the Strategic Learning cycle. It represents both its successful culmination and a source of learning for the next situation analysis.

Perhaps the most crucial activity involved in this stage is *experimentation*. In the industrial era, the creation and implementation of strategy was a kind of "Ready, aim, fire" process. This approach worked reasonably well in a relatively linear, stable, and predictable environment. But today's discontinuous environment requires what Paul Saffo of the Institute for the Future calls a "Ready, fire, steer" approach. In other words, the organization's strategic direction is developed, implemented, and then repeatedly and continuously *modified* in response to changes in the environment and in the firm's own realities. As this chapter will discuss, experimentation offers one key to making these adjustments successfully.

A readiness to experiment, to learn from the results, and to adjust your strategy accordingly is a hallmark of adaptive organizations. It mitigates the tendency for thinking to become narrowed within a set of fixed mental models, and it helps stamp out the complacent "If it ain't broke, don't fix it" attitude I've warned against. It also injects a different kind of divergent learning. The situation analysis is an intellectual voyage of discovery. Experimentation adds to this the dimension of *action* learning.

As we've seen, rigidity can be fatal when the environment shifts. Experimentation offers an antidote to the human tendency toward rigidity of thinking. As Darwin showed, the success with which life on earth has evolved to fill almost every conceivable niche in widely varying environments is based on nature's continual experimentation—the generation of an endless stream of variations through the random mechanism of the genetic lottery. In effect, nature places millions of unpremeditated bets on a proliferating array of new variations. Most fail and die out. Those that survive multiply and eventually dominate. Any species that stops adapting is doomed.

The adaptive organization employs a similar methodology. By continually experimenting, producing "mutant strains" of new products, processes, methods, and strategies, the organization maximizes its chances of developing new businesses that are capable of responding to the next change in the environment. But here is the difference from nature's blind process. Being human and therefore capable of reason, analysis, insight, and memory, the leaders of an adaptive organization can *learn* from both their mistakes and their successes, and thereby improve their odds.

This isn't always easy to do. But companies that are able to continuously experiment, learn, and adapt will be the ones that succeed over the long term.

This is no mere theory. As James C. Collins and Jerry I. Porras point out in *Built to Last*, many of the greatest moves in business history were the result not of artful strategic planning but of trial-and-error experimentation closely analogous to Darwinian variation and selection. Collins and Porras call this evolutionary process "branching and pruning." Imagine a tree in an orchard, continuously sprouting new branches (variation). If a gardener intelligently prunes the branches that are less healthy or produce lower-quality fruit (selection), then in time the tree will consist only of strong branches fully laden with delicious fruit.

The Power of Mistakes

As the Darwinian metaphor suggests, experimentation can't proceed without mistakes. In fact, the whole point of experimentation is to learn your way to success through failure. Yet here we encounter another paradox. Successful organizations are, by definition, organizations that do things right. They are filled with people who are justly proud of their technical, administrative, and managerial prowess and who have risen within the organization largely because of their ability to make things work—usually the first time. Such people set and meet high personal standards of success; they consider failure a mark of shame and do everything possible to avoid it.

All of this is natural and even admirable. Yet multiplied across the breadth of an entire company, these human qualities can produce an organization that is risk-averse, shunning uncertainty and error in favor of repeating what has worked in the past. The measurement and reward systems used by many companies encourage the same tendency. In an organization where punishment, disapproval, career stagnation, or even discharge are the likely response to mistakes, people quickly learn to avoid mistakes when they can and cover them up where they can't. And, of course, concealing a failure ensures that no one will learn from it. Thus, learning from experimentation requires a mistake-friendly, knowledge-sharing culture—something that is much easier to describe than to create and sustain.

Fostering Innovation through Experimentation

There are a number of powerful techniques that various companies have developed for fostering a culture in which constant experimentation is generated.

New-Business Venturing

In imitation of business incubators such as Idealab and CMGI, mature companies are increasingly creating their own venture capital funds and new-business incubators. These provide an environment in which both internal and external start-up businesses can be nurtured until they are able to exist on their own. As with a conventional venture capital fund, the idea is to multiply the chances of success by funding a substantial number of projects, most of which are likely to fail. Although a majority of the new businesses may never pay off, the value of the learning is immense, and a few may produce breakthroughs that pay for all the other projects many times over.

Recognizing the threat and opportunity of digital technology, Kodak created an internal venture capital fund and new-business incubator based in Silicon Valley and staffed by venture capital veterans. The fund's mandate is to create and grow new companies based on technology developed at Kodak's research labs. The fund also invests in and guides start-up companies whose technology promises to expand the imaging business. Examples of the latter include MyFamily.com, Snapfish.com, and PhotoAlley.com.

Many consider 3M the gold standard of innovation. With over 50,000 products made in 60 countries, 3M has clearly developed a powerful process for product innovation, which might be described as "internal incubation"—nurturing hundreds of prospective businesses within the walls of 3M and looking for the handful that will become the drivers of the company's future revenues and profits. It's a simple philosophy: Place a lot of bets and "double down" on the winners.

The company nurtures evolutionary research activities through a greenhouse-like organizational culture that allows the natural mutation process of "offshoot and divide" to flourish. So-called Genesis Grants are provided to pay for the early stages of R&D, and incentives for innovation include giving those who spawn a new business the opportunity to manage it as a freestanding division within the company. 3M is patient in letting the process of discovery take its course, recognizing that it may take many years for a new type of research to reach fruition—if it ever does.

Richard P. Carleton, former CEO of 3M, remarks, "It's a series of lateral developments. Offshoot and divide, offshoot and divide, that's the thing. . . . We're not choosy. We'll make any damn thing we can make money on."

Pruning is a crucial part of the 3M process, of course. Evolutionary technologies are constantly being weeded out for various reasons. Some perish for want of money, equipment, and volunteers; some are terminated because they lack energetic internal champions to defend them; other projects vanish for a time like an underground stream, only to reemerge later. In the end, the fittest survive.

Innovation through Acquisition

Cisco Systems, the worldwide leader in networking gear for the Internet, has been one of the fastest-growing and most profitable companies in the history of the computer industry. Annual revenues have grown from $69 million in 1990 to $18.9 billion in 2000.

CEO John Chambers takes an outside-in approach to innovation. Cisco grafts intellectual assets and next-generation technologies onto its corporate structure via a combination of acquisitions, alliances, and partnerships. Cisco routinely makes 15 to 20 acquisitions per year to capture intellectual assets and next-generation products, typically via smaller pre-IPO start-ups that offer promising technologies.

Recognizing that the "assets have feet," Cisco measures the success of every acquisition first by employee retention, then by new product development, and finally by return on investment. In fact, 9 of 14 CEOs from recently acquired companies hold executive positions at Cisco.

Recent events have challenged the future viability of Cisco's innovation model. The 2000–2001 slump in tech stocks has driven the value of Cisco shares dramatically downward, making them a less powerful currency for acquiring other companies. And the slowdown in growth of Cisco's sales has further weakened its ability to buy technologies it needs. As a result, Cisco's dominant market share of some technologies is beginning to erode. Will Cisco be as adept at reinventing its business model as it was at inventing it in the first place? Will Cisco's own R&D engineers be able to generate innovation internally? The next few years will answer these questions.

What all of these methods of innovation have in common is that they provide an avenue through which a company can experiment with new technologies, strategies, and processes without "betting the farm" on any single approach. In each case, a relatively small portion of the company's resources is devoted to developing each new idea. Based on results, the company will either channel more money, time, and energy into the project or let it die. As Clayton M. Christensen puts it in his book *The Innovator's Dilemma*, the successful innovators he studied "planned to fail early and *inexpensively* in the search for the market for a disruptive technology." Place a lot of small bets, and when you find the winners, let them ride.

Experiential Learning: The After-Action Review

Learning from experimentation has three basic components: conducting the experiment; studying the success and failure of the experiment; and then transferring the lessons learned throughout the organization. To methodically pursue all three steps requires a great deal of discipline. Most companies are stuck in the plan/act mode and consequently devote little time to reflection, analysis, and self-education. But when the learning is done right, it's a highly effective process that adds immeasurably to a company's effectiveness.

One of the most powerful techniques for harnessing the power of experiential learning comes—perhaps surprisingly—from a highly traditional, nonbusiness organization: the United States Army.

The idea of learning from experience presents a peculiar dilemma for the leadership of the army. After all, the ultimate form of competition for which the army was created and which provides the true test of the army's methods and strategies is an event that no one ever wants to experience—namely, a war. But in the new global environment produced by the end of the Cold War and the emergence of new kinds of international threats and challenges, the American military needed ways to test new weapons and tactics without waiting for a war to erupt.

In response to this challenge, the U.S. Army developed several new tools for developing and disseminating knowledge. At the National Training Center in the Mojave Desert, the army began fighting virtual wars—large-scale combat exercises pitting one high-tech battle unit against another, with every soldier, tank, helicopter, and plane tracked by satellite and computer. The contests are extreme and sometimes chaotic, hewing as closely to reality as possible without incurring casualties. The data generated by these virtual wars are then fed into the computer at the army's CALL center—Center for Army Lessons Learned—where they can be quantified and digested, and then shared throughout the army's ranks worldwide.

In this process of action learning, the after-action review (AAR) is a key component. An AAR is a learning review conducted immediately after a military engagement (simulated or real) in order to drive out lessons learned and identify the strengths and weaknesses of the organization as the basis for continuous improvement. In the course of an AAR, the participants' subjective interpretation of events and the computers' objective data are compared, producing insights that are often eye-opening.

An AAR typically focuses on four questions:

1. *What was the intent?* That is, what was the strategy at the time the action started? What role was supposed to be played by each unit? What was the desired outcome, and how was it supposed to be achieved?

2. *What actually happened?* In army parlance, what was the "ground truth"—the actual events as they played out in the heat of battle, with all the misunderstanding, disruption, and confusion that inevitably occur when two armies clash?

3. *Why did it happen?* This is the diagnosis. Why did the commanders' intent, the adversaries' actions, changes in the environment, and the decisions of individuals combine to produce a specific set of outcomes?

4. *How can we do better?* What lessons can be learned from the events of this action that will enable army units in similar future actions to carry out their missions in such a way as to more closely achieve the commanders' intent?

As you can see, an AAR isn't an open-ended feedback session. Rather, it's a highly structured process designed to ferret out the crucial insights to be gleaned from the battlefield experiment. It normally includes commanders from at least three leadership levels within a given unit as well as their counterparts from other units that were involved in the action. The AAR dialogue is facilitated by an experienced officer who is trained to help the participants sort out their various and often conflicting viewpoints, arrive at ground truth, and drive out the learning.

The army's AAR manual recommends that the time spent on the AAR be divided this way: one quarter to reviewing ground truth; one quarter to discussing why it happened; and fully half to discussing how to improve. It is crucial to conduct the meeting with honesty, frankness, and mutual respect among all the participants, and it is just as important to learn from successes as from failures.

The after-action review is a powerful tool for generating organizational learning from experiments and experiences. No wonder it's now being used at world-class organizations such as Motorola, Shell, and GTE Corporation, among others. Of course, in a business context, there are no (literal) battles to use as occasions for an AAR. But consider holding an AAR in the aftermath of any key event. For example:

▼ A major new-product launch or market test.

▼ The opening of a new manufacturing facility, retail outlet, or web site.

▼ A corporate reorganization, merger, or spin-off.

▼ An external or internal crisis or turning point, such as an unexpected public relations challenge.

In short, any significant event that has the potential to produce valuable learning could be a suitable occasion for the AAR exercise.

Strategic Learning 365 Days a Year

To enjoy the full benefits of Strategic Learning, don't let the process slip into dormancy between "planning seasons." Instead, take deliberate steps to make the Strategic Learning method a permanently active part of your business culture, so that the cycle of learn, focus, align, and execute is constantly at work, helping your business adapt to the ever-changing world in which it operates.

11

Strategic Learning as a Path to Personal Growth

Just as companies need a process for generating ongoing renewal, so do individuals. Strategic Learning is a process that can be used both for organizational growth and as a personal tool, for the development of more effective leadership.

Strategy and leadership are regularly discussed as if they are two separate subjects. In fact, this makes no sense. Strategy and leadership are interdependent parts of a whole. If you don't have a strategy, you can't lead; and a strategy without leadership will get you nowhere. Long-term success is *always* the result of great strategy and great leadership working hand in hand.

The importance of leadership comes home to me repeatedly as I coach executives through the Strategic Learning process. It takes strong leaders to generate great insights, make hard choices, create a clear focus, align their organizations, inspire their people, and lead change—and then to repeat this cycle over and over, so that their organizations *go on* winning. Strategic Learning is a process designed to help leaders do this. But how well it works is a function of leadership effectiveness.

At Sony Media Solutions, it was Marty Homlish's use of the "death spiral" metaphor, together with his unrelenting focus and follow-through, that produced a major profit turnaround within 10 months.

At International Specialty Products, it was Peter Heinze's bold symbolic act—adding 25 percent to the incentive pool to reward adherence to the new culture—that gave a jump start to the new strategy.

By contrast, at A-One Technologies (as described in Chapter 8), CEO Ben mandated a culture change as part of a business turnaround while personally clinging to the old ways, favoring incrementalism, bureaucracy, and decision by consensus over speed and initiative. Without effective leadership by example from Ben, A-One's turnaround would be doomed to founder.

In the new economy, effective leadership is more crucial than ever. Success in the old world was based largely on the leveraging of physical assets. In the new world, it is based mainly on the leveraging of human knowledge and creativity. To achieve this, a superior ability to bring out the best in people is essential for success. Everyone pays lip service to this truth, yet many companies have been slow to act on it. The biggest failure in organizations today is the failure to realize the full potential of their people. The winning firms of the future will be those that are able to maximize not only their ROA (return on assets) but also their ROP—return on people.

I am perplexed when I hear a CEO declare, "We'll succeed because our employees are the best in the world." For one thing, as a statement of fact this is highly implausible. Why should one company in a competitive arena have succeeded in monopolizing all the leading talent? I understand that CEOs who say something like this are trying to please their people by flattering them, but most people recognize when they are being handed a line, and they find it condescending rather than pleasing.

In any case, this slogan misses the real point. The key isn't just to hire the best people you can. That alone is not nearly enough. The key is to bring the best out of the people you have. *That's* the real difference between successful companies and the also-rans. And the companies that consistently manage to do this—that create an environment in which people are inspired to achieve at a high level—are usually the winners in the ongoing talent wars. Many of the best people in the industry gravitate to them, attracted by the promise of an exciting, creative, high-achieving workplace. Companies like Southwest Airlines generally don't have a recruitment problem, even when their rivals complain of the tight talent market. Instead, they have a *selection* problem, being blessed with many more qualified job applicants than vacancies.

The ability to develop effective leaders at every level of an organization will increasingly become the key source of competitive advantage in the years to come. But companies that overlook the importance of leadership development or fail to pursue it through a consistent, systematic process will struggle, no matter how well conceived their strategies may be.

Emotional Intelligence

"Know thyself," the Delphic oracle advised the Greeks thousands of years ago. This wisdom remains an excellent starting point for any discussion of leadership. True leadership—whether you are Gandhi, Andy Grove of Intel, or the owner of Joe's Dry Cleaning Service—begins with self-awareness. When self-awareness is combined with other important attributes, like empathy, motivation, sociability, and political adroitness, we have the foundations of an effective leader—someone with a high degree of what has come to be called *emotional intelligence.*

Most senior level executives at large, well-established companies are highly intelligent, well-educated people; that is, they have high IQs (intelligence quotients). But increasingly, research—popularized by writers such as Daniel Goleman, author of *Emotional Intelligence*—indicates that it is emotional quotient (EQ), not IQ, that sets brilliant leaders apart from the pack of merely good executives.

Let's be clear. A good IQ and strong technical skills are important for success. They help aspiring business leaders achieve in school and contribute during their early years in the workforce. But they are threshold requirements. Later in life, especially at the senior executive level, IQ is eclipsed in importance by EQ.

While it is possible to be successful without high EQ, it's extremely rare. Bill Gates, for example, takes perverse pride in being a technologically minded nerd with poor social skills, and yet he is one of the most successful businesspeople in history. But he is the rare exception. And even Gates has suffered from his relative lack of EQ. Most observers agree that a significant cause of the unfavorable ruling handed down initially in the landmark antitrust case against Microsoft was the apparent arrogance and hostility exhibited by Gates in his videotaped testimony. Gates's bullying demeanor on the witness stand was a costly mistake that an executive with higher EQ would never have made.

For most people, EQ is the sine qua non of leadership. "Without it," Daniel Goleman writes, "a person can have the best training in the world, an incisive, analytical mind, and an endless supply of smart ideas, but he still won't make a great leader." Indeed, Goleman's research suggests that EQ is twice as important as technical skills and IQ at *all* levels of a company.

What, then, is EQ? And how exactly does EQ contribute to the effectiveness of great business leaders?

The Elements of EQ

In a *Harvard Business Review* article titled "Leadership That Gets Results," Goleman identified four components of emotional intelligence: self-awareness, self-management, social awareness, and social skill.

1. *Self-awareness.* Self-awareness requires a high degree of honesty both with yourself and others. Self-aware people have a deep understanding of their emotions, strengths, weaknesses, needs, and drives. They understand how their feelings affect them, others, and job performance. The hallmarks of self-awareness are self-confidence, a realistic self-assessment, and a self-deprecating sense of humor.

2. *Self-management.* We are all deeply influenced by our emotions; it's an unchangeable fact of human nature, and a source of behavior that's both good and bad. Effective leaders, however, are able to manage their emotions, controlling and channeling them in productive and positive ways. People who are skilled at self-management are trustworthy; because they are able to control their impulses, they can consistently live up to their own standards of honesty and integrity. They are also conscientious, skilled at adapting to changing circumstances, ready to seize opportunities, and driven to achieve at a high level no matter what obstacles may arise.

3. *Social awareness.* A key aspect of social awareness is empathy, the ability to recognize and understand other people's emotions and to make decisions that take those emotions into account. In the business world, it's easy to overlook or denigrate the importance of empathy. Some leaders who pride themselves on their "toughness" and their "realism" consider empathy to be soft, irrelevant, or a sign of weakness. But empathy is an increasingly important skill in a world in which motivating and inspiring people makes the difference between success and failure.

Other aspects of social awareness are organizational awareness (the ability to read and navigate the currents of company politics) and service orientation (the ability to recognize and focus on meeting customer needs).

4. *Social skill.* This is not simply a matter of being "a nice person." Rather, social skill includes a wide range of specific abilities for dealing effectively with people. Socially skilled leaders are adept at finding common ground among diverse groups, orchestrating teams, and maintaining rapport. Recognizing that nothing important ever gets done alone, they build strong and wide-ranging networks that they can galvanize when needed. They are clear and persuasive communicators, effective at managing change and mediating conflicts, and capable of inspiring others with a compelling vision of the future.

Evidence as to the importance of EQ isn't hard to find. History is filled with the stories of leaders who lacked crucial components of EQ and therefore failed to achieve their goals, despite being gifted with high IQ and brilliant technical abilities. The story of the slow rise and rapid fall of Douglas Ivester at Coca-Cola is a good example.

Ivester's Rise and Fall

In October 1997, Roberto Goizueta, the legendary chairman and CEO of Coca-Cola, died of cancer. It took the board only 15 minutes to appoint his successor: Douglas Ivester, a brilliant financial strategist, who, as Coke's number two, had engineered much of the company's success over the previous decade.

Ivester was seen as the perfect candidate. A former auditor at the respected accounting firm of Ernst & Young, he was detail-oriented and had mastered marketing, global affairs, and public speaking—although he had a somewhat obstinate personality. His most widely acclaimed coup had taken place in the mid-1980s, when he removed the company's huge, debt-ridden bottling operation from the balance sheet and turned it into a separate public corporation, Coca-Cola Enterprises, in which the parent firm retained a 49 percent interest. This move (which came to be called "The 49-Percent Solution") saved the company millions of dollars and was widely hailed as a visionary piece of financial engineering.

Yet despite his obvious brilliance, Ivester began to struggle in his new job. In the late 1990s, Coke hit a number of bumps in the road that weren't necessarily Ivester's fault. They included a slump in earnings and a weakening stock price precipitated in part by the Asian financial crisis. But the board of directors became concerned about a more subtle problem. For all of his sterling attributes, Ivester lacked certain crucial leadership skills that Goizueta had possessed in spades, including charm, wit, and a finely tuned ear for political nuance. In short, EQ.

As Ivester began to take center stage, he sometimes appeared self-righteous, arrogant, and greedy. "I know how all the levers work," he once claimed, "and I could generate so much cash I could make everybody's head spin." In 1994, for example, in his first address to the soft-drink industry as Coke's president, he gave a speech portentously entitled "Be Different or Be Damned." In it, he likened rival firms to "parasites" and "sheep," and Coke to a lone "wolf." "I want your space on the shelves," he told them. "I want every single bit of beverage growth potential that exists." Ivester's audience was stunned by his hubris.

As CEO, Ivester's lack of EQ manifested itself in a string of small gaffes that snowballed into major public-relations headaches. These included the bungling of an attempted acquisition of French soda company Orangina; the ham-handed way that Coke responded to a contamination scare in Belgium; and Ivester's imperious tone in discussing a controversial new vending machine designed to raise the price of Coke as the weather got hotter. To make matters worse, the CEO seemed to develop a defensive bunker mentality. He refused to appoint a number two, insisted on micromanaging details himself, and reacted badly to criticism and advice. When Donald Keough, Coke's former president and chief operating officer (COO), sent him a six-page letter filled with suggestions, Ivester replied with a curt note—one line long.

The final straw came when, in the midst of an employee lawsuit alleging racial discrimination in the United States, Ivester reorganized the company and demoted Coke's highest-ranked black executive, Carl Ware. Ware, a former Atlanta politician and one of the most respected black executives in the nation, quit in protest. Of course, the press covered the story extensively. Coke's customers and employees were shocked, and the board was alarmed. Many observers shook their heads and declared that the politically astute Goizueta would never have made such a move.

Every consumer-product company lives and dies by the strength of its brand. Under Ivester, Coke's sacred, 113-year-old image was in danger of being tarnished around the globe. People began asking, "What's wrong with Coke?" Ivester called himself a substance-over-style kind of guy, and said he wasn't concerned.

On December 1, 1999, Coke's two most powerful directors, Warren Buffett and Herbert Allen, met with Ivester privately to say they had lost confidence in his leadership. Five days later, Ivester voluntarily stepped down from one of the most high-profile jobs in the business world. Shortly thereafter, Carl Ware rejoined the company as a senior vice president, and the board replaced Ivester with Douglas Daft, a leader known for his strong interpersonal skills.

Strategic Learning for Personal Renewal

Stories like Ivester's—and they are legion—serve to confirm the research suggesting that EQ is the key to leadership effectiveness. But the good news is that Goleman has offered us an answer to the age-old question: Is leadership innate, or is it a skill that can be taught and learned? His research has shown that, in contrast to IQ, which is thought to be largely determined by unchanging genetic factors, EQ can be significantly improved, provided that one is prepared to work at the task with systematic vigor, making a serious commitment of time and energy to the process. There is no doubt that some people are born with higher EQ than others. But no matter who we are, we can significantly improve our EQ if we apply the right tools in a process of lifelong learning.

This finding prompted me to pose a key question to Mike Fenlon, a close colleague at Columbia Business School with whom I have been collaborating on leadership development. Could Strategic Learning, which offers demonstrable benefits to organizations, also be used to develop leadership effectiveness in individuals? In other words, could Strategic Learning be as useful a tool for personal growth as it is for organizational renewal?

Mike and I looked critically at the underlying principles of Strategic Learning and realized that the Strategic Learning cycle could work equally well as a system for leadership development. After all, learning is at the heart of both strategy creation and leadership development. The only difference is that strategy creation involves an outside-in learning process, starting with an understanding of customers and the competitive environment, whereas leadership development involves inside-out learning, starting with an understanding of self. Like an adaptive organization, an adaptive individual must continuously learn and translate that learning into action. In both cases, Strategic Learning creates an *ongoing* process of learning and renewal.

Over the past two years, under Mike's guidance, we have systematically applied the Strategic Learning cycle to leadership development in our executive programs at Columbia Business School, with companies such as Ericsson, Deloitte Touche Tohmatsu (DTT), and CGNU, and also with participants in our open enrollment programs. The results have been truly exciting. Executives find that the process is a powerful way for them to develop greater self-knowledge and to leverage this for personal development. They particularly value the fact that it is a simple tool that they can use for themselves as a vehicle for lifelong learning. And importantly, it has helped us and the executives we work with to effectively integrate strategy and leadership. This vital integration has now become a hallmark of Columbia's teaching philosophy in executive education.

When applying Strategic Learning to personal renewal, the four basic steps of the process are applied like this (see Figure 11.1):

▼ **Learn:** Generate insights about your personal strengths and weaknesses by conducting an honest self-appraisal and by getting feedback from those around you. Develop an awareness of the values that are most important to you. Examine your environment (that is, the business and industry in which you work and the role you occupy) and identify the specific leadership challenges you face. This process of self-discovery amounts to a personal situation analysis.

▼ **Focus:** Translate your newfound insights about your strengths and weaknesses, your personal values, and the leadership challenges you face into a set of priorities and action plans for self-improvement.

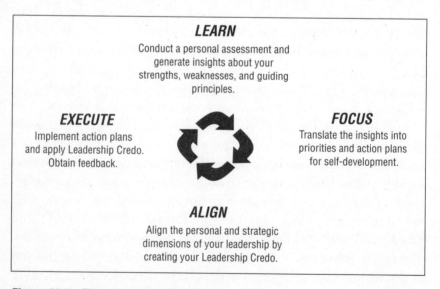

LEARN
Conduct a personal assessment and generate insights about your strengths, weaknesses, and guiding principles.

EXECUTE
Implement action plans and apply Leadership Credo. Obtain feedback.

FOCUS
Translate the insights into priorities and action plans for self-development.

ALIGN
Align the personal and strategic dimensions of your leadership by creating your Leadership Credo.

Figure 11.1   The Leadership Development Cycle
Developed in collaboration with Mike Fenlon.

▼ **Align:** In order to align your personal values and leadership philosophy with the strategic priorities and cultural values of your organization, you'll write a Leadership Credo in which you define your core principles and your theory of success for your business—"This is what I believe in, and here's how we are going to win." The Leadership Credo is the vehicle for integrating organizational strategy with leadership effectiveness.

▼ **Execute:** To complete the cycle, implement the action plans you've created and apply the Leadership Credo to your everyday life and work. In the meantime, continue to appraise your own performance, seek feedback from others, and learn from observation and experience. Repeat the cycle again and again.

As always with Strategic Learning, the last step is crucial. You should never stop learning. Indeed, many rising executives derail their careers when they stop learning, either because they think they've learned all there is to know or because they've become overwhelmed by information. The key is to keep yourself open to new ideas and innovations while having a process in place to help you digest this information in a deliberate, meaningful way.

Let's now walk through the leadership development cycle in greater detail.

Learn

The essential first step is to conduct a personal situation analysis. The aim here is the same as in a situation analysis for crafting a business strategy. Your goal is to generate the key insights that will be the platform for creating focus on the right personal development priorities and achieving superior execution. As we've noted, the process here works from the inside out. Leadership development starts by achieving a realistic understanding of self—the essence of who you are and what you believe in, your strengths and shortcomings. This requires an accurate self-assessment together with an understanding of how your personal makeup fits with the leadership challenges you face.

This is important work, requiring a combination of sensitivity, humility, and self-discipline. But it can be profoundly rewarding. Great leaders are distinguished by a deep and sure sense of self, which enables them to define themselves and their values effectively and consistently to others, in both word and deed. The result is *authenticity*, a quality without which no leader can hope to attract followers.

Achieving this level of self-awareness isn't easy. It requires a continuous process of learning, not a one-time leap. There are a number of techniques that I've found helpful in coaching executives.

The Lifeline Exercise

A good starting point is the Lifeline Exercise, which we often use during executive programs at Columbia Business School.

Here's how it works. Draw a line across a sheet of paper. This is a time line representing your life from birth up to the present. Next, insert check marks with brief descriptions of the major events and key turning points in your life. For better or worse, these watershed moments have helped define who you are and what you believe in. They may include achievements, disappointments, personal milestones, and crises you've experienced or witnessed.

Now translate this time line into a story. It's the story of your life, if you like, but one that emphasizes the moments of truth that have shaped the person you are today. Share this story with a trusted colleague—your personal truth teller. Then reverse the process and listen to your colleague's story. In so doing, not only will you help one another with the process, but you'll practice empathy, one of the basic skills of EQ.

By making your life's lessons and the values you've derived from them explicit, the Lifeline Exercise can be a liberating and insightful experience. When I did this exercise, I became acutely aware of the impact on me of a patriotic act by my father.

During World War II, there was no conscription in my native South Africa; signing up to fight for the Allies was purely voluntary. In 1942, Hitler's armies appeared to have the upper hand. My father decided it was time to leave his very young family—my sister was

10, and I was only five—and do his duty. I vividly remember watching the train carrying my father pulling away from the station, as he started off on his long journey to Europe to fight for what he believed in. None of us could be sure that he'd ever return. Even then, I was aware that he was doing this for the simple reason that he believed it was *right*.

Mercifully, my father returned unharmed in 1945, full of stories about his wartime experiences. Looking back, one great truth comes into sharp relief. This experience taught me the crucial difference between purely physical courage and moral courage. The former involves doing morally neutral things that involve physical risk—like skydiving. The latter involves doing morally right things regardless of the danger—as my father, and millions of others, did. Sadly, I've often seen people of acknowledged physical courage fail to stand up for principle and truth. Ever since childhood, I've used moral courage as the true yardstick of character.

We've seen such tests of moral courage during the many corporate downsizings of recent years. We've seen leaders being tough and taking ruthless, insensitive actions against people, showing no respect for human dignity. We've seen workers with 30 years of service being escorted off company premises with only a few hours' notice, like criminals—all in the interest of "company security." Leaders who order such actions aren't tough; they're weaklings. If they were really tough, they'd have had the moral courage to show compassion in difficult times.

As you can see, my personal definition of moral courage is something I feel strongly about—a deeply held value that, I hope, has helped to shape my behavior as an executive. The Lifeline Exercise helped me both to recognize this value and to understand its source in my childhood experiences and observations.

Many people find that sharing and reflecting on the stories that have shaped their lives provides a powerful way to explore their core values and to distill the lessons of their lives. Consider the riveting story told by one of our participants at a Columbia management program.

Colonel Toreaser A. Steele is one of the very few African-American female wing commanders in the U.S. Air Force. The daughter of sharecroppers, she was raised in a huge family in Georgia. One day when she was 10 years old, she and her grandmother were in a white-owned grocery store. Little Toreaser had a full bladder and asked to use the bathroom. Because of her race, the store owner refused. Unable to hold it in, Toreaser finally peed on the floor, and was utterly humiliated. But showing great dignity and without making a fuss, her grandmother calmly mopped up the puddle herself, comforted the little girl, and escorted her home.

The lessons from that experience linger with Wing Commander Steele today. Her grandmother taught her true toughness—the ability to roll with life's blows, even those that go to the core of your being—and true tenderness—a deep understanding of other people's needs and what it takes to sustain and nurture their sense of self-worth.

Using 360-Degree Feedback

A well-constructed 360-degree feedback instrument can be a powerful learning tool. It enables you to get feedback from peers, subordinates, and superiors on an anonymous basis.

There are many feedback instruments available on the market. Most cover the major aspects of EQ: leadership style, vision, patience, listening skills, empathy, consistency, tolerance, and other social skills. Studying others' comments about you will highlight the gaps between your self-perceptions and the ways others perceive you. These gaps are important to understand when setting priorities for self-improvement. Once again, we confront the fact that perception is reality.

Some companies are reluctant to use 360-degree feedback, worrying that it might cause embarrassment or resentment. It's true that the process requires maturity, judgment, and humility from all concerned. Expert advice and coaching are essential to help people interpret the results constructively. It's also important to repeat the measures periodically so as to measure progress.

Another important rule: The top executive team at a company should never require those below them to engage in a 360-degree feedback exercise unless they're prepared to do it first. Having experienced the process firsthand, the leaders can then legitimately ask others to do the same.

Finally, when you're on the receiving end of feedback, be sure to *thank* your colleagues for providing it and share with them your improvement priorities. This is important even when—*especially* when—some of their comments are difficult or painful to hear. By doing this, you are modeling your willingness to learn and grow as well as your readiness to trust in the honesty and integrity of others, important traits that are needed not only by company leaders but by every member of an adaptive organization.

Executive Coaching

There are few things so valuable as someone who will tell you the truth. Truth telling is an act that requires enormous trust between people. It can be difficult to find the right colleague to provide this kind of honest feedback; reporting relationships, unspoken rivalries, personal differences, and political considerations can complicate matters. Spouses and friends can sometimes be good coaches, but these relationships bring with them a lot of "baggage."

One way to get the honest feedback you need is to hire a professional executive coach. More and more business leaders are taking advantage of this service today, and if you choose the right person, it can pay handsome dividends. I've seen the benefits of coaching at work in the career of my colleague Bob Johansen, president of the Institute for the Future.

Coaching for Work and Life

Five years ago, the position of president opened up unexpectedly, and Bob was the leading internal candidate. As chairman of the Institute, I approached Bob to test his interest. He surprised me by saying he wasn't sure he wanted this role and that he needed time to reflect on the opportunity. Bob was an outstanding researcher and loved his work. He wasn't at all sure that taking on the leadership of the entire Institute was what he wanted to do with his life. Bob was already leading the largest program area at the Institute, and he didn't want to lose contact with the research work and the clients that excited him the most.

Bob and I took the opportunity to talk at length about his future plans and about his role at the Institute. We talked about leadership in general, about his personal leadership style and competencies, about how this would fit with the challenges faced by the Institute, about how he and I would work together, and, most important, about his enthusiasm for accepting the job. Bob suggested that we would need to redefine the role of president for him to be fully happy in the role, as well as to redefine the traditional ways in which the president had interacted with the board of directors. I was open to exploring both of these redefinitions, which were actually long overdue.

After careful thought, Bob decided that this was a mission that held great meaning for him, and he agreed to accept it—on the condition that he be allowed to engage a personal coach to help him learn and grow as a leader. The board readily agreed.

Bob engaged Dr. Pierre Mornell as his coach. A family psychiatrist by training, Pierre has been doing high-level executive coaching with corporate clients for more than 20 years. His background as a medical doctor, a psychiatrist, and a family therapist has proven surprisingly relevant to his work in executive coaching.

When I asked Bob how he decided when to call on Pierre in the early days of his presidency, I got a surprising answer: "I called Pierre when I had trouble sleeping at night, or when I found myself suddenly coming close to tears." These two subtle symptoms of emotional stress are the sorts of things that most executives aren't comfortable talking about, which is one reason why executive coaching is so important. When a leader experiences this kind of high-stress moment, a skilled coach can help turn it into a learning experience. In the end, both the leader and the organization benefit.

Pierre has an interesting rule of thumb about stress: "More stress, more exercise." His belief is that exercise becomes more important for executives even as budgeting the time to exercise becomes more difficult. Pierre also coached Bob to shift his exercise schedule from morning to midafternoon, a time that Bob finds much more uplifting, physically and emotionally. Just as Bob begins to droop in the afternoon, his exercise routine provides a new injection of energy. It demonstrates that executive coaching is not just about work; it is about life.

With the guidance Pierre provided, Bob has developed into an out-standing leader. He has led the Institute through an exciting period of growth, and he has thrived despite the stresses involved.

Focus

The second step in the leadership development cycle is to establish your priorities and action plans for personal growth—your own winning proposition. What are those few things you will concentrate on, day in and day out, in order to become a better leader?

To begin with, summarize the key insights about yourself and the leadership challenges you face that you generated in your personal situation analysis. Discuss these with your coach or trusted colleague (that is, your truth teller). What are the most important strengths you need to build on? What are the key weaknesses that need improvement? What are the gaps that you need to close? Concentrate on the EQ elements—those competencies that contribute most to leadership effectiveness.

Then, examine the personal values you identified in the Lifeline Exercise. Consider how these values will help to sustain and guide you in the leadership challenge you currently face. Which of your values are likely to be most severely tested in the coming months? Which may need to be adjusted or modified to enhance your effectiveness as a leader?

Finally, develop a short list of no more than five personal development priorities, together with specific actions you will take and a method for assessing your progress.

For example, suppose that one of the important insights from your 360-degree feedback survey is that you are perceived as not being a good listener and therefore lacking in empathy. You will want to make one of your personal development priorities "improving my listening skills." Your list of concrete actions in pursuit of that priority might include the following:

▼ Set up a coaching session with an expert on listening skills who will help me define and develop the right techniques for my improvement program.

▼ Share my goals with trusted colleagues and ask them to provide honest feedback on my progress.

▼ Devote half an hour of quiet time at the start of each workday to focus on the day ahead and place listening skills at the top of my mind.

▼ Practice my listening skills at every opportunity and keep a journal of my learning and progress.

▼ Meet monthly with my listening skills coach until I feel I have fully internalized my new skills. Thereafter, have an annual checkup meeting with my coach to keep reinforcing these skills.

Align

The task here is to align your sense of self and your core beliefs with the way in which you will lead your organization. The connection must be one that you can convey clearly to those around you. It is the integrity of this alignment that gives the leader authenticity and moral authority. This is the crucial point at which strategy and leadership intersect.

The Leadership Credo

A useful tool for integrating your personal leadership beliefs with the strategic goals of your organization is the Leadership Credo, a concept developed by Mike Fenlon. The Leadership Credo is a succinct statement of a leader's personal beliefs and leadership principles, the vision and winning strategy of the organization, and the cultural values that will drive its success.

Every Leadership Credo is unique, but it should provide compelling responses to the following questions:

▼ *What do I stand for as a leader?* What are the principles and personal values that clearly define who you are and guide your approach to leadership? Identify three to five values and reflect on the watershed moments in your life that have shaped them. The stories of these moments can help you articulate these values both for yourself and for others.

▼ *What is our organization's vision, and how will we win?* A leader must be able to articulate both where he or she wants to lead the organization and how it will reach its goal. The vision and the winning proposition articulated here should come directly from the firm's strategy.

▼ *What do we stand for as an organization?* What are the key values and behaviors that define our core beliefs and will help to drive our success as an organization? The leader must identify those key values—no more than five—and the related behaviors that will form the foundation for the organization's culture.

As you can see, the Leadership Credo integrates strategy and leadership. We use it regularly in the executive programs at Columbia Business School, and we've found that it serves as an excellent vehicle for leadership development.

It's important for the leader to be skilled at articulating his or her own Leadership Credo in a way that others inside and outside the organization can immediately grasp. At Columbia, we devote significant time to working with our executive participants on honing their Credos, making them as simple and clear as possible. And we often call upon members of the Ariel Group, a Boston-based group of actors, who work with the executives on using vivid imagery, metaphors, and storytelling techniques to enliven their messages and engage listeners. In the process, we've seen many a sterile, abstract document transformed into a galvanizing call to arms.

Execute

This is the learn-by-doing step in the cycle. Implement your personal improvement plan. Articulate your Leadership Credo at every opportunity. Continually appraise your own performance, seek feedback, and use it as the basis for further learning and improvement.

As always with Strategic Learning, the key is to repeat the cycle again and again. You should never stop learning. Unfortunately, many rising executives derail their careers when they stop striving for self-improvement, either because they think they've learned all there is to know or because they fail to translate their learning into meaningful leadership development.

The keys are to keep yourself open to new ideas and self-examination, to work with truth tellers you can trust to give you honest, unbiased feedback about your strengths and weaknesses, and to use the leadership development cycle as a process for incorporating what you learn into your daily practice. Those who work at this can continuously enhance their EQs and their leadership effectiveness.

"The Proof of the Pudding Is in the Eating"

I feel so strongly about the value of the leadership development cycle that I can't refrain from sharing a couple of stories that vividly illustrate how it works.

A Moment of Authenticity

When I met Jim Copeland, he was managing partner for the United States for Deloitte and Touche. He has since become the CEO of the worldwide firm. He had a distinctive personal style: slightly formal, quite reserved, perhaps a little shy. Jim was eager to have the members of his leadership team attend one of Columbia's executive programs; to demonstrate his commitment, he joined them personally.

As they often do, the Ariel Group worked with Jim and his colleagues on improving leadership communication and developing "presence." To our delight, Jim loved the exercises they taught. In fact, the day and a half he spent with them made such a big difference to his effectiveness as a communicator that he decided to make this work a continuing part of his personal development, and he asked Pat Dougan of the Ariel Group to serve as his executive coach.

Shortly thereafter, Jim became head of Deloitte worldwide. In his new role, he had to tackle a vitally important part of Deloitte's global strategy, which involved the creation of alignment among their partnerships around the world. He had to travel around the world winning the support and enthusiasm of Deloitte's people for this new way of operating—a very challenging leadership task. Fortunately, Jim's work with Pat Dougan gave him a host of new skills and techniques that helped him rise to the occasion.

Later that year, I was in the audience at Deloitte's worldwide partners' meeting. Of course, Jim spoke about the global alignment challenge, and he gave a very articulate, vivid speech that impressed the group enormously.

But then, during the question-and-answer session, someone in the audience decided to behave a little mischievously. Raising his hand, he called out, "Jim, people say you've been working with a personal coach. Are the rumors true?"

Nervous glances were exchanged around the room. Many executives would be embarrassed to admit the "weakness" of turning to a personal coach. How would Jim respond to this public challenge? Would he get angry and answer defensively or evasively?

He did none of these. Instead, Jim beamed broadly and declared, "Yes, it's absolutely true. Her name is Pat Dougan, and she's sitting in the third row here today. Pat, please stand up!" As the applause subsided, Jim went on, "Many of you know that I haven't relished giving speeches and public presentations all these years. Maybe you've noticed some improvements recently. Pat's work with me has made a huge difference. Working with a coach has helped me grow tremendously, and I strongly recommend it to all of you."

The folks at Deloitte still speak admiringly about the authenticity of Jim's gesture. This was a real leadership moment—a moment of honesty and openness that deeply enhanced his stature and effectiveness as a leader.

Jim Copeland was always an effective leader. He simply took advantage of some help to enhance one aspect of his leadership— his communication skills. By contrast, the hero of my second story had much more serious problems as a leader.

From Arrogant to Self-Aware

Walter was one of 35 participants in one of our executive education programs. All were senior managers from the same global consumer products company. They came together from around the world to work with us on Strategic Learning and leadership development.

When the program started, Walter had just been promoted to a very senior job. It was clear that he was an extremely bright man and very driven to succeed. Unfortunately, Walter's IQ was much greater than his EQ. As our sessions began, his abrasive personality became very obvious. Walter was impatient, arrogant, dismissive of others' opinions, and very demanding. During breaks, he was frequently at the front of the room, complaining to the faculty leader, "Why are we going so slowly? We could do all this in half the time! The class debates are teaching me nothing new."

On the day devoted to an overview of Strategic Learning, I became Walter's target. Every participant had received in advance a copy of a paper outlining the process, and, unlike most of the others, Walter had studied it carefully. Not surprisingly, my talk covered much of the same material. During our coffee break, Walter marched up to tell me: "I'm a senior executive, and here I am listening to you rehash ideas I read about just last week. Quite candidly, you're wasting my valuable time. If the others were too lazy to read your paper, that's their problem, not mine." I caught embarrassed glances on the faces of Walter's colleagues.

Little did we know that the seeds of a transformation had already been planted. According to our usual practice, Walter had gone through a 360-degree feedback exercise back at the office prior to starting our program. Then, as the two-week program unfolded, he worked with coaches from Columbia on studying and interpreting the comments of his colleagues. For the first time in his life, Walter bumped into the realities of how others perceived him and his leadership style.

At first, his reaction was to be arrogant and dismissive. But as the program went on, Walter began to see the importance of building his leadership competency through honest self-appraisal. Little by little, we could see him beginning to absorb and process the truth about himself and about how his hostility and arrogance were harming his effectiveness as a leader. As Walter worked through the Lifeline Exercise, we noticed lightbulbs switching on—clearly some new level of self-awareness was emerging. He became much quieter and more pensive in class, taking notes and reflecting on the discussion rather than making outbursts.

The magic moment came one afternoon when Walter approached me with a surprising request. "I wonder whether you'd be good enough to serve as a mentor for me. I'd like to hear what you think about me and get your ideas as to how I might improve my leadership effectiveness." Of course, I was delighted to agree.

Walter's self-revelations continued in the days that followed. Having seen and internalized a series of truths about himself and his life for the first time, he defined a set of personal development objectives to transform his leadership style. Witnessing the change, his colleagues who had been cool toward Walter at the start of program gradually came to embrace and even admire him. At the end of the fortnight, the class selected him to present his Leadership Credo to the group, and it was a moving experience for us all. After the program, Walter continued to work without letup on his personal improvement priorities.

Six months later, the same group reconvened for a follow-up module to brush up on their leadership skills. On the first day, Walter sought me out. He shook my hand warmly and said, "I'm so looking forward to this. I can't tell you what a change this program has made in my life." And throughout the session he was a star and a role model for the entire group.

Walter's story demonstrates more powerfully than anything I could say how effective a tool the leadership development cycle can be.

Two Real-Life Leadership Credos

As a member of the board of directors of Ocean Spray, I have had an opportunity to watch the company's new CEO in action. Rob Hawthorne joined Ocean Spray in early 2000 after an impressive career with General Mills and the Pillsbury Company. Ocean Spray is a farmer-owned cooperative that markets cranberry juice, sauce, and other products under its own well-known brand name. Unfortunately, the company had fallen on hard times during the late 1990s. It had stopped innovating, and the competition had cut its market share by a third. Furthermore, an industrywide oversupply of cranberries had driven prices to the lowest level in over 50 years. For the first time in many years, Ocean Spray found itself operating at a loss. Rob was brought in to arrest the decline and lead Ocean Spray back to profitability.

Rob has a calm and unflappable way about him, as well as considerable experience in turnaround situations. I recently asked him to share his experiences with one of my Columbia MBA classes. We particularly enjoyed his remarks about his Leadership Credo, which he agreed to share in this book.

Rob Hawthorne's Leadership Credo

Over the years, I have made many mistakes, hit a few home runs (sometimes through good luck rather than good planning), and occasionally experienced the absolute joy that comes from realizing you've made a meaningful difference in the lives of people as they work to move a company to the next level.

I've been privileged to lead a number of companies through difficult turnarounds, and occasionally I've received the kind of electric-shock therapy that comes from making decisions on the fly without enough available facts. I've earned the scars and gray hair that come to someone who cares a lot—perhaps too much. My library is filled with books on leadership and strategy. Most are worth reading; some are better than others. I have shamelessly borrowed many of the suggested techniques, disassembling and inserting them into my own leadership style. In fact, after 30 years, it would be difficult to credit the stolen pieces to their original owners . . . with one exception.

When I was president of the Pillsbury Brands Group, Kevin Cashman presented a simple concept that helped crystallize my leadership approach and style. Kevin is a psychologist and the president and CEO of Leadersource, a company that helps senior executives grow and improve their leadership effectiveness. Kevin suggested to me that great leaders always lead *from the inside out*. That is, they act and react based on their own personal principles and values.

These principles come from life experiences. They are often formed outside our business lives and then applied to guide us in our professions, pointing us in the right direction. They act as a kind of internal compass, always pointing to "true north." A principle such as "Always tell the truth" is a simple yet powerful example.

Principle-based leaders who are true to themselves tend to be genuine and believable, and their people understand this immediately. After thinking about Kevin's observation, I immediately recognized that whatever leadership success I had experienced was based on this simple concept.

My principles are not complicated. I try to live my personal and business life using openness, honesty, and integrity as touchstones. During the intense pressure of a business turnaround, adhering to these principles has helped tremendously. The trust of employees is easy to lose but tough to win back. As soon as embattled employees see their leader communicating openly, honestly, and with integrity, they begin to relax and start making better decisions. As a CEO or senior executive, you will stand a much better chance if you are open and honest at all times.

Here is my Leadership Credo.

1. What Do I Stand For as a Leader?

Openness, Honesty, Integrity

Communicating openly, honestly, and with integrity will alleviate organizational fear and build an atmosphere of trust. If you want to have a high-performing organization, this is the price of admission. Whenever I have taken on a new assignment, I ask employees three magic questions. Sitting in small (10-people) "Coffee with Rob" sessions, I ask: (1) What's working? (2) What's not and why? (3) How can I help? Then I listen.

During my first month as the new CEO of Ocean Spray, I listened to more than 300 employees in these small group sessions, and I learned a lot. People want to be heard and need feedback relative to their concerns. I would encourage you to provide what I call an assumption of positive intent. People need to know that you trust and value their perspectives. This open approach will make you a better listener.

Restless Dissatisfaction . . . a Sense of Urgency

Dissatisfaction, even in times of success, can be very positive. Healthy organizations are never entirely happy. The best test is to ask whether things are better today versus this time last year. If people say, "Of course, things are better . . . but we need to fix the issue in front of us right now," you're on the right track. Restless dissatisfaction and a sense of urgency tell me we're going to get better.

It's important to note the difference between simply administering what's already in place and real problem solving. I expect executives to lead the way in solving problems and energizing the entire organization by their example. The most coveted designation ought to be Master of Problem Solving, not MBA.

Making a Big Company Act Small

Put a skilled and determined cross-functional team on a problem, and they will solve it every time. A single person attacking the same problem may get it done through heroic effort, but it will take longer, and the organizational buy-in will be much lower. In view of that truth, why not organize your entire company, division, or department into cross-functional business teams? That is exactly what we did at Pillsbury and Ocean Spray—with impressive results. In both cases, we were able to have a big company act small, becoming much quicker and lighter on our feet. If you feel the need for speed, adopting a team-based organization will help.

The Power of Simplicity

One of the most difficult challenges a CEO faces is finding a way to express corporate goals in an easily understood manner. Taking the time to polish and hone objectives into simple, telegraphic, and instantly understandable statements will be rewarded with organizational alignment.

If you have three or four top corporate objectives, you will stand a better chance of having employees recall them than if you have 10 or 20. Also, operating on the basis of principles rather than manuals and assuming that conversations are more effective than memos will simplify your organization.

Keep it simple.

Don't Oversteer

We all operate in a state of permanent white water. In crisis mode, organizations often become paralyzed, locked in relentless analysis, and frozen by the fear of making a decision. If you can remove the fear and encourage the notion that being directionally correct is sufficient, everyone will tend to move from intransigence to warp speed.

One caveat. If the decision you make turns out to be wrong (they sometimes do), you'll be expected to make a midair correction.

Once everyone operates with the "directionally correct" and "midair correction" principles, innovation and speed will improve substantially.

Relentless Focus on Our Customers

As a leader of a consumer packaged-food company, I start every decision with the consumer in mind. High-performing companies spend time in truly understanding their consumers, penetrating all the way down to the insight level. Insights are the jewels of understanding that drive strategy and ultimately action.

2. What Is Our Organization's Vision, and How Will We Win?

At Ocean Spray, our vision is to become the best juice company in the world—not the biggest, just the best. We will do this by *building our brand*, using five key principles.

- ▼ *Innovation.* We will lead the juice drinks category with innovative new products and unique packaging concepts that will delight our customers.
- ▼ *Speed to Market.* We will shorten our innovation cycle times while servicing customers at a world-class level.
- ▼ *Taking Waste Out.* We will continuously take waste out to generate funding to build our brand.
- ▼ *Intense Customer Focus.* We will continuously generate superior, consumer-based insights as our guide to market leadership.
- ▼ *Competitively Fit Organization.* We will strive to ensure that our organization is the best prepared to compete, with the right skills and a passion for our brand.

3. What Do We Stand For as an Organization?

A grower-owned cooperative is profoundly different from a publicly traded company, yet profoundly the same. Our values and goals reflect that duality.

▼ *Build shareholder value and provide a consistent, profitable return.* As with any company, this is our primary goal. But in a cooperative, the stakes are even higher. Our business represents a way of life for generations of family farmers. This added human dimension makes winning in the marketplace a personal pursuit.

▼ *Harness diversity of opinion.* Our cross-functional design and our team attitude make us a powerhouse driven by diverse opinions. The only way to compete successfully is through the combined energy, imagination, and determination of our people, beginning with our growers.

▼ *Start with an external focus.* Every decision begins and ends with the customer, who will always be the ultimate judge of our success.

▼ *Encourage restless dissatisfaction.* Challenging the status quo and having the courage to change enable us to improve constantly. We will always stretch ourselves and our teams to accommodate new ways of thinking and acting.

The second Credo was actually not written for that purpose. Rather, it is a reprint of an essay by Carly Fiorina, chief executive of Hewlett-Packard, in which she describes a watershed event from her career at AT&T and the seven personal and business principles, distilled from such events, that have guided her career as a leader. Does the combination sound familiar? Of course—it's very similar to the Lifeline Exercise and the Leadership Credo process explained in this chapter. Without the benefit of coaching, Ms. Fiorina created her own personal version of the leadership development cycle, as reflected in her essay.

Carly Fiorina: Making the Best of a Mess

It was 1984; I was 30 years old and working at AT&T. The company's divestiture had just occurred, the Bell operating companies had just been spun off, and things were in shambles. Access Management, the division responsible for connecting long-distance calls to local phone companies, was in the worst shape. I decided that's where I wanted to work.

People thought I was nuts. Nobody knows what they're doing, people said. It's a mess. And that's exactly what appealed to me. It was a wonderful challenge. I knew I could have a big impact, for better or for worse.

Access Management was an area about which I knew absolutely nothing. I teamed up with two excellent engineers. I listened and I learned. We discovered that the bills from the local companies were AT&T's biggest single cost. And we had no idea whether we were being charged the right amount.

I've saved a picture from those days where I'm standing in a room covered floor to ceiling with boxes filled with bills. A team of us looked over every one of those bills manually for three or four months and found significant overcharges.

This is not something that most people think of as fun. Nevertheless, our goal became to verify every bill and prove every overcharge. We decided we must create a billing verification system. Eventually, this system was implemented all over the country by hundreds of employees and saved the company hundreds of millions of dollars. We had great fun accomplishing something nobody thought we could.

From this and other experiences, I have distilled seven principles for personal and business growth and success:

▼ Seek tough challenges: They're more fun.

▼ Have an unflinching, clear-eyed vision of the goal, followed by absolute clarity, realism, and objectivity about what it really will take to grow, to lead, and to win.

▼ Understand that the only limits that really matter are those you put on yourself, or that a business puts on itself. Most people and businesses are capable of far more than they realize.

▼ Recognize the power of the team; no one succeeds alone.

▼ "Never, never, never, never give in," to quote Winston Churchill. Most great wins happen on the last play.

▼ Strike a balance between confidence and humility—enough confidence to know that you can make a real difference, enough humility to ask for help.

▼ Love what you do. Success requires passion.

I learned these lessons in part by watching my parents. My father had health issues; he was told he could never play football. He went on to play terrific football. Raised in a tiny Texas town, he became a professor and federal judge. My mother had a series of stepmothers who didn't think much of developing girls and a father who wouldn't pay for her college tuition. So she ran away from home, in small-town Ohio, joined the Air Force, became an accomplished artist, and devoted herself to being interested and interesting.

I loved working the billing issue at Access Management. I did not love law school. I wanted desperately to make my father proud that his daughter would follow in his footsteps. Quitting was the ultimate personal failure in my mind and his. Yet, in the end, loving what I did was more important. But life went on. We laugh about it today, and we know we learned something valuable.

Every experience in life, whether humble or grand, teaches a lesson. The question is not if the lesson is taught, but rather if it is learned.

These two examples help to illustrate the essence of effective leadership. It starts from the inside, with a deep and secure knowledge of self. Its foundation is a set of firmly held and clearly expressed values that form the basis for all actions, thus giving the leader authenticity. It shows a keen awareness of the needs of others and a genuine readiness to listen. It provides a clear and resonant sense of direction for the organization. It speaks with simplicity. And, above all, it shows humility—a willingness to learn and grow.

Creating an Environment for Success

Having examined what Strategic Learning can do as a tool for leadership development, let's return to our broader theme—the role of Strategic Learning in helping your organization continually adapt to the changing business environment.

As you'll recall, the previous chapters of this book developed the following line of logic.

First, the way companies create their future is through the strategies they pursue. These strategies may be implicit or explicit; they may be developed in a thoughtful, systematic way or allowed to emerge haphazardly. But in one way or another, the strategy a company follows determines how effectively it uses its scarce resources and hence the degree of success it is likely to achieve.

Recognizing this truth, many companies have an explicit process for developing strategy. But due to the radical increase in speed, complexity, and uncertainty, traditional ways of doing strategy no longer work. They are mostly based on a static planning model, which focuses on one-time, A-to-B change. They tend to produce incrementalism—an extension of the past rather than an invention of the future. As a result, these processes usually produce operating plans and budgets rather than insights and strategic breakthroughs.

We need to reinvent the way we think about strategy. To be valuable in today's turbulent environment, the goal of strategy must be to provide a process for generating ongoing renewal. In short, our strategy process must help us create and lead adaptive organizations with the built-in ability to continuously scan and interpret the changing environment, generate superior insights, and act on them to produce winning strategies.

This logic, in turn, carries several crucial implications.

▼ If the creation and implementation of breakthrough strategies is to be more than an ad hoc or one-time-only exercise, we need practical tools to make it into an ongoing process, deeply imbedded in the culture of the organization.

▼ Such a process of discovery and strategic innovation is completely different from planning. It is crucial, therefore, that companies not attempt to combine the two. Strategy should come first, and planning should follow.

▼ And because, in contrast to the old era of asset-based competition, the mobilization of all of a company's creative intelligence is now essential for success, the importance of leadership as a catalyst for such mobilization has significantly increased.

Throughout this book, we've seen the strong interrelationship between strategy and leadership. A leader cannot lead without a clear and compelling strategy. Conversely, a strategy without effective leadership will take you nowhere.

So today, more than at any time in the past, effective leadership is at the core of the creation and implementation of winning strategies. This is the inner truth of Peter Drucker's dictum that the purpose of an organization is to get ordinary people to do extraordinary things. Leadership and strategy are the two closely linked forces by which that alchemy occurs.

Strategic Learning offers a set of tools that helps organizations perform this alchemy consistently. As we've suggested, Strategic Learning may be thought of as a kind of systematic R&D process for strategy. Just as the great industrial firms—GE, IBM, Siemens, Sony, 3M, Intel—have developed coherent processes to ensure that product innovation occurs regularly and in a strategic context rather than sporadically and randomly, so tomorrow's most consistently effective companies will need to make systematic strategic innovation a high priority. The Strategic Learning process offers a way to pursue this goal.

We can carry the analogy a step further. Having a systematic plan for R&D is crucially important, but by itself it's not enough to ensure a steady stream of innovative new products. It's equally essential to create an environment conducive to the creative work of your engineers, scientists, artists, designers, and other professionals.

In the same way, Strategic Learning as a process is not enough by itself to ensure that your company will be at the forefront of strategic innovation in your industry. For the process to be truly effective, the whole company must be infused with the spirit of discovery and innovation. Strategic Learning is an enabling process, of course, and as such it provides a framework within which creative thinking can occur. But for that process to work at its best, it requires an environment that fosters innovation.

Among other things, this means nurturing creativity and strategic thinking at *every* level of your organization. There's a story about a packaged-goods company that was proudly unveiling its latest product, a new pancake mix. The firm held a party at which hundreds of employees, company friends, and members of the press gathered to sample the pancakes made with the new mix. The pancakes were so good that a long line developed in front of the griddle where a chef from the company kitchen was whipping up batches of pancakes as quickly as he could. In an effort to satisfy everyone in the crowd, a strict rule of one serving per customer was enforced.

In the midst of this scene, the company CEO pushed his way to the front of the line, held out his plate, and said to the chef, "I'll have a second helping of pancakes, please."

Those nearby, bemused by the CEO's gaffe, wondered how the chef would respond. He simply shook his head. "Sorry," he replied. "Just one per customer."

The CEO bristled. "Do you know who I am?" he demanded angrily. "I'm the CEO of this company!"

Unfazed, the chef shrugged and replied, "And do you know who *I* am? I'm the fellow who hands out the pancakes!"

It's a lesson that all of us in leadership roles need to learn. The people who work for us—on the assembly line, at the customer help desks, in the warehouse, in the sales department—are the ones who hand out the pancakes. Without them, all of us at the top of the business, despite our fancy offices, our advanced degrees, our years of experience, can do nothing. The most important thing we can do to promote the success of our businesses is to support, help, and encourage our people, providing them with an environment that encourages and rewards their involvement, creativity, and sense of shared ownership.

Some business leaders assume that the most important element in promoting creativity is hiring the best people. "Find the next Thomas Edison or Steve Jobs," they assert, "and he'll produce creative breakthroughs armed with nothing more than a pen and a pad of paper." This assumption leads to a view of business as essentially a battle for talent, in which the company that does the best job of finding the best minds (either through shrewd hiring and recruitment practices or through company acquisitions) is the inevitable winner.

I disagree. Business is much less a battle for talent than *a battle for performance.* After all, in the end, we all fish for talent in the same pond. Very few of the world's gifted people are hiding under rocks; identifying and recruiting them isn't much of a mystery. And most mainstream companies in any industry are relatively comparable when it comes to salaries, benefits, and perks. Thus, it's not really practical to think that your company can monopolize the best talent in your field by virtue of a fat checkbook or a clever recruitment effort.

In any case, there's a self-correcting mechanism at work in the talent market, as there is in most markets. When any one company begins to dominate the talent pool in an industry, people naturally begin to look for opportunities elsewhere. Why join Company A as their twentieth top-flight engineer (or researcher or financial expert or film director) when you can join Company B as the number one expert or get together with a few friends and launch brand-new Company C?

So long-term success in business can't be achieved by simply focusing on getting the best people. The real secret is to inspire these talented people to perform to their full potential. And here, as demonstrated by the research of Dan Denison that we've already cited (Chapter 6), there's no substitute for clarity of purpose—what Denison calls "mission."

But there are other cultural factors that play an important role in making a company a hotbed of strategic innovation. Experience and research show that companies that follow specific practices in managing their workforces tend to be more innovative than others. Here are some of the practices I recommend to companies that are eager to make the most of the innovative potential of Strategic Learning.

Make a Commitment to Lifelong Learning on the Part of Your People

The American Society for Training and Development recommends spending 4 percent of your payroll on education. Many companies budget in line with the 4 percent guideline but actually spend less than this. As the fiscal year unfolds and financial pressures mount, managers find themselves putting off education expenditures. The trouble is that this tends to happen year after year, with the result that actual education spending averages less than 2 percent of payroll.

You should make the recommended 4 percent sacrosanct. This means you are making the promise to give your people the opportunity to regularly get away from the urgent and think about the important, to let new ideas in, and to systematically learn and grow.

More specifically, I suggest the following allocation: Set aside

2.5 percent of payroll for education and development programs that you design and offer, and give your managers personal control over another 1.5 percent. Let them accumulate their education funds in a personal account that they can spend on whatever type of learning they wish. Yes, that means permitting them to spend company funds on education that is not obviously linked to their jobs. You never know whether a course on philosophy, ancient history, cabinetmaking, or beekeeping may suggest a breakthrough idea with practical on-the-job implications. At the very least, providing this kind of educational benefit will improve morale and give your people an opportunity to open their minds in a refreshing and stimulating way—all of which is certain to redound to your company's benefit, both directly and indirectly.

Refresh Work Teams through Job Rotation

Research shows that on-the-job learning tends to decline sharply or stop altogether after the same group of people has been working together for about four years. By that time, everyone has heard everyone else's point of view, worked out all their arguments, and learned what there is to learn from the others' past experiences. Bringing fresh blood into the group recharges the learning batteries and forces everyone to grapple with new points of view and approaches.

To make job rotation attractive, your corporate culture must support and reward it. Don't let any department or division develop a reputation as your organization's Siberia, where effort goes unnoticed and unappreciated and where tackling tough challenges is a thankless task, while other departments are considered fast-track assignments that all the brightest people covet. If you let this happen, people will begin to think of parallel moves as potential career traps rather than as opportunities to learn. Instead, make a conscious effort to provide real opportunities for growth and success throughout the company, and send your most promising people everywhere. Again, you'll be creating chances for unexpected learning and strategic breakthroughs to occur.

Build Heterogeneity into the Organization

Deliberately work to ensure that work groups at every level are varied by gender, age, cultural background, learning styles, national origin, and other characteristics. And be sure to hire some mavericks and truth tellers who feel like sandpaper, and spread them around the organization. Any time a division or department begins to run like clockwork in a seemingly frictionless fashion, the danger of complacency arises. Seize the opportunity to shake things up by introducing a new face—one that looks quite different from the old ones.

Develop the International Experiences of Your People

This is increasingly hard to do today with so many dual-career couples for whom dislocations are difficult to manage, but don't give up on it. It's more important than ever to have your people conversant with the cultural, economic, political, and business differences of Europe, Asia, Africa, and the Americas. One way to make an overseas assignment more attractive is to make the "return ticket" sacred, so your managers don't have to fear that when the three- or four-year assignment is completed there'll be no job waiting for them in their home country.

When I was at Unilever, the company had a highly effective system that explicitly listed the "return ticket status" for everyone on an overseas assignment based on a negotiated agreement. For example, some were guaranteed a job at the same level or better back in their home country; others preferred to be assured of another expatriate posting. And Unilever made it a habit to slightly overdeliver on these promises (provided, of course, that job performance remained satisfactory). As a result, no one had reentry problems, and word spread throughout the company ranks that accepting a foreign berth was both safe and rewarding.

Institutionalize Time for Reflection

It's important to set aside time from the daily bustle of business to think about broader issues, free from the pressure of immediate goals. Rather than create a new meeting, take one of your regular meetings (perhaps one that has been focused on ritualistic performance reviews) and turn it into a best practices forum at which good ideas can be shared and spread. The only requirement is that everyone show up with a best practice from inside or outside the company—plus an open mind.

Many of the world's most effective companies have such programs. For example, the heads of GE's 12 key businesses meet quarterly with the sole objective of knowledge sharing and cross-fertilizing best practices. Practical benefits have arisen from these meetings. For example, a creative idea that originated in GE's European business has been applied across the company. It's the concept of "reverse mentoring" in information technology, in which high-ranking (and mostly older) managers are coupled with junior (and mostly younger) experts who teach them the mysteries of IT.

Andrea Saveri, a researcher at the Institute for the Future, has eloquently articulated the importance of such free-form learning conversations in an essay she coauthored, called "Strategy, Experience, and Meaning":

> Strategy implies a bit of distance from the field of action. It assumes a metaview of the world—the view of an observer separate from the player. It is the blessing and bane of human existence that we are, in fact, always both a player and an observer in our individual lives.
>
> In times of rapid change, when life seems to bear down with the force of a storm, the player usually rises to the occasion. He jumps into the maelstrom, depending on sensibility and intuition to negotiate the currents. All the observer can do is hold on for the ride.
>
> In quieter moments, the observer can step into the foreground, interpret the field of action, make a study of its other half, and make sense out of what has happened. For the world to have meaning, the observer must have this time to reflect.
>
> Learning ultimately occurs when these two parts sit down and have dinner together. . . . This, then, is a plea for individual and organizational attention to quiet times and quiet places. . . .

And it's a call for designing eddies in our worldwide streams, places where we can be sure we accomplish the other half of our work as a species.

It takes deliberate effort to set aside time and space for such "eddies" in the bustle of corporate life. They can take many forms: best-practice meetings, regular retreats, executive education programs, sabbaticals. The rewards may take time to emerge, but they will be enormous.

Benchmark Your Company against Noncompetitors

Measuring your company's products and processes against those of your direct competitors has very limited usefulness. Perhaps you'll be able to establish where they stand compared with your own company on some key performance measures. But you won't be able to ask them how they did it, which is the *real* learning. To do so may be illegal, and it's certainly impractical. A much better approach is to benchmark against noncompetitors who are best in class in the areas of most value to you, and then to start a learning dialogue with them. Returning once again to General Electric as a role model, GE claims to have learned much more about supply chain management from Wal-Mart than from any of its direct competitors.

One of the best approaches is what I call *intellectual bartering*—trading your best business "secrets" with a noncompeting company from which you're eager to learn. When I was at Seagram, the company's programs for career development and succession planning were rather weak. As a result, these issues were handled on a catch-as-catch-can basis rather than systematically. Searching for a way to jump-start improvement, I recalled that Tom Ostermuller, whom I had worked with when he was at McKinsey & Company, had gone on to become a senior executive at Bristol-Myers Squibb, which was known for its career development and succession planning expertise. Meanwhile, Seagram had excellent financial planning systems—something that I suspected Bristol-Myers Squibb could learn from.

I contacted Tom at Bristol-Myers Squibb, and we agreed to trade ideas in these two areas. A Seagram team spent two days with the Bristol-Myers Squibb human resources team, who conducted a kind of "open university" program for us, walking us through their career development and succession planning approach. They took a great deal of pride in showing us the ropes and in answering all our questions on human resource practices. As it happens, the Bristol-Myers Squibb folk never did follow up on the agreed quid pro quo. They were pleased simply to teach us what they knew. Thus, we at Seagram enjoyed an invaluable learning experience that ended up costing us nothing but our time.

Turn Your Company Conferences into Opportunities for Learning

Every organization has large-scale meetings of one kind or another—conventions, sales conferences, annual planning meetings, what have you. All too often, the opportunities these provide for developing and sharing knowledge go by the board. Instead, the emphasis is on preaching (exhortations to succeed), cheerleading (inspirational talks), and back-patting (awards and prizes). You may not want to eliminate these traditional elements altogether, but add educational programming as well. Use the opportunity to listen to different voices. Bring in outside speakers from worlds that are different from your own. Urge them to shake up your thinking with fresh perspectives and challenges. Hold best-practices workshops with people from around the world, and reward managers who share their divisional secrets of success as well as those who shamelessly "steal" those secrets to enhance their own division's performance.

Create a Climate of Open Communication

Why not tell your people the whole truth about what your company is doing, how well it is performing, the obstacles it faces, and the plans you are developing? In some quarters, this may be viewed as a radical notion. In many companies, employees are told less about all these matters than shareholders; sometimes they read things in the annual report that they never knew before. I've never understood this; after all, it is the employees who must somehow transform the strategies developed by management into reality. How can they do this wholeheartedly without a full understanding of the factual background that underlies those strategies?

I fervently believe that bringing out the best in people requires, above all else, a culture of openness. We talk a lot about the importance of trust. But we can't simply ask for trust; we have to earn it. And an essential step toward earning trust is showing it.

Trust your employees to be able to deal with the facts about your business in a mature, responsible, and honest fashion. We like to boast about the "risk-taking" business cultures we are building. If this is so, then take risks on the side of openness with your employees. Hold regular informational meetings with your people, right down to the folks on the shop floor, in the mail room, and in the company cafeteria. Share the latest numbers with them, explain what they mean, and discuss the opportunities and dangers you face.

Deal frankly with failures. No one expects company managers to be godlike and infallible, and the chances are good that the rumors being whispered about your latest mistakes are worse than what really happened. When you try to withhold the truth, you're encouraging the development of a culture of denial, sending the message, "We're not truth tellers here." Instead, set an example of insisting on "ground truth" (as in the army's after-action reviews), even when this may cast you or your company's leadership in a less-than-flattering light. Squelch gossip about missteps by telling people honestly what happened, what went wrong, and how you plan to recoup and move forward.

Above all, tell people what the company's plans are and where they fit in. You'll almost certainly find that they respond to honest communication with a higher level of commitment, involvement, productivity, and creativity.

Leadership philosophies like the ones outlined here have the effect of planting Strategic Learning in a garden surrounded by other healthy plants—practices that encourage a culture of innovation, learning, openness, and sharing. Don't think of Strategic Learning as a ritual or a technique, or even a collection of techniques, that you can plug into a company as a quick fix for what ails you. Instead, think of it as a guiding framework and a way of leading your organization with continual learning and adaptation as the core philosophy. Nurtured in this spirit, Strategic Learning will grow faster and stronger than ever—and so will your company.

SOURCES

INTRODUCTION   A Journey of Discovery

Page 3: "The following statistics . . . provide a call to action": Richard Foster and Sarah Kaplan, *Creative Destruction*. New York: Currency Books, 2001, pages 7–11.

Page 4: "As a result, technical advances no longer happened randomly": Lester Thurow, *Building Wealth: The New Rules for Individuals, Companies, and Nations in a Knowledge-Based Economy*. New York: HarperBusiness, 2000, page 18.

Page 4: "Business more than any other occupation": Quoted by Drake Beil in "Create a Culture of Innovation," *Honolulu Advertiser*, July 17, 2000.

Page 6: "The ability to learn faster than competitors": Arie de Geus, "Planning as Learning," *Harvard Business Review*, March–April 1998.

CHAPTER 1   The New Playing Field

Page 14: "That's an information-based service as much as a product": Brent Schlender, "The Odd Couple," *Fortune*, May 1, 2000, page 116.

Page 16: "Robert Reich, the former secretary of labor": Robert B. Reich, *The Future of Success*. New York: Alfred A. Knopf, 2000, pages 27–40.

Page 16: "This is a tricky balance": Clayton M. Christensen, *The Innovator's Dilemma*. Boston: Harvard Business School Press, 1997.

Page 18: "In a speech given to industry analysts in December 1999": Quoted in *PRNewswire*, December 7, 1999.

Page 18: "Jung quickly earmarked $60 million": Nanette Byrnes, "Avon's New Calling," *Business Week*, September 18, 2000.

Page 19: "The plan is to have 30,000 eRepresentatives by year-end 2001": Interview, Leonard Edwards, March 8, 2001.

Page 22: "By 1989 its sales reached an all-time high of $627 million": *S&P Creditwire*, January 5, 1995.

Page 23: "In 1996, the company was sold for $135 million": *Hoover's Online*, 2001. Hoover's Company Information, www.hoovers.com.

CHAPTER 2   The Challenge of Change

Page 29: "The crowds would 'mostly hoot and holler' when he performed his jumps": Richard Fosbury, Interview on CNNSI, www.CNNSI.com.

Page 30: "Research by Mike Tushman of the Harvard Business School": M. I. Tushman, W. H. Newman, and E. Romanelli, "Convergence and Upheaval: Managing the Unsteady Pace of Organizational Evolution," *California Management Review* 29, no. 1 (Fall 1986).

Page 30: "In 1900, the average life expectancy in the United States": National Center for Health Statistics, www.cdc.gov/nchs.

Page 32: "First, you must do a nice-looking watch": Dick Tracy's Cellular Swatch Watch," *New York Times*, June 26, 2000.

Page 33: "As the prolific and insightful management thinker Charles Handy has noted": Charles Handy, *The Empty Raincoat*. London: Arrow Business Books, 1994, pages 49–64.

Page 38: "Intel succeeds because it is guided by the spirit of cofounder Andy Grove": Andrew S. Grove, *Only the Paranoid Survive*. New York: Bantam Doubleday Dell, 1996.

Page 38: "Our success is the result of anxiety": Lee Kuan Yew and Louis Kraar, "A Blunt Talk with Singapore's Lee Kuan Yew," *Fortune*, August 4, 1997.

CHAPTER 3   The Search for an Answer

Page 43: "All the lessons of war can be reduced to a single word": Basil H. Hart, *Strategy*. New York: Penguin Books, 1991, page 334.

Page 44: "Henry Mintzberg, author of the classic management text": Henry Mintzberg, *The Rise and Fall of Strategic Planning*. New York: The Free Press, 1994, pages 24–26.

Page 47: "Our predicament is the growing gap": Paul Saffo, Esther Dyson, Charles Handy, and Peter M. Senge, "Looking Ahead: Implications of the Present," *Harvard Business Review*, September 1, 1997.

Page 51: "In *The Origin of Species*, his groundbreaking study": Charles Darwin, *The Origin of Species*. New York: Grammercy Books, 1979, page 125.

CHAPTER 5   Winning the Battle for Insight: Doing a Situation Analysis

Page 82: "Marketing . . . is understanding the behavior of customers": John Deighton, e-mail to the author, May 7, 2001.

CHAPTER 6   Defining Your Focus

Page 107: "Dan Denison, formerly a professor at the University of Michigan Business School": "Why Mission Matters," *Leader to Leader*, Summer 2000, pages 46–48.

Page 109: "Nothing is more brick-and-mortar than real estate": Interview, John Gilbert, III, March 1, 2001.

Page 110: "Our customers are not in the technology business": Robert Slater, *Saving Big Blue*. New York: McGraw-Hill, 1999, page 239.

Page 115: "According to Michael P. Delain, GE Appliances' quality manager": Claudia H. Deutsch, "New Economy, Old-School Rigor," *New York Times*, June 6, 2000, page C1.

Page 118: "George A. Miller's classic research": George A. Miller, "The Magical Number Seven Plus or Minus Two: Some Limits on Our Capacity for Processing Information," *Psychological Review* 63 (1956), pages 81–97.

Page 126: "To define a clear vision and inspire your people": Carly Fiorina, presentation at 1999 Strategic Learning Conference, The Conference Board, March 29, 1999.

CHAPTER 7   Aligning the Organization

Page 131: "For any strategy to succeed": These principles of organizational alignment have been well researched and documented by such scholars as Jay Galbraith, Nadler and Tushman, and Don Hambrick.

Page 139: "Overall crime in New York is down": New York City web site, www.nyc.gov.

Page 146: "As Michael Porter of the Harvard Business School has pointed out": Michael Porter, "What Is Strategy?" *Harvard Business Review*, November–December 1996.

CHAPTER 8   Transforming the Culture

Page 149: "The so-called onion model of culture": With variations, this model is described by several writers, including Geert Hofstede in *Cultures and Organizations: Intercultural Cooperation and Its*

Importance for Survival (New York: Harper Collins, 1994, page 9), and Edgar H. Schein in *The Corporate Culture Survival Guide* (San Francisco: Jossey-Bass, 1999, page 16).

Page 153: "Behavioral psychologist B. F. Skinner has pointed out": B. F. Skinner, *About Behaviorism*. New York: Vintage Books, 1976, pages 223–227.

Page 155: "As Edgar H. Schein puts it": Schein, *Survival Guide*, page 187.

Page 159: "[Such firms] have turned the typical logic of strategic management on its head": Charles O'Reilly III and Jeffrey Pfeffer, *Hidden Value: How Great Companies Achieve Extraordinary Results with Ordinary People*. Boston: Harvard Business School Press, 2000, pages 7–8.

Page 160: "We can't share knowledge, we can't reach out to customers": Slater, *Saving Big Blue*, pages 104–105.

Page 160: "If the CEO isn't living and preaching the culture": Ibid., page 93.

Page 161: "These change agents, he wrote to the staff, should be": "Road Map for the Revolution," *Think Twice* [IBM internal publication], December 1993.

Page 162: "Never start with the idea of changing culture": Schein, *Survival Guide*, page 189.

Page 165: "Toyota's real strength resides in its ability to learn": Alex Taylor III, "How Toyota Defies Gravity," *Fortune*, December 8, 1997.

Page 166: "The Atlanta Gas Light Company . . . provides a good illustration": Atlanta Gas Light Company, Annual Report, 1993.

Page 168: "The real task . . . is to behave your way into a new way of thinking": Richard Pascale, e-mail to the author, June 14, 2001.

Page 169: "Harley-Davidson . . . uses a value statement": Rich Teerlink and Lee Ozley, *More Than a Motorcycle*. Boston: Harvard Business School Press, 2000, page 250.

CHAPTER 9 Overcoming Resistance to Change

Page 186: "Change Leadership: Getting from A to B": D. Nader and M. Tushman, *Competing by Design*. New York: Oxford University Press, 1997.

Page 189: "The research of Warner Burke": W. Warner Burke, *Managing Change: Interpretation and Industry Comparison*, Introduction.

Page 191: "Equation for successful change": M. Beer, *Organization Change and Development: A Systems View*. Santa Monica, CA: Goodyear Publishing, 1980. Adapted from R. Beckhard and R. T. Harris, *Organizational Transitions*. Reading, MA: Addison-Wesley, 1987.

Page 208: "Leadership means setting an example": Lee Iacocca, *Iacocca: An Autobiography*. New York: Bantam Books, 1984, page 241.

Page 208: "Now there's a company that doesn't understand equality of sacrifice": Ibid., page 245.

CHAPTER 10 Implementing and Experimenting

Page 212: "As Collins and Porras point out": James C. Collins and Jerry I. Porras, *Built to Last*. New York: HarperBusiness, 1994.

Page 214: "It's a series of lateral developments": Ernest Gundling, *The 3M Way to Innovation*. New York: Kodansha International, 2000, page 69.

CHAPTER 11 Strategic Learning as a Path to Personal Growth

Page 222: "It is emotional quotient (EQ), not IQ, that sets brilliant leaders apart": Daniel Goleman, *Emotional Intelligence*. New York: Bantam Books, 1995.

Page 223: "A person can have the best training": Daniel Goleman, "What Makes a Leader?" *Harvard Business Review*, November–December 1998, page 94.

Page 223: "Goleman identified four components of emotional intelligence": Daniel Goleman, "Leadership That Gets Results," *Harvard Business Review*, March–April 2000, pages 78–90.

Page 242: "Rob Hawthorne's Leadership Credo": Interview, Robert Hawthorne, August 20, 2001.

Page 247: "It was 1984": "Making the Best of a Mess," *New York Times*, September 29, 1999. Copyright 1999 by Carly Fiorina. Reprinted with permission.

CHAPTER 12 Creating an Environment for Success

Page 253: "The American Society for Training and Development recommends spending": ASTD, *State of the Industry Report*, 2001.

Page 256: "Strategy implies a bit of distance": Andrea Saveri, "The Work of Global Interconnection: Strategy, Experience and Meaning," Institute for the Future Outlook Project, Report SR-672b, June 1999, page 26. Reprinted by permission.

INDEX

ABOUT THE AUTHOR

Willie Pietersen was raised in South Africa and received a Rhodes Scholarship to Oxford University. After a period spent in the practice of law, he embarked on an international business career. Between 1974 and 1994, Pietersen ran multibillion-dollar divisions of several major global corporations, including Unilever, The Seagram Company, and Sterling Winthrop. In 1998, Pietersen was named Professor of the Practice of Management at the Columbia University Business School. He serves as an advisor and consultant to many global companies, including Sony, Ericsson, Deloitte and Touche, SAP, and The Chubb Corporation, and is Chairman of the Menlo Park–based think tank, Institute for the Future.

Willie Pietersen may be contacted at StratLearnCycle@aol.com.